THE INTERNATIONAL MONETARY FUND

Financial Medic to the World?

THE INTERNATIONAL MONETARY FUND

Financial Medic to the World?

A PRIMER ON MISSION, OPERATIONS, AND PUBLIC POLICY ISSUES

Edited by
Lawrence J. McQuillan
and
Peter C. Montgomery

HOOVER INSTITUTION PRESS
Stanford University   Stanford, California

URL: http://www-hoover.stanford.edu

Hoover Institution Press Publication No. 456

Cover image of international money © 1998 PhotoDisc

First printing, 1999
05   04   03   02   01   00   99   9   8   7   6   5   4   3   2   1

Manufactured in the United States of America
The paper used in this publication meets the minimum requirements
of American National Standard for Information Sciences—Permanence
of Paper for Printed Library Materials, ANSI Z39.48–1984. ⊚

Library of Congress Cataloging-in-Publication Data
The International Monetary Fund—financial medic to the world? :
a primer on mission, operations, and public policy issues / edited by
Lawrence J. McQuillan and Peter C. Montgomery.
       p.   cm.
   Includes bibliographical references and index.
   ISBN 0-8179-9642-7
   1. International Monetary Fund.   I. McQuillan, Lawrence J.,
1961–   .   II. Montgomery, Peter C.
HG3881.5.I58I574   1999
332.1′52—dc21
                                                    99-11874
                                                      CIP

Contents

PART FOUR: RECENT INTERNATIONAL MONETARY FUND FINANCING INITIATIVES 91

Mexico

East Asia

Russia

Response

PART FIVE: MISSION CREEP   159

Human Rights

Government Corruption

Geopolitics and International Security

Thoughts on Mission Creep

PART SIX: ABOLISH THE INTERNATIONAL MONETARY FUND? 193

Figures and Tables

Preface

The Hoover Institution generates ideas on public policy reforms that seek to improve the human condition. Hoover also serves as a commentator, not only on society's current circumstances but also on ideas for reform.

Another dimension of the Hoover Institution's role is educating the public on policy issues. With this volume, the Institution launches a book series that will capture the discussion surrounding significant contemporary public policy issues and deliver that discussion to the public in a concise and understandable format. Thus, this volume represents a synthesis of Hoover's objectives to research and to educate.

The International Monetary Fund—Financial Medic to the World? is a useful compendium providing both background information and current policy discussions on an organization that a large segment of society knows little about. In combing through the extensive writings on the International Monetary Fund (IMF), the editors—Hoover Institution research fellow Lawrence J. McQuillan and public affairs fellow Peter C. Montgomery—chose articles and opinion pieces that represent a diversity of views on the origins, operations, and effectiveness of the IMF. The book specifically examines the mission and operations of the IMF, now more than fifty years old, and the effects of its financing programs and loan conditions on the countries accepting IMF funding. The editors look at the historical record as well as recent IMF activity in Mexico, East Asia, and Russia and present a dialogue on "mission creep." Finally, the book presents opposing viewpoints on whether the IMF should continue to exist.

The Hoover Institution endeavors to promote a wider discussion of important policy issues. Greater knowledge, more analytic thinking, and a national dialogue will contribute to reasoned and informed policy decisions. Hoover is committed to playing a prominent role in this process.

Part of promoting a wider discussion of today's policy issues involves using modern technology to disseminate knowledge and encourage a national dialogue. To this end, we are launching a new site on the World

Wide Web, www.imfsite.org, to make available the information in this book; the web site will also include other pertinent material, supplementing the information in the book for those interested in additional treatments. Furthermore, we will make an effort to add new material as future writings are released on the topic.

Many Hoover supporters have been enthusiastic about the effort to cast our net widely, using technology to our greatest advantage. I would like to especially acknowledge Overseer William K. Bowes Jr. for his interest and support of our communication strategies.

In addition to the editors, Lawrence McQuillan and Peter Montgomery, I want to thank Michael Walker, managing editor of the *Hoover Digest*, Patricia Baker, executive editor of the Hoover Press, and the superb staff of the Hoover Press for producing such a fine volume.

John Raisian
Director
Hoover Institution

Introduction

When pollsters asked children in Thailand about the International Monetary Fund, 30 percent described it as an unidentified flying object. Similarly, a December 1997 *Time* magazine profile of the fund depicted the IMF as a flying masked action hero dropping money over East Asia. These images of the IMF, as a mysterious outside force reshaping the global economy, are perhaps similar to the views held by most people. Adding to the mystery is the fund's long-standing practice of not releasing internal documents to the public, which discourages transparency and an independent assessment of fund operations. All of this is beginning to change.

Although the IMF is still not a household word, since 1997 it has been the focus of unprecedented media coverage, academic analysis, and fund introspection. A search of a leading library database reveals that 414 magazine, newspaper, and journal articles were written on the IMF from 1995 through 1996. Over the next two years, this number jumped to 1,560, a 277 percent increase. What explains this rise to prominence of a previously obscure international financial organization? The answer is money, and lots of it, given to some of the world's most populous and wealthy nations who are experiencing their worst recessions since World War II. Worse yet, critics charge that IMF money and advice is not helping.

The IMF currently has financing arrangements with fifty-nine countries—roughly a third of its membership and over a quarter of all countries in the world. In East Asia alone, its major lending initiatives affect 315 million people. Since August 1997, Thailand has received $4 billion in IMF credits, Indonesia $12 billion, and South Korea a record-breaking $21 billion. Russia has taken an additional $11 billion. IMF loan commitments around the world now total $86 billion, and a newly authorized 45 percent increase in its capital base ensures greater lending in the future. Furthermore, the negotiations to establish loan conditions place the fund in the role of a shadowy surrogate government influencing economic policy for supposedly sovereign nations. This role does not endear the IMF to citizens with fresh memories of colonial times. All of this is orchestrated from fund headquarters in Washington, D.C., with a staff of twenty-six hundred people.

Given the unprecedented level of IMF intervention in the world economy and the continuing struggles of borrowing countries, many observers are asking some basic questions: What are taxpayers receiving in exchange for their contributions to the IMF? Does the fund promote international economic stability, as it contends, or does it produce financial chaos? Should the IMF be strengthened or should it be abolished and replaced by market-based alternatives? This book examines these basic questions of mission, operations, and public policy.

OVERVIEW OF THE BOOK

The International Monetary Fund — Financial Medic to the World? assembles sixty-two pertinent and influential magazine, newspaper, and journal articles, opinion pieces, and government documents, representing a cross section of views, into an anthology that examines the history, operations, and performance of the IMF. Part 1 presents a brief overview of the origins of the fund, including a discussion of the competing British and American plans and the final agreement reached at Bretton Woods, New Hampshire. Part 1 also presents the fund's description of its organization and operations along with six selections written by outside analysts that address important questions concerning fund operations.

Given this institutional overview, part 2 looks at the effectiveness of IMF financing programs. The first selection, written by an IMF staff economist, reviews the leading studies on the effect of fund programs. The conclusions may surprise you. Next, using the historical record, critics question the usefulness of the IMF and propose fundamental reforms.

Part 3 explores the history, operations, and effectiveness of IMF "conditionality," the often austere terms and conditions of IMF loans. Does conditionality entice recipient governments to implement politically difficult but needed economic reforms or does it contribute to financial crises and political inaction? Or, alternatively, does conditionality have little effect due to lack of enforcement?

Part 4 examines the pros and cons of recent IMF financing initiatives in Mexico, East Asia, and Russia. Are the current problems in East Asia and Russia the result of earlier IMF activities in Mexico? Are fund policy prescriptions tailored to the unique circumstances of each country or are they "off-the-shelf" remedies that more often than not prolong and deepen financial crises?

Part 5 explores "mission creep" at the fund, specifically, the extent to which financing decisions are, or should be, influenced by considerations of human rights, government corruption, and geopolitics and international security.

Part 6 explores the fundamental question: Is the IMF ineffective, unnecessary, and obsolete or is it indispensable for international financial stability? Should the IMF be abolished or should it be strengthened? Read the arguments and decide for yourself. For convenience, complete bibliographic information on the studies referenced in the selected readings is included at the end of the book.

PART ONE

THE ORIGINS AND OPERATIONS OF THE INTERNATIONAL MONETARY FUND

The first half of the twentieth century experienced two world wars and a global depression. The European continent suffered greatly in both wars, and the United States was devastated by the Great Depression. From these conditions arose a desire to create a new international monetary system that would address balance of payments deficits, substantially preserve national independence yet eliminate "beggar-thy-neighbor" trade policies such as competitive devaluations, and encourage stable exchange rates without being wholly reliant on gold to back currencies. The discussions that ensued led to a gathering of forty-four nations in July 1944 in Bretton Woods, New Hampshire, to draft the Articles of Agreement for the International Monetary Fund and the International Bank for Reconstruction and Development (the World Bank). The Bretton Woods conference created an institutional structure to address the concerns of the time—one that the framers hoped would lead to global prosperity.

Part I looks at the origins and operations of the IMF. Leland Yeager presents a brief overview of the background and purposes of the fund. Next, the most widely cited article on fund operations answers the question What is the International Monetary Fund? The article, written by the IMF, explains quotas and voting rights, organizational structure, exchange arrangements, the source of IMF funds, the operation of financing programs, and interest charges.

The remaining six selections address important questions concerning IMF operations. The first selection, written by Lawrence McQuillan, questions the claim that U.S. contributions to the fund are costless. The next piece, written by David Sanger, examines who actually controls the IMF. Is it a majoritarian organization or an arm of the U.S. Treasury? Next, Judy Shelton argues that there is a better alternative to the "mixed" exchange-rate regime currently supervised by the fund. The remaining three selections, written by Louis Uchitelle, David Sacks and Peter Thiel, and Roland Vaubel, look at how IMF financing programs operate in the real world and expose the huge subsidies that borrowers receive from member governments through IMF loans.

THE HISTORY OF THE INTERNATIONAL MONETARY FUND

1–22 July 1944

The IMF is established at the United Nations
International Monetary and Financial Conference
held in Bretton Woods, New Hampshire.
The Articles of Agreement are signed
by forty-four nations.

27 December 1945

Articles of Agreement enter into force after
ratification by twenty-nine countries.

8–18 March 1946

Board of governors holds first meeting in
Savannah, Georgia, to adopt bylaws and elect
first executive directors. Governors decide to
locate the fund's headquarters in
Washington, D.C.

6 May 1946

Twelve executive directors hold first meeting
in Washington, D.C.

1 March 1947

Operations begin.

8 May 1947

First drawing (by France).

The International Monetary Fund: Background and Purposes

Leland B. Yeager

This selection was excerpted from Leland Yeager's book *International Monetary Relations: Theory, History, and Policy*, published in 1976. Leland Yeager is the Ludwig von Mises Distinguished Professor Emeritus of Economics at Auburn University and Paul Goodloe McIntire Professor of Economics Emeritus at the University of Virginia.

The IMF resulted from lengthy discussions of separate American, British, Canadian, and French proposals drafted during World War II. The British "Keynes Plan" envisaged an international clearing union that would create an international means of payment called "bancor." Each country's central bank would accept payments in bancor without limit from other central banks. Debtor countries could obtain bancor by using automatic overdraft facilities with the clearing union. The limits to these overdrafts would be generous and would grow automatically with each member country's total of imports and exports. Charges of 1 or 2 percent a year would be levied on both creditor and debtor positions in excess of specified limits. This slight discouragement to unbalanced positions did not rule out the possibility of large imbalances covered by automatic American credits to the rest of the world, perhaps amounting to many billions of dollars. Part of the credits might eventually turn out to be gifts because of the provision for canceling creditor-country claims not used in international trade within a specified time period. The rival American plan took its name from Harry Dexter White of the U.S. Treasury. White rejected the overdraft principle and the possibility of automatic American credits in vast and only loosely limited amounts. Instead, he proposed a currency pool to which members would make definite contributions only and from which countries might borrow to tide themselves over short-term balance of payments deficits. Both plans looked forward to a world substantially free of controls imposed for balance of payments purposes. Both sought exchange-rate stability without restoring an international gold standard and without destroying national independence in monetary and fiscal policies. According to the usual interpretation, the British plan put more emphasis on national independence and the American plan on exchange-rate stability reminiscent of the gold standard. The compromise finally reached resembled the American proposal more than the British.

The Articles of Agreement of the International Monetary Fund (and also the articles of its sister institution, the International Bank for Reconstruction and Development [the World Bank]) were drafted and signed by representatives of forty-four nations at Bretton Woods, New Hampshire, in July 1944. By the end of 1945, enough countries had ratified the agreement to bring the fund into existence. The board of governors first met in March 1946, adopted bylaws, and decided to locate the fund's headquarters in Washington, D.C. One year later the fund was ready for actual exchange operations.

According to its Articles of Agreement, the purposes of the International Monetary Fund are to promote international monetary cooperation, facilitate the expansion of international trade for the sake of high levels of employment and real income, promote exchange-rate stability and avoid competitive depreciation, work for a multilateral system of current international payments and for elimination of exchange controls over current transactions, create confidence among member nations and give them the opportunity to correct balance of payments maladjustments while avoiding measures destructive of national and international prosperity, and make balance of payments disequilibriums shorter and less severe than they would otherwise be.

Recognizing that these goals could not all be achieved promptly, Article XIV of the agreement provided for a postwar "transitional period" during which the member countries might violate the general ban on exchange controls over current account transactions. No definite length for the transition period was stated, but countries maintaining exchange controls more than five years after the start of fund operations (that is, beyond 1952) were expected to consult the fund about them every year. Actually, consultations about general economic policies have become an annual routine with all members, not just with members in violation of the standard decontrol obligations. Such consultations, requiring voluminous documentation, have even become the main activity of the fund, the one using up the most man-hours.

The "purposes" just mentioned are vague. More specifically, the fund provides drawing rights (in effect, loans) to help its members meet temporary deficits without resort to exchange controls, exchange-rate adjustments, or internal deflation. Member countries are supposed to "live with" or "ride out" purely temporary deficits, drawing on the fund when necessary to supplement their own accumulated reserves of gold and foreign exchange. The fund is not meant to use up its resources, however, hopelessly palliating "fundamental disequilibrium." A country faced with a "fundamental" deficit in its international transactions may be expected to seek a remedy in devaluing its currency. An opposite situation of "fundamental" balance of payments surplus would presumably call for upward revaluation. Such adjustments were expected to be infrequent.

[Editors' note: For a description of the conceptual role of IMF financing programs in the context of balance of payments accounts, see the appendix starting on page 230.]

THE INTERNATIONAL MONETARY FUND AT A GLANCE

Current Membership

182 countries

Governing Bodies

Board of governors, interim committee,
and executive board

Managing Director and
Chairman of the Executive Board

Michel Camdessus, from France,
assumed office in January 1987

First Deputy Managing Director

Stanley Fischer, from the United States,
assumed office in September 1994

Staff

Approximately 2,600
from 122 countries

Total Quotas

$205 billion

Total Loan Commitments
as of 31 December 1998

$86 billion

What Is the International Monetary Fund?

International Monetary Fund

This selection was excerpted from an IMF booklet *What Is the International Monetary Fund?* published in 1998.

The IMF's membership now numbers 182 countries. Membership is open to every country that conducts its own foreign policy and is willing to adhere to the IMF charter of rights and obligations. All major countries are now members of the IMF. The formerly centrally planned economies of Eastern Europe and the former Soviet Union have become members and are at various stages of completing their transition to market economies. Members can leave the IMF whenever they wish. Cuba, Czechoslovakia (now the Czech Republic and Slovak Republic), Indonesia, and Poland have in fact done so in the past, although all except Cuba eventually rejoined the institution.

QUOTAS AND VOTING

On joining the IMF, each member country contributes a certain sum of money called a quota subscription, as a sort of credit union deposit. Quotas serve various purposes. First, they form a pool of money that the IMF can draw from to lend to members in financial difficulty. Second, they are the basis for determining how much the contributing member can borrow from the IMF or receives from the IMF in periodic allocations of special assets known as SDRs (special drawing rights). The more a member contributes, the more it can borrow in time of need. Third, they determine the voting power of the member. The IMF itself, through an analysis of each country's wealth and economic performance, sets the amount of the quota the member will contribute. The richer the country, the larger its quota. Quotas are reviewed every five years and can be raised or lowered according to the needs of the IMF and the economic prosperity of the member. In 1946, the then thirty-five members of the IMF paid in $7.6 billion; by 1999, IMF members had paid in $205 billion. A proposal

TABLE 1.   IMF Quotas, Governors, and Votes as of 4 January 1999

Member	Quota (billions of U.S. dollars)	Quota (percent of total)	Governor	Votes (number)	Votes (percent of total)
LARGEST QUOTAS					
United States	$37.43	18.25%	Robert E. Rubin	265,518	17.78%
Germany	11.63	5.67	Hans Tietmeyer	82,665	5.53
Japan	11.63	5.67	Kiichi Miyazawa	82,665	5.53
France	10.46	5.10	D. Strauss-Kahn	74,396	4.98
United Kingdom	10.46	5.10	Gordon Brown	74,396	4.98
Saudi Arabia	7.24	3.53	Ibrahim A. Al-Assaf	51,556	3.45
Italy	6.48	3.16	Carlo A. Ciampi	46,157	3.09
Canada	6.10	2.97	Paul Martin	43,453	2.91
Russia	6.09	2.97	Viktor Gerashchenko	43,381	2.90
Netherlands	4.86	2.37	A. H. E. M. Wellink	34,692	2.32
China	4.78	2.33	Dai Xianglong	34,102	2.28
SMALLEST QUOTAS					
Tonga	$0.0071	0.003%	K. T. Fakafanua	300	0.02%
Bhutan	0.0064	0.003	Sonam Wangchuk	295	0.02
Kiribati	0.0056	0.003	Beniamina Tinga	290	0.02
Micronesia	0.0049	0.002	John Ehsa	285	0.02
Marshall Islands	0.0035	0.002	Ruben R. Zackhras	275	0.02
Palau	0.0032	0.002	T. E. Remengesau Jr.	272	0.02

SOURCE: International Monetary Fund, "IMF Quotas, Governors, and Voting Power, General Department and Special Drawing Rights Department," available from http://www.imf.org/external/np/sec/memdir/members.htm; Internet; accessed 13 January 1999.

to raise quotas to about $280 billion is awaiting approval by at least 85 percent of the IMF's membership. The United States, with the world's largest economy, contributes most to the IMF, providing about 18 percent of total quotas (about $37 billion); Palau, which became a member in December 1997, has the smallest quota, contributing about $3.2 million [see table 1, which was created by the editors].

The founding nations reasoned in 1944 that the IMF would function most efficiently and decisions would be made most responsibly by relating members' voting power directly to the amount of money they contribute to the institution through their quotas. Those who contribute most to the

IMF are therefore given the strongest voice in determining its policies. Thus, the United States now has more than 265,000 votes, or about 18 percent of the total; Palau has 272, or 0.02 percent of total votes.

ORGANIZATION

Many people view the IMF as an institution of great authority and independence and assume that it decides the best economic policies for its members to pursue, dictates these decisions to the membership, and then makes sure its members conform. Nothing could be further from the truth. Far from being dictated to by the IMF, the membership itself dictates to the IMF the policies it will follow. The chain of command runs clearly from the governments of member countries to the IMF and not vice versa. In setting out the obligations of individual members to the IMF, or in working out details of lending arrangements with a member, the IMF acts not on its own but as an intermediary between the will of the majority of the membership and the individual member country.

The top link of the chain of command is the board of governors, one from each member, and an equal number of alternate governors. As the governors and their alternates are ministers of finance or heads of central banks, they speak authoritatively for their governments. The oddly named interim committee (it has existed since the 1970s) gives them advice on the functioning of the international monetary system, and a joint IMF/ World Bank Development Committee advises them on the special needs of poorer countries. Since governors and alternates are fully occupied in their own capitals, they gather only on the occasion of annual meetings to deal formally and as a group with IMF matters.

During the rest of the year, the governors communicate the wishes of their governments for the IMF's day-to-day work to their representatives who form the IMF's executive board at headquarters in Washington. The twenty-four executive directors, meeting at least three times a week in formal session, supervise the implementation of policies set by member governments through the board of governors. At present, eight executive directors represent eight individual countries: China, France, Germany, Japan, Russia, Saudi Arabia, the United Kingdom, and the United States. Sixteen other executive directors represent groupings of the remaining countries. The executive board rarely makes its decisions on the basis of formal voting but relies on the formation of consensus among its members, a practice that minimizes confrontation on sensitive issues and promotes acceptance of the decisions ultimately made.

The IMF has a staff of about twenty-six hundred, headed by a managing director, who is also chairman of the executive board, which appoints him. By tradition, the managing director is a European or at least a non-American. (The president of the World Bank is traditionally a U.S. national.) The international staff comes from 122 countries and comprises mainly economists but also statisticians, research scholars, experts in public finance and taxation and in financial systems and central banking, linguists, writers and editors, and support personnel. Most staff members work at IMF headquarters in Washington, though a few are assigned to small offices in Paris, Geneva, Tokyo, and at the United Nations in New York or represent the IMF on temporary assignment in member countries. (At present, seventy "resident representatives" are assigned to sixty-four member countries.) Unlike executive directors, who represent specific countries, staff members are international civil servants; they are responsible to the membership as a whole in carrying out IMF policies and do not represent national interests.

EXCHANGE ARRANGEMENTS

In its early years, all members joining the IMF undertook to follow the same method of calculating the exchange value of their money. They did so according to what was called the par (equal) value system. In those days, the United States defined the value of its dollar in terms of gold, so that one ounce of gold was equal to exactly $35. The U.S. government stood behind this definition and would exchange gold for dollars at that rate on demand. On joining the IMF, all other members had to define the exchange value of their money in terms of gold (of the weight and fineness in effect on 1 July 1944) or in terms of the U.S. dollar. Members kept the value of their money within 1 percent of this par value, and if they felt a change would help their economy, they discussed the contemplated change with other members in the forum of the IMF and obtained their consent before implementing it. The par value system had the advantage of keeping currencies stable and predictable, a great help to international investors, traders, and travelers, but over the years it also developed

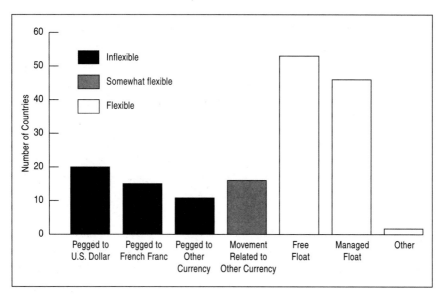

FIGURE 1.   How Members Determine Exchange Values

a number of disadvantages. It was a wrenching experience, attended by great political risk, for a government to change the par value of its currency, and each change in the par value of a major currency tended to become a crisis for the whole system. The par value system served the world well for about twenty-five years. It came to an end in the early 1970s, however, when U.S. gold reserves proved inadequate to meet the demand for gold in exchange for the dollars presented by those who regarded gold at $35 an ounce to be an irresistible bargain.

Since the abandonment of the par value system, the membership of the IMF has agreed to allow each member to choose its own method of determining the exchange value of its money. The only requirements are that the member no longer base the value of its currency on gold and that it inform other members about precisely how it is determining the currency's value. The choice is wide [see figure 1]. Many large industrial nations allow their currencies to float freely; their money is worth whatever the markets are prepared to pay for them. Some countries try to manage the float by buying and selling their own currencies to influence the market (a practice known inelegantly as a "dirty float"). Other countries peg the value of their money to that of a major currency or group of currencies so that, for example, as the French franc rises in value, their own currency rises too. Many European countries currently keep the value of their individual currencies within a predetermined range of other currencies in the group. The European Economic and Monetary Union, however, launched on 1 January 1999, requires, for eleven members of the European Union, transition to a single currency, the euro.

SOURCE OF FINANCE

The quota subscriptions (or membership fees) referred to earlier constitute the largest source of money at the IMF's disposal. Quotas are now in theory worth about $205 billion, although in practice this sum is deceptively large. Because member countries pay 75 percent of their quotas in domestic money, and because most national currencies are rarely in demand outside the countries issuing them, approximately half of the money on the IMF's balance sheets cannot be used. Although there are occasional exceptions, only twenty or so currencies are borrowed from the IMF in the course of a typical year, and most potential borrowers from the IMF want only the major convertible currencies: the U.S. dollar, the Japanese yen, the deutsche mark, the pound sterling, and the French franc.

As each member has a right to borrow from the IMF several times the amount it has paid in as a quota subscription, quotas may not provide enough cash to meet the borrowing needs of members in a period of great stress in the world economy. To deal with this eventuality, the IMF has had since 1962 a line of credit, now worth about $24 billion, with a number of governments and banks throughout the world. This line of credit, called the *general arrangements to borrow*, is renewed every five years. The IMF pays interest on whatever it borrows under these arrangements and undertakes to repay the loan in five years. These arrangements have been strengthened by a decision on the *new arrangements to borrow*, which brings the total of the two arrangements to $40–$45 billion.

FINANCIAL ASSISTANCE

The IMF lends money only to member countries with payments problems, that is, to countries that do not take in enough foreign currency to pay for what they buy from other countries. The money a country takes in comes from what it earns from exports, from providing services (such as banking and insurance), and from what tourists spend there. Money also comes from overseas investment and, in the case of poorer countries, in the form of aid from better-off countries. Countries, like people, however, can spend more than they take in, making up the difference for a time by borrowing until their credit is exhausted, as eventually it will be. When this happens, the country must face a number of unpleasant realities, not the least of which are commonly a loss in the buying power of its currency and a forced reduction in its imports from other countries. A country in that situation can turn for assistance to the IMF, which will for a time lend it foreign exchange to help it put right what has gone wrong in its economic life, with a view to stabilizing its currency and strengthening its trade [see figure 2, which was created by the editors to explain the fund's lending facilities].

A member country with a payments problem can immediately withdraw from the IMF the 25 percent of its quota that it paid in gold or a convertible currency. If the 25 percent of quota is insufficient for its needs, a member in greater difficulty may request more money from the IMF and can over a period of years borrow cumulatively three times what it paid in as a quota subscription. This limit, however, does not apply to loans under the IMF's special facilities, including the supplemental reserve facility (SRF), created in December 1997 to provide short-term financing to members faced with a sudden and disruptive loss of market confidence (Korea was the first country to use the SRF).

In lending to a member more than the initial 25 percent of quota, the IMF is guided by two principles. First, the pool of currencies at the IMF's disposal exists for the benefit of the entire membership. Each member borrowing another's currency from the pool is therefore expected to return it as soon as its payments problem has been solved. In this way, the funds can revolve through the membership and are available whenever the need arises. Second, before the IMF releases any money from the pool, the member must demonstrate how it intends to solve its payments problem so that it can repay the IMF within its normal repayment period of three to five years (which in certain cases can be extended up to ten years). The logic behind these requirements is simple. A country with a payments problem is spending more than it is taking in. Unless economic reform

FIGURE 2.   IMF Financing Facilities

General Balance of Payments Assistance Facilities (General Resources Account)

REGULAR FACILITIES

Reserve tranche: Equal to the difference between a member's quota and the fund's holdings of its currency in the general resources account. A member may withdraw up to the full amount of its reserve tranche at any time subject to a "balance of payments need," which is not challenged by the IMF. This withdrawal does not constitute a use of IMF credit and is not subject to charges or an obligation to repay with hard currency.

First credit tranche: Equal to 25 percent of a member's quota. First credit tranche drawings are contingent on a member's demonstration of "reasonable efforts to overcome their balance of payments difficulties" (low-level conditionality).

Second–fourth (upper) credit tranches: Drawings above 25 percent of quota. Upper credit tranche drawings are made in installments or phased and are released when performance targets are met (high-level conditionality). Such drawings are associated with standby and extended arrangements.

Standby arrangement (SBA): SBA gives a member the right to draw, usually quarterly, a specified amount during a prescribed period provided that performance criteria are met. These arrangements are for short-term assistance and typically cover a twelve- to eighteen-month period (although they can extend up to three years). Repayments are made within three years and three months to five years of each drawing.

Extended fund facility (EFF): Similar to SBA except that the assistance is generally for longer periods and for larger amounts. EFF arrangements are for medium-term assistance, usually three years, but can be extended for a fourth and are designed to correct balance of payments difficulties resulting from structural problems. The phasing and performance criteria are comparable to those for SBA, although phasing on a semiannual basis is possible. Repayments are made within four and a half to ten years of each drawing.

Supplemental reserve facility (SRF): Additional resources available under SBA or EFF, for up to one year, for a member experiencing exceptional short-term balance of payments difficulties resulting from a sudden loss of market confidence reflected in its capital account and currency reserves. Financing is available in two or more tranches; the first tranche is available at the time of approval and normally coincides with approval of the corresponding SBA or EFF. Repayments are made within one and a half years of each disbursement,

FIGURE 2. *(continued)*

with a possible one-year extension subject to approval. Borrowers pay a surcharge of at least three hundred basis points.

SPECIAL FACILITIES

Compensatory and contingency financing facility (CCFF): The export compensatory element provides financing to a member experiencing a balance of payments need related to a temporary shortfall in export earnings. The cereal element compensates for a temporary increase in cereal import costs. The contingency element helps a member with a current IMF arrangement keep its adjustment program on track when faced with unforeseen adverse external shocks.

Buffer stock financing facility (BSFF): Provides financing for a member's contribution to an approved international buffer stock, provided the member demonstrates a balance of payments need.

SPECIAL MECHANISMS

Emergency financing mechanism (EFM): A set of procedures to facilitate rapid executive board approval of IMF financial support while ensuring proper conditionality. EFM is used in circumstances where a member faces an external accounts crisis.

Support for currency stabilization funds: IMF financial support, within the framework of an upper credit tranche, for a member's establishment of a currency stabilization fund designed to bolster confidence, for a transitional period, in an exchange-rate-based stabilization strategy.

Emergency assistance: Emergency financial assistance to a member facing balance of payments difficulties caused by a natural disaster or a postconflict situation. Assistance is usually limited to 25 percent of quota, provided that the member is cooperating with the IMF to find a solution to its problems. In most cases, emergency assistance is followed by an arrangement with the IMF under one of its regular facilities.

CONCESSIONAL FINANCING FACILITIES (highly concessional IMF loans and grants to countries. These are not purchases by one country of another country's currency)

Enhanced structural adjustment facility (ESAF): A highly concessional loan (0.5 percent annual interest rate) to a low-income member facing protracted balance of payments problems. ESAF supports medium-term, three-year adjustment programs that emphasize macroeconomic and structural reforms.

FIGURE 2.   (*continued*)

Semiannual disbursements are dependent on meeting performance targets regarding key quantitative and structural variables. ESAF loans are repaid in ten equal semiannual installments, beginning five and a half years and ending ten years after the date of each semiannual disbursement.

Heavily indebted poor country (HIPC) debt initiative: Exceptional assistance intended to help eligible countries who follow sound reform policies reduce their external debt burden to sustainable levels. The IMF provides grants to HIPCs that are used to retire ESAF obligations incurred during six-year debt-restructuring programs.

SOURCES: David M. Cheney, ed., "Financial Facilities and Policies: IMF Financing Helps Members Pursue Sound Policies," in *IMF Survey Supplement on the Fund* (Washington, D.C.: International Monetary Fund, 1997), pp. 12–15; David M. Cheney, ed., "Debt Strategy: IMF Strategy Emphasizes Adequate Financial Support," in *IMF Survey Supplement on the Fund* (Washington, D.C.: International Monetary Fund, 1997), pp. 15–17; and IMF press release number 97/59, "IMF Approves Supplemental Reserve Facility," 17 December 1997, available on-line at http://www.imf.org/external/np/sec/pr/1997/pr9759.htm.

takes place, it will continue to spend more than it takes in. Since the IMF has an obligation to the whole membership to preserve the financial integrity of its transactions, it lends only on condition that the member use the borrowed money effectively. The borrowing country therefore undertakes to initiate a series of reforms that will eradicate the source of the payments difficulty and prepare the ground for "high-quality" economic growth. Along with its request for a loan, the potential borrower presents to the IMF a plan of reform, typically undertaking to reduce government expenditure, tighten monetary policy, and deal with certain "structural" weaknesses (such as the need to privatize inefficient public enterprises). More recently, the IMF's experience with its member countries' adjustment efforts has shown that reforms need to be broader and deeper to achieve high-quality growth. This means more attention to ensuring that countries have adequate social safety nets in place to cushion the effects of adjustment on the poor parts of the population, good-equality government spending (including more attention to spending on health and education), and good "governance" (with minimal scope for corruption and with openness of fiscal policy and policymaking).

The specifics of each IMF-supported adjustment program are selected by the member, and hence the program of reform is the member's, not the IMF's. The IMF's main concern is that the policy changes are sufficient to overcome the member's payments problem and do not cause avoidable harm to other members. Depending on the seriousness of the payments problem and the amount the member wishes to borrow, the executive directors, representing the entire membership, judge whether the reform measures are in fact sufficient and whether the IMF can reasonably expect repayment.

If the executive directors are satisfied that the reforms will solve the problem, the loan is disbursed in installments (usually over one to three years) tied to the member's progress in putting the reforms into effect. If all goes well, the loan will be repaid on time, and the member, with necessary reforms now in place, will come out of the experience economically stronger.

[Editor's Note: A country borrows (or draws) from the fund's general resources account by using its own currency to buy (purchase) the currency of another member country at an exchange rate dominated in SDRs, the fund's own unit of account. A drawing on the IMF by a country raises the fund's holdings of the country's currency but reduces its holdings of other currencies by an equal amount. The composition of the fund's resources changes but not the total amount as measured in SDRs. Countries are charged a fee for each drawing. The country repays the drawing over a specified period by using member currencies acceptable to the fund to repurchase its own currency at the prevailing SDR exchange rate.]

CHARGES

If a member borrows money from the IMF, it pays various charges to cover the IMF's operational expenses and to recompense the member whose currency it is borrowing. At present, the borrower pays in service charges and commitment fees about ¼ of 1 percent of the amount borrowed and in interest charges about 4½ percent (except for the structural adjustment mechanism for which interest charges are much less and the supplemental reserve facility for which interest charges are considerably higher). An IMF member earns interest on its quota contributions only if other members borrow its currency from the pool. How much the member earns varies but lately has been about 4 percent of the amount of its currency that other members have borrowed from the IMF. Both the interest charges a borrower pays to the IMF and the recompense a creditor receives from the IMF are slightly below market rates in keeping with the cooperative spirit of the institution.

The next six selections, written by outside analysts, address important questions concerning IMF operations and their effect on donor and recipient countries. Specifically, the selections examine member contributions to the IMF, fund decision making, exchange-rate arrangements, the operation of financing programs, and the subsidization of interest rates.

■ Are U.S. contributions to the IMF costless?

International Monetary Fund Quotas and the Federal Budget

Lawrence J. McQuillan

Lawrence McQuillan, coeditor of this volume, is a research fellow at the Hoover Institution at Stanford University.

Although the International Monetary Fund had at least $31 billion available for lending (see figure 3), it nevertheless sought a quota increase of 45 percent under its Eleventh General Review of Quotas. On 23 October 1998, Congress approved the requested $15 billion U.S. quota increase

FIGURE 3.   IMF Financial Position as of 20 July 1998

Currency Holdings from Members' Quotas (billions of U.S. dollars)	$195
Unusable currency holdings due to some members' weak balance of payments and currency reserve positions	−65
Usable Currency Holdings	130
Members' currency purchases (outstanding credit)	−70
Available Resources	60
Undrawn credit commitments	−17
Uncommitted Resources	43
Reserves	−12
Resources Available for Operations	$31
Additional Resources Available to the IMF	
General Arrangements to Borrow (line of credit from twelve countries)	$22.7
Special Arrangement with Saudi Arabia (line of credit)	$2.0
Gold Holdings (IMF controls 9.6 percent of the world's gold holdings)	$32.0
New Arrangements to Borrow (line of credit from twenty-five countries; in effect as of 17 November 1998)	$22.7

SOURCE: Harold J. Johnson, *International Monetary Fund: Observations on Its Financial Condition,* testimony before the Joint Economic Committee, 23 July 1998 (Washington, D.C.: U.S. General Accounting Office, 1998).

from $37 billion to $52 billion. How will this increase affect the federal budget? Not at all, according to U.S. Treasury secretary Robert Rubin. "Over the last 50 years, our contribution to the IMF has not cost the taxpayer one dime." How can this be true? The answer is hidden in the arcane procedures of Washington budgeting.

When $15 billion is transferred from the U.S. Treasury to the IMF, the fund, in return, credits the U.S. Treasury with 11 billion in special drawing rights (SDRs), the fund's own money. Technically, this swap is considered a fair exchange with no federal budget implications. The transfer, however, does impose several real costs on society.

First, the Treasury must acquire $15 billion through taxation or borrowing, both of which reduce the amount of funds available to private citizens and distort market incentives. Second, the United States earns interest only on that portion of its quota that has been borrowed by other IMF members from the pool of currencies. Lately, IMF interest rates have been less than 4 percent, well below alternative market rates. Third, the United States can withdraw at its discretion only that portion of its cash contribution equivalent to the dollar borrowings of other IMF members (the reserve tranche). Fourth, federal contributions to the IMF come with an opportunity cost—money retained by the fund is not available for alternative federal spending programs.

Although many in Washington argue that U.S. contributions to the IMF are costless, there are in fact real costs imposed on U.S. taxpayers. Once again, there is no free lunch.

■ Who controls the IMF?

Runaway Agency or U.S. Pawn?

David E. Sanger

This selection was excerpted from an article by New York Times staff reporter David Sanger, "As Economies Fail, the IMF Is Rife with Recriminations," published in the Times on 2 October 1998.

Everywhere else in the world, politicians and businessmen insist that one of the biggest problems with the IMF is that, contrary to the view of the Congress, it acts as the United States Treasury's lap dog. Ask in Djakarta or Moscow, and the response is the same: The fund never ventures far without looking back for the approving nod of its master.

That view may not be far wrong. In ordinary times, the United States largely leaves its hands off, as the fund's executive board—made up of twenty-four representatives of the 182 member nations—delves into the intricacies of budget policy in Greece or banking regulation in Argentina. "Surveillance" of the world's economies is the fund's main activity.

When the United States weighs in, however, is when the fund is called on to rescue a country in deep trouble. Only then does the fund—and the Treasury—have the leverage to extract commitments in return for billions in aid. In theory, the American influence is limited: It has an 18.5 percent vote in the fund. Germany, Japan, France, and Britain have about 5 percent each. But in practice the United States usually gets its way, exercising its influence behind the scenes, often in interactions between Mr. Fischer [first deputy managing director of the IMF] and Mr. Summers [deputy secretary of the U.S. Treasury].

The bailouts of Russia and South Korea were prime examples of how Washington muscles into the fund's turf as soon as major American strategic interests are involved. Last Christmas [1997], as South Korea slipped within days of running out of hard currency to pay its debts in December, it sent a secret envoy, Kim Kihwan, to work out a rescue package. "I didn't bother going to the IMF," Mr. Kim recalled recently. "I called Mr. Summers's office at the Treasury from my home in Seoul, flew to Washington and went directly there. I knew that was how this would get done."

Within days the Treasury dispatched David Lipton, its most experienced veteran of emergency bailouts, who is leaving his post as undersecretary for international affairs this month to shadow the IMF's negotiations with the government in Seoul.

Mr. Fischer was displeased. "To make a negotiation effective, it has to be clear who has the authority to do the negotiating," he said.

■ Is there a better alternative to the "mixed" exchange rate regime currently supervised by the IMF?

Time for a New Bretton Woods

Judy Shelton

This selection first appeared in the *Wall Street Journal* on 15 October 1998. Judy Shelton is an economist and serves on the board of Empower America.

It has become all the rage among finance ministers, central bankers, international bureaucrats—even politicians—to talk about the need to reform the "global financial architecture," just as a past generation did at the Bretton Woods monetary conference. It sounds bold, decisive. And with the world teetering on the edge of a financial cliff and staring into the dark economic abyss below, you can expect to keep hearing the word *imperative* as well.

But the rhetoric does not match the reality. When Treasury secretary Robert Rubin calls for stronger government regulation of global finance or President Clinton intones about having to temper "the unruly energies of the global economy," they are not proposing a new Bretton Woods agreement. They are not talking about restoring a fixed exchange-rate system to provide a stable monetary foundation for international trade, much less considering an international monetary system anchored by a dollar convertible into gold. They are merely invoking the powerful imagery of that conference to underscore the seriousness of their intent to protect the world from what they view as the excesses of runaway capitalism.

MONETARY STANDARD

It makes no sense, though, to talk about redesigning the financial architecture without first dealing with the more fundamental problem of defining a monetary standard for measurement. What is the global unit of account for signaling value across borders? How can you expect sound investment flows and a high-performance global economy in the absence of a rational international monetary regime? At a time when developing nations are opting to withdraw from the global economy and abandon free market capitalism rather than be further victimized by currency chaos, Messrs. Clinton and Rubin can ill afford to avoid these questions.

For all the barbs hurled at Indonesia and South Korea for indulging in "crony capitalism," and despite the harsh criticism leveled at Japan for not sufficiently stimulating its economy through government spending, the current economic crisis is largely the result of a world monetary system that has utterly broken down. Price signals are distorted by gyrating currencies that create a house of mirrors atmosphere for asset valuation, leaving investors without an accurate reflection of global economic opportunity and risk. Misdirected capital flows and economic dislocations stem from distorted perceptions about the relative returns from seemingly productive investment projects.

The Clinton administration's wish list for improving the financial workings of the global economy includes such reforms as "increased transparency," tighter government surveillance of financial activities, and additional resources for the International Monetary Fund. Steps have also been taken to bump up government loan guarantees and strengthen the social safety net with financing from the World Bank. These objectives are in keeping with the view that the same Keynesian mechanisms that serve to "tame the cycles of boom and bust" in the domestic economies of advanced nations should be implemented on a global scale. But they have dubious merit if the goal is to perpetuate democratic capitalism around the world. What the world really needs is global monetary reform similar to what was set out at Bretton Woods, New Hampshire, in 1944.

That conference was the culmination of a planning process begun more than two years earlier. Treasury secretary Henry Morgenthau asked his assistant Harry Dexter White to prepare a paper outlining the possibilities for coordinated monetary arrangements among the United States and its allies; ideally, the plan would evolve into a postwar monetary system based on an "international currency." The request was made at 2 A.M. on 14 December 1941—one week after the attack on Pearl Harbor.

White responded with a draft proposal emphasizing that the primary goal should be to stabilize the exchange rates of the Allied countries in order to encourage the flow of productive capital: "The advantages of obtaining stable exchange rates are patent. The maintenance of stable exchange rates means the elimination of exchange risk in international economic and financial transactions. The cost of conducting foreign trade is thereby reduced, and capital flows much more easily to the country where it yields the greatest return because both short-term and long-term investments are greatly hampered by the probability of loss from exchange depreciation. As the expectation of continued stability in foreign exchange rates is strengthened there is also more chance of avoiding the disrupting effects of flights of capital and of inflation."

White viewed protectionism as "World Enemy No. 1" in the economic sphere and argued that weaker nations needed reassurance that the future would not mean a return to the prewar "every nation for itself" pattern of competitive depreciation that led to economic chaos and widespread depression. A stable international monetary system would serve as the stepping-stone away from "shortsighted disastrous economic nationalism" and provide the foundation for a more prosperous world.

Today we again face the problem of economic chaos and possible global depression. But instead of seeking to establish an orderly monetary system so free markets can function properly, our leaders are advocating complex regulatory schemes to enhance the role of government in private commerce. Mr. Rubin passed up the chance to press for international monetary reform last week, commenting only that whatever exchange rate regime a nation chooses—fixed or floating—the nation must be "committed" to it. Yet it is the prevailing do-your-own-thing approach to currency relations that has disrupted financial flows and now threatens to reverse the economic gains from international trade.

You cannot build a new global financial architecture on a foundation of quicksand. Individuals who bring their goods and services to the marketplace need a meaningful unit of account and reliable store of value so they can make logical economic decisions. Entrepreneurial endeavors should not be undercut by monetary manipulation. Government officials who insist on maintaining "flexibility" in the name of national autonomy are resorting to the last refuge of scoundrels. The only ones who are particularly concerned about "sovereign monetary authority" are the sovereigns themselves, not the citizens. Hardworking men and women simply want a form of money they can trust.

Trust is the determining factor for the credibility of a currency. The objective of global monetary reform is not to transfer control over currencies at the national level to a supranational central bank with discretionary authority. The goal is to shift economic power away from government and back to the people by guaranteeing the value of money through the rule of law, not the rule of men.

The best way to do that is to adopt a global gold standard. The Bretton Woods system was a gold exchange standard, not a gold standard. Only the United States was required to convert its currency into gold at a fixed rate, and only foreign central banks were allowed the privilege of redemption. If you corrected for those two flaws—by requiring all countries to maintain convertibility and by granting every individual the right to redeem—you would be back to the classic international gold standard. A modern version would provide the world with a common currency anchored by gold and redeem the promise of global capitalism.

It was not nostalgia that prompted Federal Reserve chairman Alan Greenspan to mention in testimony before Congress that the systemic risks posed when currency mismatches lead to insolvency do not occur under a gold standard. Mr. Greenspan noted that episodes involving the "misuse of capital and its consequences" due to misjudgments by investors were limited and temporary during the latter part of the nineteenth century and the early twentieth century. Yet international capital flows were largely uninhibited during that period. "In an environment where gold standard rules were tight and liquidity constrained," Mr. Greenspan explained, "imbalances were generally aborted before they got out of hand."

The discipline of the gold standard was abandoned following World War I as politicians sought more flexibility to achieve economic objectives—driven by motives similar to those of Mr. Clinton and Mr. Rubin in their efforts to "put a human face on the global economy." But anyone who has seen the damage wrought on citizens of developing nations as the result of today's disorderly, undisciplined, disparate approach to currency relations has reason to doubt the ultimate wisdom of such pronouncements.

So let's have no more gratuitous allusions to Bretton Woods that neglect to focus on the need for a sound monetary regime to serve the needs of an open global economy dedicated to free trade. We must go beyond Bretton Woods and back to the future with a new gold standard.

■ How do IMF financing programs operate in the real world?

A Bad Side of Bailouts: Some Go Unpenalized

Louis Uchitelle

This selection was originally published in the New York Times on 4 December 1997. Louis Uchitelle is a staff reporter for the Times.

Much of the $55 billion that has been pledged by the international community to South Korea—like the $40 billion for Indonesia and the $17 billion for Thailand before it—will ultimately go to lenders who dished out huge sums for risky projects that failed to pay off.

The rescue plan centers on shaky Korean banks. The nation's industrialists, who borrowed billions of dollars from them for new factories and such, have not made enough profit to repay their debts.

The banks, of course, got their money in part from Korean depositors. Other money came from foreigners—big European, American, and Japanese banks, for example—that lent enthusiastically to the Korean banks, in hopes of sharing in the profits.

The bailout money, from the International Monetary Fund, the World Bank, and individual countries, will be channeled through the Korean government and its central bank in great measure to the private banking system. In some cases, foreign creditors may be paid off directly. Mostly, the money will go to salvage some institutions and to close others while paying off creditors. The bailout will, in effect, repay the depositors and the foreign lenders. At the end of last year [1996], South Korean banks owed nearly $60 billion to foreign banks, according to the Bank for International Settlement.

"We keep blaming this crisis on corruption and bad banking practices," said Jeffrey Sachs, a Harvard economist. "But this all happened in the private marketplace. It was so often a case of big foreign lenders pushing their money on the Koreans and the Korean banks enthusiastically taking it in."

Of course, some of the bailout money is earmarked for specific projects, such as public works. That is particularly true of the World Bank's $10 billion contribution. But money that the Korean government is now spending on such projects will simply be freed up for the financial rescue.

All of the Asian aid packages, already totaling more than $100 billion, are prompting many economists and investment bankers to argue anew that bailouts, even when they accomplish their immediate goals, set a bad precedent. By making the lenders whole, they encourage more careless lending and fresh crises.

"If we practice bailing out countries whenever they get into trouble," said Richard Cooper, a Harvard economist, "then lenders everywhere will come to count on that and they will continue to make loans they should not make."

That view, widely held, is producing numerous proposals for change. Mr. Cooper suggests that new regulations should be adopted by all countries that would cause the owners of banks—the shareholders—to lose their investments in such situations. That would make lenders more cautious, reducing bank failures and the need for bailouts. Robert Hormats, a vice president of Goldman, Sachs, argues that developing countries should adopt capital controls, dictating how loans can be dispersed, particularly those from abroad. That, too, could force lenders to be more cautious.

Henry Kaufman, an economist and money manager, says a new layer of international supervision and lending standards is needed. "There is simply no effort today to manage global liquidity," he said.

A national bailout is the only tool readily available today to reverse financial crises that a government cannot handle on its own. These crises are almost always rooted in the unrealistic view of lenders and borrowers that they will profit. When those profit hopes were dashed in Asia in recent months, devaluations, bankruptcies, and bank failures followed.

The IMF will feed the $55 billion to South Korea in stages. The money will go to the Ministry of Finance or the central bank, where it will augment Korean government funds. The additional funds may help restore confidence in the country and stabilize the slide in its currency.

Or it may be used to directly solve the banking crisis.

A Korean bank, for example, may have made a five-year, $100 million loan to an auto company, which has defaulted. The bank may have received its funds from $100 million in six-month loans from American and Japanese banks.

As long as the Korean economy seemed sound, even booming, the foreign banks were willing to roll over these short-term loans. Indeed, they were eager to do so because they were lending to Korean banks at much higher rates than they would charge domestic customers. But in the current crisis the American and Japanese banks, fearful of losing money, want quick repayment. And new lending from abroad dries up.

With the IMF bailout, the foreign banks may choose to roll over their loans, expecting that, in time, they will be repaid in full. That happened in Mexico. The $48 billion that was made available to the country, $20 billion of it from the United States, reassured most foreign investors, and they left their money in place. But the big Mexican debtor was the government, while in Asia's crisis, the private sector owes the money.

If the foreign banks—American and Japanese in this example—insist on quick repayment, the Korean government can do this as well, with its newfound money. Or the process can be less direct. The Ministry of Finance can buy the bad loans from the Seoul bank. The Seoul bank, in turn, buys foreign currency with the proceeds and repays the American and Japanese banks.

A similar reimbursement process functions for Korean depositors whose money has gone to bad loans. The Korean government can replenish the deposits, in whole or in part, by buying up the bad loans, using general funds to do so. In this case, the IMF bailout adds to the government's available funds.

But for Joseph E. Stiglitz, chief economist at the World Bank, the bailout solution is unlikely to deter the unrealistic lending practices that inject money from all parts of the world into a Korea or a Thailand.

"To the extent that private investors who made bad decisions are bailed out," he said in a speech, "their incentives will be distorted, exacerbating the problems governments face in trying to stabilize capital flows."

■ How big a subsidy do borrowers receive from member governments through IMF loans?

The IMF's Big Wealth Transfer

David Sacks and Peter Thiel

This selection first appeared in the *Wall Street Journal* on 13 March 1998. David Sacks is a research fellow at the Independent Institute in Oakland, California. Peter Thiel heads Thiel Capital International LLC, a hedge fund based in Palo Alto, California.

In March 1998, as a result of the crisis in Asia, President Clinton pushed Congress to spend an extra $18 billion on International Monetary Fund "loans." The administration has promised the American taxpayer that these bailouts won't cost anything because, in the past, troubled trade partners have repaid. A case in point is Mexico, which paid back its $40 billion loan from early 1995 ahead of schedule. So what's the problem?

There are several, actually.

First, the fact that Mexico repaid its debt does not imply that anyone else will. In fact, the IMF already has a number of deadbeat debtors on its dole, such as Russia and Kenya.

It's elementary that a loan is either repaid or defaulted on. But that binary choice certainty tells us nothing about the relative likelihood of these possibilities. Implying that a repaid loan had a payback probability of 100 percent is like implying that a defaulted loan had a payback probability of 0 percent. If that were true, nobody would make bad loans.

And this is the second big problem with claims that these bailouts are cost-free, even if they're repaid.

PROSPECTIVE RISK

Capital markets evaluate credit risks based on the likelihood of repayment, before a loan is made. The higher the prospective risk of default, the higher the interest rate. To wit, Brazilian bonds are riskier than Swiss bonds and therefore Brazilian borrowers must compensate investors with higher yields.

In assessing a loan's prudence, the critical question is whether the interest rate is commensurate with the risk. To the extent that the IMF sets below-market rates, the recipient governments effectively receive handouts from the United States and Western Europe.

And this is what is taking place. Recent IMF packages to South Korea, Thailand, and Indonesia involve interest rates ranging from 4.6 percent to 4.8 percent on dollar-denominated debt with a maturity of three years. Even the U.S. government has to pay substantially more (about 5.5 percent) for debt of that term. What this means is that, even if there were no risk of default at all, American taxpayers would still be losing money because the rates at which they are lending dollars are lower than the rates at which they are borrowing dollars.

The world's bond traders have priced East Asian credit risk rather differently from the IMF. In December 1997, while negotiations were taking place with bank creditors in New York, the state-guaranteed Korean Development Bank attempted to issue $2 billion worth of bonds at a 500-basis-point premium over U.S. Treasurys (offering annual yields of 10.5 percent in dollars). This premium was too low, and the paucity of buyers forced lead underwriter J.P. Morgan to cancel the offering. At the time, secondary South Korean sovereign debt was trading at a spread of 900 basis points over U.S. Treasurys (about 14.5 percent). On the dates of their respective IMF bailouts, the credit ratings for Thai and Indonesian debt were even lower.

These so-called IMF loans, then, actually offered extraordinarily generous rebates of about 10 percent below market rates. On the $117 billion lent to East Asia under IMF auspices thus far, the region is saving about $12 billion a year in interest payments. Over three years, South Korea, Thailand, and Indonesia will have received a direct wealth transfer of at least $35 billion, mostly from U.S. and Western European taxpayers.

But this $35 billion figure actually understates the true scale of the transfer. Investors priced South Korea's debt at a yield of 14.5 percent only because there was a good chance the IMF would come in sooner or later and rescue them. Absent the market-distorting activities of the IMF, the risk premium on this sovereign debt would have been even greater.

More specifically, much of this $35 billion will amount to a wealth transfer from middle-class Westerners to East Asian governments, banks, and their rich equity owners and from there to wealthy Western and Japanese investors who risked capital in foolish ways (or perhaps not so foolish since there was a good chance they would be bailed out in the end). The whole series of transactions amounts to a remarkably regressive tax.

Curiously, the U.S. government lends money through the IMF at far lower rates of interest than it charges to most domestic loans to Americans. In the case of loans guaranteed by the Small Business Administration, for example, the prevailing interest rate hovers around 10.75 percent; university students must pay about 9 percent on college loans; and veterans must pay about 7 percent on federally guaranteed mortgage loans. All of these borrowers are safer credit risks than East Asian governments.

These numbers explain why the prevailing pro-IMF rationalizations start with the premise that circumstances are highly abnormal. In one of the more common apocalyptic scenarios being peddled by proponents of the IMF bailout, the crisis in Asia triggers a domino effect, leading to a bank collapse in Japan, a recession in Western Europe, and economic catastrophe in the United States.

"ASIAN FLU"?

The problem with this doomsday scenario is that it depends on the Clinton administration's characterization of the market meltdown as an "Asian flu"—a bug that strikes without cause and could strike the United States. It doesn't, and it won't. The debacle in Asia was caused by "crony capitalism," an oxymoron describing the ways in which politicians infect markets by distorting prices and artificially creating winners and losers. Investors were encouraged to take enormous gambles in real estate, finance, and other industries — and when these gambles produced big losses, the current crisis ensued. We don't face this problem in the United States, so we shouldn't fear being infected by Asia's ills.

Most peculiarly, the IMF's remedies seem designed to avoid a theoretical economic disaster by replicating the policies that led to an actual economic disaster. After all, the difference between the crony capitalism of East Asia and the crony capitalism of the IMF is primarily quantitative: Whereas the governments in East Asia subsidized companies and industry sectors, the IMF operates on a much grander scale by subsidizing entire countries. The IMF, despite its efforts to push economic reforms, rewards bad regulatory regimes in the same way East Asia's crony capitalism rewarded bad investments. There is good reason to be wary of a cure whose side effects include generating more of the same disease.

■ That IMF borrowers pay uniform interest rates raises the following question.

Why Should the IMF Lend at Subsidized Interest Rates?

Roland Vaubel

This selection was excerpted from "The Political Economy of the IMF: A Public Choice Analysis," published in *Perpetuating Poverty: The World Bank, the IMF, and the Developing World*, edited by Doug Bandow and Ian Vasquez (1994). Roland Vaubel is a professor of economics at the University of Mannheim in Germany.

Member governments can borrow from the IMF at favorable interest rates instead of resorting to the international capital market. According to its Articles of Agreement (V.8.d and XX.2), the fund has to charge uniform interest rates to all borrowers, effectively paying the largest subsidies to the least creditworthy. The IMF also tends to give the greatest benefits to long-term debtors because, contrary to the Articles of Agreement (V.8.b), the rates are normally independent of loan duration. The uniformity of interest charges not only aggravates the moral hazard problem but also results in adverse selection of borrowers, a "lemon" problem.

Under the Bretton Woods system, the aim of maintaining stable exchange rates was used to justify cheap IMF credits. Many IMF borrowers, however, especially during the Bretton Woods era, were perfectly capable of acquiring foreign exchange via the market.

If, however, a member government is not creditworthy, the question becomes why it should be granted loans at all. There are two possible answers: to overcome imperfections of the capital market or to provide development aid. With imperfect information, the capital market would function imperfectly as well. However, if the IMF really has better information than potential private lenders about the true creditworthiness of its member governments, it could try to improve the market's information rather than to extend credit itself. Surely the fund has an obligation to make such information public for the protection of other lenders. Alternatively, subsidized IMF lending is a poor form of development aid since the IMF's criterion for extending credit (i.e., balance of payments difficulties) is not a suitable indicator of need.

Moreover, the interest rate subsidy creates an incentive to delay adjustment once a credit has been obtained—Article V, Section 7.b of the Articles of Agreement specifies that each member is normally expected to repay its credits (even before maturity) "as its balance of payments and reserve position improves." That runs directly counter to the objective laid down in Article I.vi that the fund should "shorten the duration . . . of disequilibrium in the international balances of payments of members."

The interest rate subsidy might be regarded as an insurance benefit against economic instability, but "premiums" do not differ according to risk. From 1960 to 1982, for example, forty-two member countries accounted for 78 percent of all standby and extended credits from the IMF. That is not an outcome to be expected if members had been hit by random accidents. In fact, cross-sectional regressions by Lawrence Officer and Peter Cornelius showed that, between 1974 and 1980, the flow of IMF credits to member governments tended to be significantly correlated with the outstanding stock of previous IMF credits. Richard Goode presented a list of twenty-four countries that have obtained fund credits for more than ten *consecutive years*. The maximum is twenty-seven years (Chile and Egypt). He also reported that, in 1974–1984, drawings from non-oil-producing countries accounted for 85 percent of fund credit.

In short, the IMF is a continuous provider of aid, in the form of subsidized insurance, to a limited group of member governments. That raises four questions:

- Why do donor governments grant this form of aid?

- Why do they give the largest subsidies to the most negligent members?

- Why is the insurance offered to governments rather than to individuals?

- Why is the subsidy confined to insurance with an international public monopoly, the IMF?

The government treasury origins of the IMF are indicative. As John Makin has noted, the IMF serves the interests of the treasuries of its member governments by flexibly accommodating their borrowing and debt-servicing "needs" at minimum cost. By charging low and uniform interest rates, the IMF protects its members against market judgments and helps insure them against the electoral damage that a visibly poor credit standing might otherwise cause. The policy conditions imposed by the IMF may also be unpopular, but political leaders have occasionally made them scapegoats for unpopular economic reforms. The IMF at least provides politicians with a choice between high-risk premiums (lack of creditworthiness) in the private capital market and the IMF's policy conditions.

The IMF's professional staff also has a vested interest in subsidized, uniform interest rates. Low rates increase the demand for IMF credits. Uniform rates help avoid conflict with potential borrowers. For similar reasons, national social insurance systems and public insurance schemes for export credits and foreign investment do not usually charge premiums according to risk. Moreover, paying larger subsidies to the least creditworthy allows the fund, like national social insurance schemes, to justify its activities on humanitarian grounds. As is well known from social insurance economics, however, the poor are often not the worst risks. The debt crisis of the 1980s is a case in point: The governments of the richer developing countries, such as Mexico, proved to be the least creditworthy.

PART TWO

THE EFFECTIVENESS OF INTERNATIONAL MONETARY FUND FINANCING PROGRAMS

If John Maynard Keynes's book *The General Theory of Employment, Interest, and Money* is the most influential work in macroeconomics, the second-most influential work could be a little-known article by IMF staff economist Jacques Polak titled "Monetary Analysis of Income Formation and Payments Problems."[1] This 1957 article develops the analytic framework, known as financial programming, used by the fund to craft its loan programs. The IMF currently has sixty-two financing programs around the world totaling $86.2 billion (see table 2).

Financial programming consists of a set of simple equations that relates the monetary sector of an economy to the balance of payments. Conceptually, the model tells the IMF what macroeconomic adjustments and financial assistance are needed to establish a country's balance of payments equilibrium. One major operational advantage of this framework is that it requires few data series. This is important since many developing countries lack sophisticated national income accounting systems. The major operational disadvantage of the framework, as noted by Sebastian Edwards, professor of economics at the University of California at Los Angeles, is "how little financial programming has changed in thirty years. It is not an exaggeration to say that fund economists use today a very similar analytical apparatus to that used by their colleagues twenty-five or thirty years ago" despite major innovations in macroeconomic theory.[2]

Part 2 examines the effectiveness of IMF financing programs. In "The Macroeconomic Effects of Fund-Supported Adjustment Programs," IMF staff economist Mohsin Khan reviews thirteen statistical studies on the impact of fund programs on borrowing countries' balance of payments, current account deficits, inflation, and growth. Khan finds that there is no consensus that the IMF has any positive effect.

1. Jacques J. Polak, "Monetary Analysis of Income Formation and Payments Problems," *IMF Staff Papers* 6 (November 1957): 1–50.

2. Sebastian Edwards, "The International Monetary Fund and the Developing Countries: A Critical Evaluation," in *IMF Policy Advice, Market Volatility, Commodity Price Rules, and Other Essays*, ed. Karl Brunner and Allan H. Meltzer, Carnegie-Rochester Conference Series on Public Policy, vol. 31 (Amsterdam: North-Holland, 1989), pp. 10–11.

TABLE 2.   Standby, Extended Fund Facility, and Enhanced Structural Adjustment
Facility Arrangements as of 31 December 1998

Arrangement	Financing Programs (number)	Amount Approved by IMF Executive Board (billions of U.S. dollars)	Undrawn Balance (billions of U.S. dollars)
Standby	12	$46.3	$17.8
Extended	15	34.4	20.7
Enhanced	35	5.5	3.0
Total	62	86.2	41.5

SOURCE: International Monetary Fund Treasurer's Department. Available on-line at http://www.imf.org/external/np/tre/tad/index.htm.

In "Eligibility for IMF Credits," Roland Vaubel argues that governments are largely responsible for balance of payments problems by maintaining overvalued currencies, excessive money growth, and imprudent budget deficits. Irresponsible domestic policies, not temporary external shocks, explain the persistent demand for IMF assistance. Next, in "Why the IMF Is Ineffective," Bryan Johnson and Brett Schaefer look at the historical record and conclude that IMF financing programs breed dependency and fail to improve the economies of less-developed countries. Based on this "mediocre record," Jeffrey Sachs calls for an overhaul of the fund in "IMF, Reform Thyself."

The Macroeconomic Effects of Fund-Supported Adjustment Programs

Mohsin S. Khan

This selection was excerpted from an article published in *IMF Staff Papers* in June 1990. Mohsin Khan is the director of the IMF Institute, a department of the IMF that provides training in macroeconomic analysis and policy for officials of member countries.

A question that is frequently raised in connection with fund-supported programs is whether such programs have been effective in achieving their macroeconomic objectives. Some writers have argued that, at best, fund programs do little in the way of improving the economic picture, while others have gone as far as to say that programs worsen the situation by inducing stagflation. Providing a clear-cut answer to this question turns out to be no easy task. There is at present little agreement in the profession either about how to estimate the macroeconomic effects of programs or about what impact past programs have actually had on the principal macroeconomic variables the fund typically is concerned with. Although there have been a number of studies on the subject over the past decade, one cannot say with certainty whether programs have "worked" or not.

Before turning to a discussion of the alternative methodologies used in the evaluation of programs, it is important to define how the effects of programs ought to be measured. At the most general level, it has been argued that macroeconomic performance under a program should be compared to the "counterfactual"—defined as the macroeconomic performance that would have taken place in the absence of a program (see Guitián 1981). The counterfactual is perhaps the most appealing yardstick against which to assess program performance and the standard most widely employed in economics to measure the impact of government policy interventions. What would have happened in the absence of a fund-supported program is by no means the only standard against which to judge the outcomes of programs, but in many cases it is the most appropriate one. However, the counterfactual cannot, by definition, be observed and must be estimated or approximated. The various approaches used in evaluation studies should thus be judged in terms of how good they are in providing estimates of the counterfactual.

The literature suggests that four distinct approaches have been applied to the evaluation of fund-supported adjustment programs: (1) the *before-after approach*, which compares macroeconomic performance during a program and performance prior to the program; (2) the *with-without approach*, which compares macroeconomic performance in countries with programs and performance in a "control group" of countries without programs; (3) the *actual-versus-target approach*, which compares actual macroeconomic performance under the program and the performance specified in its targets; and (4) the *comparison-of-simulations approach*, which compares the simulated performance of fund program–type policies and simulated performance with some other set of policies.

In the discussion that follows, the studies are grouped according to the approach that was employed by them.

BEFORE-AFTER APPROACH

In the literature on the effects of fund-supported programs, the before-after approach has been the most popular. The first study to use this approach was by Reichmann and Stillson (1978). These authors examined a total of seventy-nine fund-supported programs implemented during 1963–72 and compared the behavior of the balance of payments, inflation, and growth during the two-year periods before and after the implementation of the program. Using nonparametric statistical tests, they found that there was a significant improvement in the balance of payments in only about one-fourth of all programs. In a majority of cases (over 70 percent) there was no significant change in the balance of payments. Of the twenty-nine programs involving countries with high inflation during the program period, the rate of inflation fell in six of eleven programs for which there was a notable deceleration in the rate of domestic credit expansion; in the nine programs involving a devaluation, there were five in which inflation was higher. Finally, growth performance was examined for seventy programs, and it was concluded that, on balance, fund-supported programs did not exert adverse effects on growth rates. In 40 percent of programs the growth rate declined after the inception of the program relative to the previous two years' average rate of growth, but at the same time growth was higher in 47 percent of the programs.

A similar procedure was followed by Connors (1979), who examined a total of thirty-one programs in twenty-three countries that were adopted during the 1973–77 period. He compared periods of one year before and after the programs. Also using a nonparametric rank test, Connors concluded that fund programs had no discernible effects on the ultimate targets—growth, inflation, and the current account deficit—or on important intermediate targets, such as the ratio of the fiscal deficit to gross domestic product (GDP).

The relationship between fiscal variables and fund program performance was examined in more detail by Kelly (1982). The methodology was primarily of the before-after variety, and in order to take into account possible lags in adjustment, comparisons were made over both one-year and three-year periods. In a sample of seventy-seven programs (covering thirty-three countries) during 1971–80, Kelly observed that when a one-year comparison was used, the fiscal deficit was reduced in 56 percent of the cases and that the current account and fiscal deficits moved in the same direction in 62 percent of the programs examined. This last result was also supported by regression analysis that showed a positive and statistically significant relationship between changes in the ratio of the fiscal deficit to gross national product (GNP) and changes in the ratio of the current account to GNP. Furthermore, in about half the cases there was a decline in the average growth rate over a three-year period and an increase or no change in the other half.

A study by Killick (1984) also attempted to capture the effects of lags by comparing the behavior of the balance of payments, the current account, growth, and inflation a year before the program with the behavior both one and two years after the program. Killick employed nonparametric statistical tests to gauge the effects of thirty-eight programs covering twenty-four countries during the period 1974–79. In contrast to other studies, Killick found that the balance of payments and the current account deteriorated irrespective of the time period over which the comparison was made. However, the difference between the preprogram and postprogram values of these variables was not statistically significant. Inflation was reduced, but the effects on growth were ambiguous. In the first year after the program the rate of growth was higher, but by the second year the positive effect had eroded and the net effect was zero.

Zulu and Nsouli (1985) also constructed before-after measures of program effects in their study of thirty-five programs implemented in 1980–81 for twenty-two African countries. They found that growth was lower or the same in the year after the program in about 60 percent of the cases. For the current account and inflation targets, the split was even—with as many programs showing an improvement in the current account and inflation performance as those showing a worsening or no change.

The most recent study using the before-after approach was that by Pastor (1987) for eighteen Latin American countries during 1965–81. Using one-year comparisons and on the basis of alternative statistical tests, Pastor concluded that fund programs led to a significant improvement in the balance of payments but that apparently there was no effect on the current account, inflation, or the rate of growth of nominal GDP.

WITH-WITHOUT APPROACH

The with-without approach is designed to overcome the inability of the before-after approach to distinguish between program and nonprogram determinants of macroeconomic outcomes. The basic reasoning behind this approach is as follows. Assume countries with and without programs are subject to the same nonprogram determinants—that is, they face the same external environment. Then, so the argument goes, by comparing before-after changes in outcomes in program countries to those in the control group of nonprogram countries, the effects of nonprogram determinants will cancel out—leaving the difference in group performance to reflect only the effects of fund-supported programs. Put in terms of the counterfactual, the idea is to use the observed performance of nonprogram countries as an estimate of what the performance of program countries would have been in the absence of a fund-supported program.

The with-without group approach was first used in two studies by Donovan (1981, 1982), which analyzed a sample of programs implemented from 1970 to 1980. The control group of countries without programs was taken to consist of all nonoil developing countries, and the comparisons were carried out over one-year and three-year time horizons. In the first study (Donovan 1981), which covered a sample of twelve programs (for twelve countries) implemented during 1970–76, the improvement in the rate of growth of exports was consistently higher for program countries than for all nonoil developing countries. The increase in the rate of inflation for program countries was about half that of the control group during the first year, and although it rose when three-year comparisons were undertaken, it was nevertheless well below the average increase in the rate of inflation of all nonoil developing countries. The outcome for growth was not as clear-cut. In the one-year comparison there was a sharp improvement in growth in program countries relative to the control group, but in the three-year comparisons growth in countries fell by more than it did in nonprogram countries.

In Donovan (1982) the sample of programs was expanded to seventy-eight, covering the period 1971–80, and the same analysis as in the first study was undertaken. The balance of payments and the current account positions of program countries were found to improve relative to the control group in both the one-year and three-year comparisons. The increase in inflation in program countries was about half that of nonoil developing countries in the one-year comparisons and fell to one-third in the three-year comparisons. However, in contrast to the results of the first study, the rate of growth of real GDP fell by more than the average decline experienced by nonoil developing countries in the one-year comparisons but by less in the three-year comparisons.

Loxley (1984) applied the same types of tests as Donovan (1982) to a group of thirty-eight least-developed economies (defined as countries with per capita incomes of $690 or less in 1980) that had programs with the fund during 1971–82. His results, however, were less definitive than those obtained by Donovan, in that the least-developed countries with programs did no better, on average, in terms of current account, balance of payments, and growth performance relative to other least-developed countries without programs, the program countries examined by Donovan, and all nonoil developing countries. The improvement was statistically significant only in the case of inflation and then only in the three-year comparisons.

Gylfason (1987) also used a version of the with-without approach in his study of thirty-two programs implemented during 1977–79. The reference group included the developing countries that had experienced balance of payments difficulties during 1975–77, and nonparametric statistical tests were used to determine if the behavior of the macroeconomic variables for program countries over a three-year period was significantly different from that of the reference group. First, there was an improvement in the balance of payments in program countries relative to the outcomes in the control group. Second, inflation in program countries did not fall but rather remained approximately the same as the average rate of inflation in the group. Third, the growth rate was not significantly affected by the program.

This pattern of results was basically replicated by Pastor (1987) for Latin American countries. Employing the same statistical methodology as Gylfason, Pastor also found that the balance of payments performance of program countries was significantly better than that of nonprogram countries and that the differences in inflation and growth performance were not statistically significant.

While the with-without approach copes with some of the problems of the before-after approach, it is by no means ideal. The problem is that program countries differ systematically from nonprogram countries prior to the program period, and this difference matters for performance evaluation. In short, program countries are not randomly selected. Instead, they are adversely selected in the sense of having relatively poor economic performance prior to the program period. This is not surprising since, after all, a basic requirement for fund financial support is that the country have a balance of payments need. This requirement alone suggests that program countries would be expected to have weaker than average external positions when the program was implemented. In any case, nonrandom selection of program countries means that simple with-without estimates of program effects may be biased. Intuitively, the bias occurs because, under nonrandom selection, the with-without estimator attributes differences in outcomes exclusively to program status, when in fact the difference in starting positions itself is a cause of differences in subsequent performance between the two groups. Furthermore, the direction of the bias can go either way. If past economic difficulties signal less-serious current difficulties, even in the absence of a program, then the with-without approach will overstate the beneficial effect of a fund-supported program. Conversely, if past difficulties signal even more serious present difficulties, then the effect of programs will be understated. There are ways, however, as discussed by

Goldstein and Montiel (1986), to modify the with-without approach to reduce some of the biases.

Goldstein and Montiel (1986) applied the generalized evaluation estimator to a sample of sixty-eight programs for fifty-eight developing countries implemented during 1974–81. These authors found that program countries systematically demonstrated weaker performance—that is, higher inflation, slower growth, and larger current account and overall balance of payments deficits—than nonprogram countries in the preprogram period. Adjusting for these preprogram differences in performances and taking into account the effects of policy instruments on targets, Goldstein and Montiel used regression analysis to estimate the program effects. Two interesting sets of results emerged from this study. First, there were no statistically significant effects of programs on the current account and balance of payments, on the rate of inflation, or on the growth of real output. Second, the estimated program effects under the generalized evaluation estimation were quite different from those obtained with the standard with-without estimator. The latter indicated an improvement in the current account, a slight worsening of the balance of payments, a reduction in inflation, and a rise in the growth rate associated with programs. When the generalized evaluation estimator is used, the improvement in the current account ratio disappears, the deterioration in the balance of payments ratio is magnified, and the favorable outcomes for inflation and growth are reversed.

ACTUAL-VERSUS-TARGETS APPROACH

Another strand in the literature on program effects compares actual outcomes for certain key macroeconomic variables to the targets for such variables specified by the authorities and the fund at the inception of the program. This approach has not been as frequently used as the other two approaches. Reichmann (1978), for example, studied twenty-one programs for eighteen countries that were in effect during 1973–75 and compared the outcomes to targets for the balance of payments, inflation, and growth. He found that the balance of payments targets were met or exceeded in nearly two-thirds of the programs. The targets for inflation were, however, exceeded in over half the programs. Greater success was achieved in the case of the rate of growth, with 62 percent of programs meeting the targets.

In a similar vein, Beveridge and Kelly (1980) surveyed the fiscal content of all 105 programs supported by the fund that were approved during 1969–78. Their focus was on intermediate targets—domestic credit expansion, government revenues and expenditures, and deficit financing—rather than on the final macroeconomic objectives. Nevertheless, the results for the intermediate targets are informative since achieving these is generally a necessary condition for meeting the ultimate targets for the balance of payments, inflation, and growth. Beveridge and Kelly showed that almost all programs contained government revenue and expenditure forecasts and that both actual expenditures and revenues tended to differ from these forecasts. A shortfall in revenues occurred in about 40 percent of the cases, while expenditures were above projected values in nearly 60 percent of the programs. Consequently, the overall fiscal deficit targets were achieved in only about half the programs, as were the domestic credit ceilings. Finally, governments were more successful in meeting domestic nonbank financing limits than foreign financing targets. The former were satisfied in almost 70 percent of the programs, but foreign financing of the fiscal deficit exceeded the target in over 60 percent of the cases.

Zulu and Nsouli (1985) also analyzed actual outcomes and targets in their study of programs in African countries approved in 1980–81. They found that the current account targets were met in 38 percent of programs, and the inflation targets in about 48 percent of the cases, but growth targets were only achieved in less than 20 percent of the programs.

COMPARISON-OF-SIMULATIONS APPROACH

Unlike the other three approaches, the comparison-of-simulations approach does not infer program effects from actual outcomes in program countries. Instead, it relies on simulations of economic models to infer the hypothetical performance of fund-type policies or policy packages and alternative policy packages. If the aim of the exercise is to evaluate the results of a specific fund-supported adjustment program, then the use of actual program outcomes is indispensable. However, if the purpose is to evaluate the design and effectiveness of fund-supported programs in general, then examining the likely effects of alternative policy packages can be quite useful and revealing.

Khan and Knight (1981), for example, constructed a small dynamic econometric model and estimated its parameters on a pooled cross-sectional, time-series sample of twenty-nine developing countries, most of which had programs with the fund. They then investigated the hypothetical effects of a stabilization program that pursued an external balance target using policies that figure prominently in fund-supported programs—namely, domestic credit restraint and reductions in government expenditures. The simulation experiments showed that such a program produced a sharp price deflation in the first year, followed by a temporary burst of inflation as prices rose back to their equilibrium level. Output, however, contracted sharply in the first year, then rose temporarily above its full-employment level, approaching that equilibrium level gradually over a period of several years.

In a further study, Khan and Knight (1985) extended their simulation analysis to a comparison of alternative policy packages. Specifically, they compared the results for the balance of payments, inflation, and real output growth of a package of demand-management policies (that is, a onetime reduction in the rates of growth of nominal domestic credit and nominal government expenditures, plus a devaluation) with a combined package of demand-management and structural policies (that is, the above-mentioned demand-management policies, plus a set of structural policies that would gradually raise the rate of growth of capacity output). The demand-management package improved the balance of payments almost immediately but at the cost of a temporarily higher rate of inflation and a short-run reduction in growth. The simulations of the combined package showed that structural policies could help to partially offset any short-term adverse effects on growth that might result from demand restraint as well as the inflationary consequences of devaluation. Furthermore, the longer-run effects of fund-type policies on the balance of payments, inflation, and growth were more favorable than the short-run effects.

A summary of the results obtained by the various studies that have evaluated the effects of fund-supported adjustment programs on the principal macroeconomic objectives is contained in table 3. Overall, these studies yield three conclusions. First, there is frequently an improvement in the balance of payments and the current account, although a number of studies show no effects of programs. Second, inflation is generally not affected by programs. Finally, the effects on the growth rate are uncertain, with the studies showing an improvement or no change being balanced by those indicating a deterioration in the first year of a program.

TABLE 3. Summary of Studies on the Effect of IMF Programs

Study	Time Period	Number of Programs	Number of Countries	Method [a]	EFFECTS ON [b] Balance of Payments	Current Account	Inflation	Growth
Reichmann and Stillson (1978)	1963–72	79	...	Before-after (2-year)	0	...	0	+
Reichmann (1978)	1973–75	21	18	Actual-versus-target	+	...	+	+
Connors (1979)	1973–77	31	23	Before-after	0	0	0	0
Donovan (1981)	1970–76	12	12	With-without	...	...	−	+
Donovan (1982)	1971–80	78	44	With-without	+	+	−	−
Killick (1984)	1974–79	38	24	Before-after	0	0	−	0
Zulu and Nsouli (1985)	1980–81	35	22	Actual-versus-target	...	0	−	−
				Before-after	...	+	−	0
Goldstein and Montiel (1986)	1974–81	68	58	Before-after	−	−	−	−
				With-without	−	+	−	+
				Generalized evaluation	−	−	+	−
Gylfason (1987)	1977–79	32	14	With-without	+	+	0	0
Pastor (1987)	1965–81	...	18	Before-after	+	...	0	0
Khan and Knight (1981)	1968–75	...	29	Comparison of simulations	+	+	−	−
Khan and Knight (1985)	1968–75	...	29	Comparison of simulations	+	+	−	−
Loxley (1984)	1971–82	38	38	With-without	0	0	−	−

[a] Comparison over one-year periods, unless otherwise noted.

[b] Direction of change; (+) indicates positive effect, (−) indicates negative effect, 0 indicates no effect.

ANALYSIS AND CRITICISM OF FINANCING PROGRAMS

Eligibility for IMF Credits

Roland Vaubel

This selection was excerpted from "The Political Economy of the IMF: A Public Choice Analysis," published in *Perpetuating Poverty: The World Bank, the IMF, and the Developing World*, edited by Doug Bandow and Ian Vasquez (1994). Roland Vaubel is a professor of economics at the University of Mannheim in Germany.

Even with today's flexible exchange rates, eligibility for IMF credits continues to depend on the state of the balance of payments. Article V, Section 3.b.ii, of the IMF's Articles of Agreement states the following:

> A member shall be entitled to purchase the currencies of other members from the fund . . . subject to the condition [that] it has a need to make the purchase because of its balance of payments or its reserve position or development of its reserves.

That condition is regarded as fulfilled if, for example, the country's gross hard currency reserves have declined. But a drop in foreign exchange reserves can be deliberately induced—in the case of fixed exchange rates, by increasing the domestic component of the monetary base, and in the case of adjustable parities, by revaluing the domestic currency. Neither choice of economic policy indicates an emergency situation.

In fact, there is considerable evidence that IMF borrowers are largely responsible for their own balance of payments problems. Sebastian Edwards's study of twenty-three developing countries under fixed exchange rates in 1965–72 confirms that excess supply of money tended "to result in international reserves dropping below desired levels." An unpublished IMF study conducted in 1981 even concluded that, in 1964–73, overexpansionary demand policies were the principal cause of balance of payments problems in borrowing countries, while exogenous factors were least important. A study by Thomas Reichmann shows that overexpansionary demand policies were the major factors in fifteen of twenty-one developing countries that had standby arrangements with the IMF during 1973–75.

An analysis by Mohsin Khan and Malcolm Knight concluded that over the whole period of 1973–80, the budget deficit (relative to gross domestic product) was the second most important factor, after their terms of trade, in explaining developing countries' current account balances. An internal IMF working paper by Donal Donovan demonstrated that overexpansionary monetary and fiscal policies also contributed to a country's debt-servicing problems. In the five years before the debt crisis of the 1980s, the rescheduling countries shared the following characteristics:

- Considerably higher rates of net credit expansion to government (13.4 percent annually) than the nonrescheduling countries (5.9 percent annually)

- Considerably higher rates of M2 monetary expansion (31.9 percent annually) than the nonrescheduling countries (22.8 percent annually)

- Not surprisingly, considerably higher consumer price inflation (23.8 percent annually) than the nonrescheduling countries (14.3 percent annually)

If it is true that the IMF wants to maximize its lending and supervision, it cannot be interested in legal restrictions on eligibility that might effectively bar potential borrowers. The criterion of balance of payments need is not an effective barrier. The IMF admits that "the requirement of need is in the nature of a portmanteau concept. It is a term of art rather than of law. . . . Reliance on judgmental factors is unavoidable." The governments of the typical borrower countries obviously share an interest in lending conditions that are as easy as possible to meet. But that arrangement is also advantageous for the influential creditor countries since it permits them to use IMF lending in pursuit of their own foreign policy objectives, as the United States did in 1982 when the debt crisis caused the Reagan administration to reverse its opposition to an IMF quota increase.

Why the IMF Is Ineffective

Bryan T. Johnson and Brett D. Schaefer

This selection was excerpted from *The International Monetary Fund: Outdated, Ineffective, and Unnecessary*, a Heritage Foundation report published on 6 May 1997. Bryan Johnson is a policy analyst and Brett Schaefer is a research fellow at the Heritage Foundation in Washington, D.C.

Much about the international economy has changed since the end of World War II. In addition, much of what the IMF has done has resulted in failure. The IMF remains ineffective because

IMF lending is more likely to create long-term dependency than to act as short-term assistance. IMF lending, as defined by its articles, is supposed to be short term. But according to economist Doug Bandow, most countries actually become long-term users of IMF loans. A review of IMF lending activities reveals an increasing reliance on the fund by less-developed countries.

For example, between 1965 and 1995, 137 countries received loans from the IMF. For 81 of these countries, the number of times they borrowed from the IMF between 1981 and 1995 increased an average of nearly 50 percent over the number of times they borrowed between 1965 and 1980. Only 44 countries reduced the number of times they borrowed during the same periods; 12 maintained activities at similar levels. This means the IMF is extending loans to more countries with greater frequency than it has in the past, thereby involving greater total amounts of assistance than was the case before 1980. Thus, the IMF has not been able to ensure that its loans to less-developed countries are indeed in the short term. Instead, these loans have been more likely to create long-term dependence.

The IMF has failed to help less-developed countries improve economically. In addition to weakening much of the world economy generally, IMF lending has hurt less-developed countries specifically. For example, a review of IMF loan recipients indicates that most are no better off economically today (measured in per capita wealth) than they were before receiving these loans. In fact, many are poorer: Forty-eight of the eighty-nine less-developed countries that received IMF money between 1965 and 1995 are no better off economically than they were before; thirty-two of these forty-eight countries are poorer than before; and fourteen of these thirty-two countries have economies that are at least 15 percent smaller than they were before their first IMF loan or purchase.

The economies of some recipient countries have performed especially poorly. For example:

1. From 1968 to 1995, Nicaragua received approximately $185 million in IMF loans. In 1968, per capita gross domestic product (GDP), measured in constant 1987 U.S. dollars, was $1,821; in 1993, it was only $816, or 55 percent less than it had been before Nicaragua received any loans.

2. From 1972 to 1995, Zaire received approximately $1.8 billion in IMF loans. In 1972, per capita GDP, measured in constant 1987 U.S. dollars, was $683; in 1993, it was only $317, or some 54 percent less than it had been before Zaire received any loans.

The inescapable conclusion is that IMF efforts to encourage economic growth have been dismal failures. Whether this has been caused by the recipient countries' poor adherence to IMF policy prescriptions or by flaws within these prescriptions themselves does nothing to alter this conclusion.

Harvard economist Jeffrey Sachs believes both may be at fault: "Countries that comply with IMF/WB [World Bank] programs seem to outperform countries that do not. At the same time, however, even countries in compliance with IMF/WB programs experience poor to mediocre growth performance."

IMF, Reform Thyself

Jeffrey D. Sachs

This selection was originally published in the *Wall Street Journal* on 21 July 1994. Jeffrey Sachs is the director of the Harvard Institute for International Development.

On the fiftieth anniversary of the founding of the International Monetary Fund at the Bretton Woods conference, it is time to ask whether the IMF fulfills its mandate of "providing (member countries) with opportunity to correct maladjustments in their balance of payments without resorting to measures destructive of national or international prosperity." The answer is that the fund's record is mediocre at best. It's time for an overhaul.

To understand the basic problem with the IMF, it is useful to compare it with a U.S. bankruptcy court.

When Macy's went into bankruptcy in January 1992, it needed three main things: a standstill on debt servicing; new working-capital loans to stay in operation until it could be restructured; and a plan of restructuring, including changes in operations and in the balance sheet. The standstill was automatic, upon filing of the bankruptcy petition. The new working capital was provided in a $600 million loan just three weeks after filing because the new lenders were given priority in the repayments of the loans. Restructuring began immediately and was successfully completed with Federated's takeover of Macy's operations.

Notice several things. The judge did not decide whether to grant a debt standstill; the bankruptcy law provided for that. The judge did not provide the $600 million out of taxpayer dollars; the law provided for "administrative priority" to attract new private lenders. The judge did not design Macy's restructuring plan or put court officials into senior advisory positions in the department stores. The judge only oversaw the preparation of the plan to make sure that it conformed with the law.

When a debtor government goes into bankruptcy, by contrast, the IMF plays the combined role of bankruptcy judge, lender, adviser, and plan designer and all behind closed doors. Bankrupt governments can't go to the markets to get new working capital since there is no system of priority lending. Governments don't receive a standstill on debt servicing as a matter of law. They may receive a partial standstill (on loans to other governments) but only after a long wait and after an IMF green light. In most countries, the IMF staff basically writes the plan of adjustment and hands it to government officials for signing. Strong governments can occasionally resist. But countries have no way to submit their own plans to the IMF executive board. Only the IMF staff can bring program proposals to the board.

The IMF's monopoly position has had all of the classic effects that we expect from protected, coddled bureaucracies. Its programs are routinized, uninspired, and generally fall far short of what could be accomplished. The most novel and successful stabilization programs of the past ten years, whether in Argentina, Bolivia, Estonia, Israel, Mexico, or Poland, are those that were designed mainly by country teams, often over the IMF's initial objections (though the IMF later claimed credit).

In the vast majority of smaller and poorer countries, the stabilization episodes have been IMF designed and administered—with poor results. The record of failures in Africa is notorious. The Yugoslav financial tinderbox was allowed to burn in the late 1980s with miserable IMF advice. Since 1990, the fund has lost crucial opportunities in the postcommunist countries, leaving many of these countries to suffer excessive declines in living standards and unnecessary financial destabilization.

The IMF failures betray a common pattern. The IMF is against stabilizing the exchange rate as a part of an anti-inflation program, even though a pegged, convertible exchange rate was part of all of the success stories just mentioned. The IMF is almost always against the early provision of working capital, in order to protect its own money. Macy's waited three weeks for an infusion of funds; Russia had to wait more than a year.

The IMF takes little care to provide a standstill on debt servicing, letting countries be destabilized by prebankruptcy debt claims. The IMF is rarely energetic in overseeing debt-restructuring deals, often simply standing by while individual creditors try to free ride on the concessions of others. And the IMF pays little attention to institutional reform of the monetary and financial system. Sure, it sends technical advisory missions, but it puts little emphasis on central bank independence or the development of financial markets for treasury debt.

Any serious overhaul of the IMF will end its monopoly position. We need Chapter 11–type procedures to enable countries in restructuring to borrow fresh working capital from the private markets rather than taxpayer dollars under IMF control. The trick would be to assign those new loans priority in the timing of the government's debt repayments.

Similarly, a revamped IMF should oversee the process of implementing a workout program, but, like a bankruptcy judge, it should mainly serve to bring the interested parties together in a law-bound setting to achieve an efficient workout, rather than to provide the monopoly of technical expertise on how to carry out the reforms. There is a world market for such expertise — in investment banks, consulting firms, accounting firms, and the like. Let all of this expertise, including the IMF staff itself, face the world market test.

Finally, the IMF's secrecy must be ended. Virtually every loan document and bit of policy advice is stamped "confidential," and since the start of operations in 1946 not a single confidential document has been declassified. Representative Barney Frank (D., Mass.) has been pushing hard to open up IMF documentation by making authorization of new U.S. funds for the IMF contingent on a more open policy. The IMF management has agreed to some initial steps in releasing some documents, though much more will be needed to ensure a real turnaround of the fund.

PART THREE

THE ROLE OF CONDITIONALITY

When Harry Dexter White returned to Washington, D.C., from Bretton Woods with the Articles of Agreement in hand, one of the first issues raised by Congress during the ensuing ratification debates was the perceived absence of language requiring the IMF to impose loan conditions on borrowing countries. White assured Congress that the proposed articles gave the fund authority to administer "conditionality" and that it would do so in order to guarantee the responsible use of IMF resources.

Meanwhile, in London, John Maynard Keynes was defending the articles before a reluctant British Parliament, which feared the agreement permitted the IMF to impose loan conditions that would usurp its sovereign right to craft domestic economic policies free from foreign intervention. Lord Keynes assured Parliament that domestic policies would be "immune from criticism by the fund" and that Great Britain would be able to borrow liberally while maintaining its independence.[1] Thus, from the beginning, IMF conditionality has engendered controversy, confusion, division, and debate—all of which continue today.

Part 3 examines the role of conditionality in IMF financing programs. The first selection, written by Scott Sidell, provides a brief history of conditionality and describes the early emphasis on demand-management tools and the more recent integration of supply-side policies. The next article, "Conditionality: Fostering Sustained Policy Implementation," presents the fund's position. The IMF contends that conditionality reduces the frequency and severity of balance of payments deficits and promotes the efficient use of fund resources. This, in turn, ensures prompt repayment, which facilitates the revolving nature of IMF credit. Irrespective of these lofty goals, Sebastian Edwards demonstrates, in "Recent Experience with Conditionality," that countries seldom honor their loan terms. This finding is remarkable since it is based on the fund's own data, never before released to outside analysts.

In "Problems with Conditionality," Doug Bandow argues that IMF loan conditions, to the extent that they are implemented, often exacerbate the

---

1. Louis W. Pauly, *Who Elected the Bankers? Surveillance and Control in the World Economy* (Ithaca, N.Y.: Cornell University Press, 1997), p. 83.

problems of borrowing countries. Furthermore, when the IMF suspends assistance as a result of noncompliance, governments quickly institute minimal policy changes to get the money flowing again instead of the major institutional reforms needed for long-term growth and development. Next, Roland Vaubel explains why conditionality is not *ex ante* rule based and transparent. Finally, the *Wall Street Journal* offers an explanation for the fund's preference for austere conditions. IMF staffer Bob Russell replies.

CONDITIONALITY OVERVIEW

Levels of Conditionality

Low conditionality involves a country merely establishing that it has a "balance of payments need," coupled with a declaration, which the fund does not ordinarily challenge, that it is taking measures to correct the problem.

High conditionality involves designing a specific set of measures to eliminate a country's balance of payments problem, fund agreement that the program will be adequate for that purpose, and the country's commitment to implement the program.

Provisions of Financing Programs

Preconditions are actions taken by a country before the IMF executive board will authorize a program.

Performance criteria are benchmarks that, if violated by a country, lead to suspension of further loan disbursements by the fund until a new agreement is reached.

Policy understandings are actions that a country agrees to take but that do not have any explicit sanction associated with nonperformance.

Typical IMF Financing Preconditions and Performance Criteria

- General commitment to cooperate with the IMF in setting policies
- Reducing government spending, budget deficits, and foreign (external) debt
- Reducing the rate of money growth to control inflation
- Ending government monopolies (i.e., privatization)
- Deregulating industries and reforming the banking sector
- Redirecting domestic credit from the public to the private sector
- Ending government wage, price, and interest-rate controls and government subsidies
- Raising real interest rates to market levels
- Removing barriers to export growth
- Lowering tariffs, ending quotas, and removing exchange controls and discriminatory exchange rates
- Maintaining adequate levels of international reserves
- Devaluing the currency for countries in "fundamental disequilibrium"

Brief History of Fund Conditionality

Scott R. Sidell

This selection was excerpted from Scott Sidell's book *The IMF and Third-World Political Instability: Is There a Connection?* published in 1988. Sidell is a financial market analyst in the trading and securities division of a major U.S. bank headquartered in New York City.

In 1944, the IMF was jointly established by forty-four member nations in an effort to promote international monetary stability and to facilitate the expansion and balanced growth of world trade. Article I of the fund's charter called on the IMF to make financial resources available to members, on a temporary basis and with adequate safeguards, to permit them to correct payments imbalances. In 1952, the principle of conditionality was implicitly incorporated into the fund's lending policies. Conditionality was conceived to encourage policies that would make it more likely for a member country to be able to cope with its balance of payments problem and to repay the fund within three to five years.

The inception of the practice of conditionality accompanied the birth of the "standby arrangement." In its infancy, the standby arrangement was intended to be a precautionary device to ensure access on the part of members who had no immediate need for such resources in the near future. The standby arrangement, however, matured quickly into a device for linking economic policies to financial assistance. The standby arrangement can be described as a "line of credit outlining the circumstances under which a member can make drawings on the fund" (Guitian 1981, 14).

On 20 September 1968, the fund decided to incorporate the practice of conditionality explicitly into its charter. Before this date, the concept of conditionality had generally been referred to in a vague manner. The amendments to the fund's Articles of Agreement in 1968 ended this confusion by introducing, for the first time, clear language that outlined the fund's position with respect to conditionality.

Until the mid-1970s, the typical conditions placed on the use of fund resources involved policies that influenced the level and composition of aggregate demand. During this period, excess demand was perceived as the most important cause of inflation, currency overvaluation, and ultimately payment difficulties. The expeditious elimination of excess demand was viewed as an essential condition for restoring payments equilibrium. This position has often been referred to as the *monetarist approach*.

The monetarist approach views excess demand as the root cause of inflation and exchange-rate disequilibrium. Its goal is the rapid alleviation, typically in one year or less, of inflation and the restoration of exchange-rate equilibrium vis-à-vis policies that alter the size and composition of aggregate demand. Monetarist policies generally call for

1. Control of the money supply

2. Reduction of the government deficit

3. Exchange-rate devaluation

4. Deregulation of prices

5. Reduction of consumer subsidies

6. Elimination of tariff and nontariff trade barriers

In the mid-1970s, the monetarist strategy gave way to a more structural, longer-run approach. The introduction of this new approach to payments adjustment was precipitated by the growing recognition, both within and outside the fund, that payment imbalances could no longer be expected to be corrected within one year. In response to this recognition, the fund increased its support for programs that called for adjustment over a longer period. In 1974, the fund established the "extended fund facility," which was designed to provide members with up to three years of financial support. In addition, the fund decided in 1979 to allow standby arrangements to be extended for up to three years. This development was accompanied by growing support for more comprehensive programs designed to affect the balance of payments through changes in supply as well as in demand. These programs continued to rely on the typical monetarist instruments but in a more gradual manner. In addition, they called for more-structural, supply-oriented policies such as reducing the size of the public sector, channeling resources away from the public sector and into the private sector, creating financial intermediaries, promoting savings, and discouraging wasteful investment by increasing real interest rates. To facilitate the success of these enlarged programs, the fund increased by six times the amount of resources that member countries were allowed to borrow. The "enlarged access policy" of 1981 authorized members to accumulate a maximum of up to 600 percent of their donation (quota) to the fund.

Conditionality: Fostering Sustained Policy Implementation

International Monetary Fund

This selection first appeared in the IMF publication *1998 IMF Survey Supplement on the Fund.*

When it provides financial support to a member country, the IMF must be sure that the member is pursuing policies that will ameliorate or eliminate its external payments problem. The explicit commitment that members make to implement remedial measures in return for the IMF's support is known as *conditionality*. This commitment also ensures that members are able to repay the IMF in a timely manner—which allows the IMF's limited pool of financial resources to revolve and be available to other members with a balance of payments problem. IMF financing, and the important catalytic effect it has in securing other financing, enables the country to adjust in an orderly fashion, without resort to measures that would be inimical to its own or other countries' prosperity.

Conditions for IMF financial support may range from general commitments to cooperate with the IMF in setting policies to the formulation of specific, quantified plans for financial policies. IMF financing from its general resources in the "upper credit tranches" (that is, where larger amounts are disbursed in return for implementation of remedial measures) is phased. The IMF requires a "letter of intent," which outlines a government's policy intentions during the period of the adjustment program; policy changes to be taken before approval of the arrangement; performance criteria, which are objective indicators for certain policies that must be satisfied on a quarterly, semiannual, or in some instances a monthly basis for drawings to be made; and periodic reviews that allow the executive board to assess the consistency of policies with the objectives of the program.

CONDITIONALITY IS FLEXIBLE

Although IMF conditionality employs specified performance criteria, it does not rely on a rigid set of operational rules. The executive board's guidelines on conditionality

- Encourage members to adopt corrective measures at an early stage
- Stress that the IMF pay due regard to members' domestic social and political objectives, as well as economic priorities and circumstances
- Permit flexibility in determining the number and content of performance criteria
- Emphasize that IMF arrangements are decisions of the IMF that set out—in consultation with members—the conditions for its financial assistance

CONDITIONALITY IN PRACTICE

The IMF takes a pragmatic approach to helping members formulate economic reform programs, recognizing that no one model suits all members. Each IMF-supported program is designed by the member country in close collaboration with the IMF staff. The process involves a comprehensive review of the member's economy, including the causes and nature of the balance of payments problems and an analysis of the policies needed to achieve a sustainable balance between the demand for, and the availability of, resources.

IMF-supported programs emphasize certain key aggregate economic variables—domestic credit, the public sector deficit, international reserves, and external debt—and crucial elements of the pricing system—including the exchange rate, interest rates, and, in some cases, commodity prices—that significantly affect the country's public finances and foreign trade and the economy's supply response.

During a standby or extended fund arrangement or during an arrangement under the enhanced structural adjustment facility, a member's reform program is monitored by the IMF through performance criteria selected according to the economic and institutional structure of the country, the availability of data, and the desirability of focusing on broad macroeconomic variables, among other considerations. Performance under IMF-supported reform programs is also monitored through periodic reviews by the IMF executive board.

GROWTH-ORIENTED ADJUSTMENT

While macroeconomic policies designed to influence aggregate demand continue to play a key role in IMF-supported adjustment programs, it is widely recognized that measures to strengthen the supply side of the economy are frequently essential to bring about a sustained return of external viability and sound growth. IMF-supported policy adjustments by member countries to enhance the growth potential and flexibility of their economies include measures to remove distortions in the external trade system and in domestic relative prices, measures to improve the efficiency and soundness of the financial system, and measures to foster greater efficiency in government spending. Structural reforms in these areas have been particularly important in programs under the extended fund facility and the enhanced structural adjustment facility. Given the emphasis on structural reforms in IMF-supported programs, close collaboration with the World Bank has been important.

TRADE-RELATED CONDITIONALITY

In October 1997, the board considered a staff report on trade reform in medium-term IMF-supported programs. Directors felt that trade liberalization should play an important role in IMF-supported programs. They agreed that, in addition to promoting efficient resource allocation, trade reform was important in fostering transparency and good governance and in reducing the scope for administrative discretion, incentives to lobby for protection, and opportunities for rent seeking. The analysis of countries' trade policies in the report was based on an index of trade restrictiveness, which directors generally welcomed as a valuable tool for classifying the relative restrictiveness of trade regimes.

Many directors supported front-loaded liberalization measures and the use of prior actions, performance criteria, structural benchmarks, and reviews to monitor implementation of trade reforms. Other directors cautioned that trade-related conditionality should be applied flexibly and should take into account each country's initial conditions, the degree of political support, and the authorities' own commitment to reforms. For trade reform to succeed, directors remarked, it should be broadly based and should initially replace nontariff barriers with tariffs, while eliminating customs duties exemptions and trade-related subsidies, all of which would tend to strengthen the government's fiscal position or at least avoid revenue losses.

SOCIAL SAFETY NETS

Adjustment programs typically have an impact on income distribution, employment, and social services. While sound macroeconomic policies and effective structural reforms promote sustained growth and employment, the adjustment process itself may involve short-term social costs for vulnerable groups. Measures built into IMF-supported programs address these costs. In collaboration with the World Bank staff, the IMF staff analyzes the social implications of reform measures and advises the authorities on how best to design social safety nets and target them to assist the neediest groups.

Recent Experience with Conditionality

Sebastian Edwards

This selection was excerpted from "The International Monetary Fund and the Developing Countries: A Critical Evaluation," published in *IMF Policy Advice, Market Volatility, Commodity Price Rules, and Other Essays*, edited by Karl Brunner and Allan Meltzer (1989). Sebastian Edwards, formerly World Bank chief economist for Latin America and the Caribbean, is the Henry Ford II Professor of International Economics at the Anderson Graduate School of Management, University of California at Los Angeles.

The year 1983 marked the beginning of the IMF involvement with the debt problem. That year thirty-four upper-tranche programs involving conditionality (standby and extended fund facility programs) were arranged. In the vast majority of cases these programs involved countries seriously affected by the debt crisis. In this selection I review the experiences of these thirty-four programs, concentrating on the programs' contents and on the relation between targets and actual outcomes, emphasizing the evolution of three final targets: the current account, inflation, and output growth.

Figure 4 lists the countries that had upper-tranche programs arranged in 1983. In 1982 all these countries faced severe external imbalances, with the average ratio of current account deficit to GDP amounting to more than 10 percent. Moreover, the vast majority of them faced serious debt problems; eight of these countries—Argentina, Brazil, Chile, Ecuador, Mexico, Morocco, Philippines, and Uruguay—are included in the IMF list of the fifteen highly indebted countries.

In accordance with the Articles of Agreement the programs sought an adjustment that would generate balance of payments viability. Given the global nature of the problem and contrary to the historical experience, these programs could not rely on increased private capital inflows to achieve viability. Consequently, in all cases rapid and significant current account turnarounds were sought. For the sample as a whole the programs targeted a reduction of the current account deficit from 10.2 percent of GDP in 1982 to 7.1 percent of GDP in 1983 and to 6 percent of GDP in

FIGURE 4.   Countries with IMF Conditionality Programs Approved in 1983

Argentina	Guatemala	Morocco	Togo
Bangladesh	Haiti	Niger	Turkey
Brazil	Kenya	Panama	Uganda
Central African	Korea	Philippines	Uruguay
Republic	Liberia	Portugal	Western Samoa
Chile	Malawi	Senegal	Zaire
Dominican Republic	Mali	Solomon Islands	Zambia
Ecuador	Mauritius	Sri Lanka	Zimbabwe
Ghana	Mexico	Sudan	

NOTE: These are countries that had upper-credit tranche programs—either standby or extended fund facility—arranged in 1983. A number of these countries had programs before 1982, and some also had programs approved after 1983.

SOURCE: *IMF Annual Reports.*

1984. Of course, for the individual countries the targets varied quite dramatically. The programs also set inflation and output growth targets.

The programs sought to achieve their objectives by a combination of expenditure-reducing and expenditure-switching policies, as well as by the implementation of structural reforms aimed at increasing the overall efficiency of the economies. For a broad description of the policy content of these programs, see table 4. Almost every program contained credit ceilings and a devaluation component. This contrasts sharply with previous fund programs. According to Reichman and Stillson (1978) only about one-half of the upper-credit tranche programs arranged between 1963 and 1972 contained credit ceilings as performance criteria, and one-third of the programs included a devaluation component. By contrast, according to Loser (1984) 50 percent of the upper-tranche programs arranged during 1977–80 included a devaluation component.

In the 1983 programs the traditional fiscal, monetary, and exchange-rate measures were supplemented by a battery of other policies, including measures geared toward reducing the extent of indexation and micro-economic-oriented policies (see table 4). Notice that in only about one-half of the cases were structural reforms—that is, trade or financial liberalization—contemplated. Moreover, in a number of cases the fund

TABLE 4. Policy Content of High-Conditionality Programs, 1983–85

	Percentage of Programs to Which Policy Applies (out of thirty-four programs)
FISCAL POLICY	
Control of Public Expenditures	
Current Expenditures	76
Public-sector wages	74
Subsidies	44
Investment Expenditures	68
Revenues	
Enlarging Tax Base	68
Higher Tax Rates	74
Public Enterprises	
Pricing Reform	79
Administrative Reforms	47
General Reform	59
MONETARY POLICY	
Control of Money and Credit Aggregates	97
Control of Credit to Government and Public Sector	100
Hike in Interest Rates	74
EXCHANGE RATE POLICY	
Devaluation	79*
WAGE-PRICE POLICY	
Wage Indexation	44
Pricing Rationalization	62
Adjustment of Producer Prices	59
DEBT MANAGEMENT	
Rescheduling	56
Coordinated Financing	38
Regularization of Arrears**	62
TRADE REFORM	
Tariff Liberalization	35
Relaxing Exchange Restrictions	41
FINANCIAL SECTOR POLICY	
Financial Liberalization	44
TAX REFORM	59

* Programs that did not include exchange-rate component corresponded to those with institutional constraints, such as belonging to a monetary union or not having a national currency.

** All countries with arrears are included here.

SOURCE: International Monetary Fund.

programs called for a hike in trade taxes as a way to strengthen the fiscal side and reduce the fiscal imbalance.

How well did the 1983 programs fare? Table 5 contains data on the evolution of three key final targets—the current account, inflation, and output growth. As can be seen, on average, the current account improved somewhat while inflation increased quite significantly. With respect to output growth, after a steep reduction in 1983, there was a small improvement in 1984 and 1985. However, before-and-after type of comparisons are not fully satisfactory. This is particularly true for the debt crisis period, during which, given the sudden halt in capital inflows, these countries had no alternative but to engineer a rapid current account turnaround. In fact, countries that did not have fund programs also experienced major current account improvements.

An informative exercise consists of comparing targets and outcomes. The comparison of intermediate targets—many of which are actually performance criteria—and the actual behavior of the policy variables provides important elements to evaluate conditionality. The compliance percentage of three key policy variables—the ratio of government deficit to GDP, the rate of growth of domestic credit, and the rate of growth of domestic credit to the public sector—are compared in table 6. As can be seen, these debt-related variables experienced a fairly low rate of compliance. This is particularly the case for the deficit target, which in no year reached a 50 percent rate of compliance.

It is interesting to compare the rate of compliance of fiscal targets in 1983–85 to those obtained in the past. Beveridge and Kelly (1980), for example, report that in 48 percent of upper-credit tranche programs implemented between 1969 and 1978, the target of overall fiscal deficit as percent of GDP was achieved. This figure is higher than that for 1983–85 reported in table 6. There are a number of possible explanations for this difference in the degree of success of the programs. First, a large number of program countries were affected by negative terms of trade shocks in 1983–85, which made the achievement of the targets more difficult than anticipated. A second possible explanation for the poor rate of achievement of intermediate targets is related to the debt crisis. There is wide agreement now that the debt crisis has introduced a serious incentive problem for the highly indebted less-developed countries. Under the current situation of

TABLE 5. Current Account, Inflation, and Growth for the 1983 Program Countries (in percent)

	1981		1982		1983		1984		1985	
	Average	Median	Average	Median	Average	Median	Average	Median	Average	Median
Current Account/GDP	11.6	11.2	10.2	9.5	7.4	5.8	6.0	4.2	6.7	6.0
Inflation	28.9	18.1	24.5	12.0	40.3	12.4	47.7	14.7	38.1	10.5
Growth	1.7	2.4	0.2	0.2	−0.1	−0.5	2.0	2.2	2.5	3.0

SOURCE: International Monetary Fund.

TABLE 6. Compliance with Conditionality for Thirty-four Programs Approved in 1983 (percentage of countries that comply)

	1983	1984	1985
Government Deficit to GDP	30.3	18.8	43.5
Changes in Domestic Credit	54.8	46.4	40.9
Changes in Net Domestic Credit to Government	72.0	52.8	52.4

SOURCE: International Monetary Fund.

debt overhang, while the costs of the adjustment are fully borne by the highly indebted country, its benefits in the short run are (almost) fully received by the creditors in the form of higher debt repayment. Naturally, under these circumstances the program countries have little incentive to comply with conditionality. In this context it may be argued that many recent fund programs have failed to recognize that under this type of incentive problem a revised type of conditionality is called for.

A serious consequence of the low rate of compliance has been that in recent years there has been a significant increase in the number of programs that have been interrupted, as well as in the number of waivers approved by the fund.

Table 7 contains information on the percentage of final targets that have been achieved in the period 1983–85. These results indicate that programs have been less successful than in the past. In relative terms, the current account target was met more frequently than the inflation targets, and these, in turn, were met more often than the growth targets.

TABLE 7. Conditionality and Program Results (percentage of countries that met or exceeded program's target)

	1983*	1984*	1985*
Current Account Target	55	52	50
Inflation Target	48	41	36
Growth Target	14	39	32

* The number of countries included are twenty-seven in 1983 and 1984 and twenty-two in 1985.
SOURCE: International Monetary Fund.

ANALYSIS AND CRITICISM OF CONDITIONALITY

Problems with Conditionality

This selection was excerpted from "The IMF: A Record of Addiction and Failure," published in *Perpetuating Poverty: The World Bank, the IMF, and the Developing World*, edited by Doug Bandow and Ian Vasquez (1994). Bandow is a senior fellow at the Cato Institute in Washington, D.C., and a former special assistant to President Ronald Reagan.

There are several problems with IMF lending, though the organization makes it hard to judge its activities. Jeffrey Sachs, director of the Harvard Institute for International Development, for instance, has complained about IMF secrecy that "makes it extremely difficult for outside observers to prepare a serious quantitative appraisal of IMF policies." The details of IMF standby agreements are not reported, and the organization refuses to release audits of its loans. Ultimately, however, the best test of the IMF's achievements is whether borrowers seem to be making progress as a result of the fund's activities. Alas, the fund appears to flunk that test, for several reasons.

INAPPROPRIATE CONDITIONS

The IMF has often focused on narrow accounting data, causing its advice to have perverse consequences. As a condition for a loan the IMF will, for instance, demand that a nation reduce its current account deficit — so the borrower restricts imports. Insistence that a country cut its budget deficit may cause the government to raise taxes, slowing growth. In fact, the IMF has explicitly lobbied for higher levies, pushing the administration of Argentina's president Carlos Menem to increase the value-added tax, for instance, and advocating that Mauritius adopt "a series of new taxes." Even where the budget deficit does not actually grow as the economy shrinks, the fund has succeeded in reducing the budget deficit only by reinforcing the very borrower policies, such as high taxes, that block growth.

There are obviously some cases in which the IMF does push for sensible reform. However, the "toughness" of the fund's conditionality has varied over time. Economist John Williamson reported that analysis showed "enormous variation between one program and another." Among the factors causing the fund to vary its conditions was, admitted Williamson, pressure "to lend money in order to justify having it."

Moreover, even setting some useful conditions may have little impact if other policies still cause serious distortions in the borrowing country. Observed Raymond Mikesell, who in 1983 estimated that more than half of the less-developed countries were following self-destructive interventionist economic policies, "The continued existence of these conditions [such as price controls] in a substantial proportion of the [less-developed countries] suggests that not enough attention is being given to policy reform in the negotiation and implementation of the IMF conditionality programs."

LACK OF ENFORCEMENT

Moreover, the IMF, like the World Bank, does not do enough to enforce its conditions. If a country violates its agreement with the IMF, the organization may simply grant a waiver, modifying the offending conditions. Or the fund may suspend the loan, only to later negotiate a new agreement. Money will start to flow again, the borrower will violate the new conditions, the IMF will hold up payments, the loan will be renegotiated, and the process will begin anew. How else can one explain seventeen different arrangements with Peru between 1971 and 1977, eight separate standby programs for Brazil between 1965 and 1972, decades' worth of credit for Zaire, and so on? In fact, the largest Third World borrowers between 1947 and 1987 were India, Brazil, Argentina, Mexico, and Yugoslavia, all of which maintained state-managed economies throughout the period despite the fund's loan conditions.

The IMF seems to measure success by making loans. The assumption is that financial input into poor countries automatically translates into growth output; thus, to not extend credit is to fail. Members of President George Bush's administration obviously had a similar view; Treasury secretary Nicholas Brady, for instance, proposed a new World Bank fund supported by the IMF. President Bill Clinton, a fervent backer of increased aid for Moscow, appears to share the same credit-equals-growth assumption. Yet shoveling more money into essentially insolvent states that have squandered billions in prior loans makes no sense. IMF conditionality would likely be more effective if the fund's refusal to make new loans were based on factors other than a country's inability or unwillingness to repay past IMF loans.

STATIST SUBSIDIES

As noted earlier, however sensible the IMF's conditions, they mean little when a nation's overall policy climate is badly askew. In general, the fund asks countries to take too few of the steps necessary to promote growth; nevertheless, the left still regularly attacks the fund for allegedly advocating capitalism. But John Williamson [senior fellow at the Institute for International Economics] has defended the IMF against the criticism that it is too market oriented.

> It has also been charged that the Fund is biased against socialism. That the Fund welcomes those governments that are willing to work with market forces cannot be doubted. At the same time, the Fund clearly does not have an evangelical zeal for spreading "the magic of the market" parallel to that of, say, the Reagan administration. Its attitude, it would claim, is nonideological: it seeks to promote economic rationality, and it just happens that under a wide range of circumstances the readiest means to that end involves harnessing, instead of fighting, market forces.
>
> What is surely true is that the Fund does not refuse to provide financial assistance to members with left-wing governments. On the contrary. [In 1982] some 16.5 percent of IMF credit was directed to the six communist member countries (China, Kampuchea, Laos, Romania, Vietnam, and Yugoslavia . . .) and Michael Manley's Jamaica was at one stage the heaviest *per capita* borrower from the Fund. . . . Moreover, the

Fund continued to give the Allende government [of Chile] the benefit of the doubt in drawing from the Compensatory Financing Facility.

The IMF similarly disclaims a bias against collectivist systems: "The fund has had programs in all types of economies and has worked with their authorities, identifying the best way to achieve external balance or exercising its function of surveillance over the payments and exchange system. . . . In many instances, fund-supported programs have accommodated such nonmarket devices as production controls, administered prices, and subsidies." Yet how is a country with such policies going to achieve self-sustaining economic growth? It is hard to take seriously an organization's claim to be "prodevelopment" when it regularly pours large sums of money into the worst economic systems on earth. One friend of the fund has argued "that to the extent that programs succeed in their objective of establishing macroeconomic stability in the economy, they can be expected to have a positive impact on growth in the longer run." But how often has the IMF been able to transform *dirigiste* policies that are bad in almost every way?

In an assessment of lending to communist states, for example, Valerie Assetto wrote that "Romania's economic reforms were superficial and actually worked to increase the power of the state. The ensuing economic crisis quickly eclipsed the 'reform' movement, and it quietly expired. Fund and [World] Bank support of the Romanian development effort continued throughout this period." Similarly, she found that the "Yugoslav authorities actually retreated slightly from the market orientation of the 1960s" despite generous assistance in following years. As late as 1990 Michel Camdessus, managing director of the IMF, lauded the fact that the IMF remained engaged in Yugoslavia, supporting "a comprehensive and bold program to stop inflation in its tracks and to reform the economy over the medium term." Yet economists Jeffrey Sachs and David Lipton blamed the fund's conditions—particularly its commitment to continued devaluations—for helping to "cause Yugoslavia to drift from high inflation to hyperinflation."

At times it would appear that the more perverse the policies, the more generous the IMF. The problem is not just the former Soviet bloc, but the many Third World regimes that followed statist economic policies for decades. For instance, India collected more money than any other developing state from the IMF, which acted more as a lender of first rather than last resort, during its first forty years. Yet while India was borrowing pro-digiously from the IMF (and other multilateral institutions), it was pur-suing a Soviet-style industrialization program. Catherine Gwin of the Carnegie Endowment for International Peace observed the country's eco-nomic orientation:

> India's economy is continental in scope; highly industrialized and ex-tremely poor; centrally planned—some would say overly planned; ad-ministratively encumbered and rampant with corruption; caste-bound and socialist-inspired; determinedly self-reliant; and, though guided by principles of social democracy, protective of the interests of politically powerful, propertied groups.

India has also devoted a large portion of its budget, well supplemented by foreign aid, to its military. In the fall of 1981, for instance, India was simultaneously negotiating with France for a $2 billion Mirage jet deal and with the IMF for a $3.6 billion loan.

In the 1970s, the Mexican government was destroying its economy even as it was a regular IMF customer. When Mexico's threatened default on its vast international obligations essentially set off the debt crisis in 1982, the IMF came to the rescue, a role extolled by the fund. Yet the loans did little to improve Mexico's economic performance; that nation did not begin making major market-oriented reforms until the end of the decade after squandering billions more of foreign money on counterpro-ductive state-led development schemes.

The IMF has some thirty-two programs operating in Africa, yet no-where have national economic policies been worse or past lending more misguided. In 1974, for instance, the IMF negotiated a loan to Tanzania, which agreed to adopt a package "of compromises that might be called socialist realism," in the words of one observer. But the government, which had ruined the economy through such policies as forced agricultural collectivization (the *ujaama* program), refused to cut spending, and the IMF terminated the program, having done no more than subsidize the leading example of "African socialism." In 1983, Reginald Herbold Green, of the Institute of Development Studies, concluded that "IMF *influence* on Tanzanian action has, to date, been fairly modest. Direct impact since 1976 has, arguably, been negative. Indirect effects are hard to assess."

Kenya, which borrowed roughly $130 million in 1988 and owed more than $380 million total at the end of 1989, was then building a sixty-story, $200 million office building—complete with a larger-than-life statue of President Daniel arap Moi—in Nairobi. Earlier lending programs to Kenya also proved disappointing. In his analysis of IMF lending to these two African states, Stanley Please of the World Bank was particularly critical of Tanzania's failure to review programs that were not working. In his view, Kenya suffered from some of the same difficulties, and, he concluded, "the problem of the inadequate use of pricing and the overextension of the public sector" was "a pervasive one in Africa."

Only after its Marxist revolution did Ethiopia begin borrowing from the IMF, yet it was the government's collectivization of agriculture that dramatically worsened the famine during the mid-1980s. The loans to Ethiopia exhibited another damning aspect of IMF lending. The fund underwrites any government, however venal and brutal. Naturally, the loans are not earmarked for repression. But the IMF extends credit directly to governments, and money is fungible. Whether Ethiopia took its IMF cash and directly bought bombs for use against Eritrean rebels or shifted its accounts around in Addis Ababa first made no real difference; in either case, the fund (as well as other lenders, such as the World Bank) was an accomplice to murder. Another good IMF customer was Nicolae Ceausescu's Romania, which, in contrast to so many other poor nations, regularly paid its debts. China owed the fund $600 million as of the end of 1989; in January 1990, just a few months after the blood had dried in Beijing's Tianamen Square, the IMF held a seminar on monetary policy in the city. Other clients include or have included Burma, Pinochet's Chile, Laos, Nicaragua under Somoza and the Sandinistas, Syria, Vietnam, Zaire, and so on—the IMF has rarely met a dictatorship that it didn't like.

Conditionality in Practice

Roland Vaubel

This selection was excerpted from "The Political Economy of the IMF: A Public Choice Analysis," published in *Perpetuating Poverty: The World Bank, the IMF, and the Developing World*, edited by Doug Bandow and Ian Vasquez (1994). Roland Vaubel is a professor of economics at the University of Mannheim in Germany.

WHY DISCRETIONARY EX POST CONDITIONALITY?

The fund imposes its conditions after the member country has gotten into trouble. The requirements are supposed to prevent borrowers from hanging on to their subsidized IMF credits longer than necessary. But the fund could more effectively accomplish its goals if the conditions addressed the causes of the crisis. Nations that have negligently, or even deliberately, created a difficult situation should be barred from receiving IMF credits at all. *Ex ante* conditions could, for example, include a requirement that domestic credit expansion may not exceed the growth of production potential, that the budget deficit may not exceed a certain percentage of the gross national product, that the rules of the General Agreement on Tariffs and Trade must be strictly observed, and that there may be neither controls on capital movements nor expropriation of investors.

Of course, such *"ex ante* conditionality" would greatly limit the number of member countries entitled to borrow from the IMF. It would reduce the power of fund officials. Such reform, moreover, would be in the interests of neither borrower governments inclined toward negligence nor lender governments that like to use the IMF to promote foreign policy goals or satisfy domestic interest groups.

Even in the case of purely ex post conditionality, moral hazard could be reduced if the IMF would at least issue—and apply—strict rules for its conditions. The governments of typical debtor countries would then have no hope of getting away with weak conditions thanks to good relations with IMF officials or special negotiating skills. At present, however, the IMF practices ad hoc conditionality, or a case-by-case approach. Fund

officials oppose strict rules about the application of IMF conditions because they limit the fund's discretionary power. Influential lenders and
borrowers feel the same way.

WHY IS THE IMF'S CONDITIONALITY NOT MORE TRANSPARENT?

If the IMF adjustment programs are justified on the grounds that they
constitute "new knowledge" and thus an international public good, their
terms should be made known. Publication might also increase the probability of the fund and its borrowers adhering to their programs, which
seem to be less and less effective.

Why are agreements not published? Secrecy helps a borrower government that does not intend to meet the stipulated conditions save face. If a
borrower intends to fulfill the conditions, secrecy enables it to make the
IMF a scapegoat for additional reform measures the IMF did not demand.
IMF officials avoid unwanted public supervision and a serious assessment
as to the effectiveness of IMF programs. Broken conditions suggest that
the fund is ineffectual. If, by contrast, the fund's conditions are minimal
and therefore easy to fulfill, it would become evident that the IMF has
little impact on borrowers' policies.

Monitoring by the IMF, the banks, and the general public would also
be easier and more effective if policy conditions were simple and few. But
the fund seems to prefer a multitude of policy conditions. Moreover, policy
targets, to be effective, must relate to easily controllable variables—either
policy instruments or close intermediate economic targets. Otherwise, it
is not clear whether a violation is due to policy failures or unforeseeable
disturbances. Without controllability, there can be no responsibility. Targets for relatively uncontrollable variables are not only likely to be missed,
as IMF experience shows, they are also unlikely to exert much influence
on the conduct of economic policy.

The fund's policy targets, however, tend to include remote, endogenous variables, such as the current account balance, that depend heavily
on any number of uncontrollable factors. A public choice perspective
suggests that the IMF staff prefers those sorts of requirements because they
reduce potential outside control and criticism of the fund's effectiveness.
Further, a multiplicity of conditions, without weights attached to them,
makes it difficult to evaluate the efficiency of any program, raises the cost

of monitoring for external observers, and permits the fund to attribute the low degree of successful program implementation to target conflicts.

The fund's desire to protect itself against outside monitoring may also explain why it prefers highly variable ad hoc conditions to simple rules. Once more, the customary borrowers and the most influential lenders share the IMF staff's interest. The choice of remote endogenous target variables can serve a similar purpose. Missing a target can almost always be attributed to unforeseeable disturbances. In that way, the debtor governments can conceal their noncompliance and the IMF staff can conceal the ineffectiveness of its conditions.

WHY ARE CONDITIONS PROCYCLICAL?

Several authors have noted that IMF conditionality varies procyclically: It is stricter when the world is in a recession than when there is a boom. The period from 1979 to 1982 is a particularly good example. There is also econometric evidence that tightening of conditionality reduces the volume of IMF credits. One need not be a Keynesian to criticize the procyclical effect of such variations in conditionality. Why does the IMF reinforce the cycle?

Fund officials have a vested interest in lending extensively and imposing strict economic policy conditions because both constitute an exercise of power and a source of prestige. At a time of worldwide recession, when the demand for IMF credits increases, fund officials can maximize their authority by tightening lending conditions but not more than is compatible with some increase in credit volume. In boom times, in contrast, the decline in demand for credits leads to eased conditions—as exemplified by the structural adjustment facility and the enhanced structural adjustment facility.

Varying conditionality thus becomes a substitute for altering interest rates since the rates the IMF can charge are fixed in advance. If that explanation is correct, it follows that Richard Cooper's 1983 proposal for countercyclical use of IMF conditionality is not feasible because it runs counter to the bureaucratic interest of the IMF staff.

The IMF Wrinkle

Wall Street Journal Editorial

This selection was originally published in the *Wall Street Journal* on 10 April 1998.

Michel Camdessus, who's asking the U.S. taxpayer for a fresh $18 billion for the International Monetary Fund, personally takes home $224,650 a year as head of that august body. A fund station chief, say the guy in Djakarta telling President Suharto what hoops to jump through, makes roughly $120,000. The average professional staff member makes $94,341.

The president of the United States is paid $200,000. A congressman voting on the IMF package makes $136,673. The highest-paid—not average—congressional staff members make $123,000. The IMF staff, though, has a wrinkle. The president, the congressmen, and the Capitol Hill staffers have to pay taxes out of their salaries. The folks at the IMF don't.

U.S. nationals working for the IMF at its Washington headquarters, for example, of course must file tax returns and pay Uncle Sam. But what happens next is a bureaucrat's dream. The IMF compensates its employees—wherever they work—for income taxes paid. There is also a generous bundle of perquisites and allowances that ensures that IMF staff under their tax-exempt umbrella can live in tasteful quarters abroad and send their children on an IMF ticket to assorted private schools and universities.

What all this means is that IMF staffers, in prescribing policies for the world at large, do not have to live with their own medicine. They are personally shielded from many of the very policies they like to inflict on others worldwide. From their Washington headquarters they roam the globe, prescribing tax hikes for Thailand, devaluations for Indonesia, and bailouts they describe as costing nothing but for which U.S. taxpayers bear the risk of lending money to a growing list of sinking economies. When the working day's done, however, and it's time for take-home pay, IMF staff can count on steady salaries in U.S. dollars, net of taxes.

It's a point that just might help clarify matters in a debate over IMF funding that has left many members of Congress bored or simply baffled by the intricacies of Mr. Camdessus's many projects. Mr. Camdessus is looking for a 45 percent increase in funding and hopes to have at his command a capital base of some $285 billion; his $18 billion sailed through the Senate on an 84-16 vote. House majority leader Dick Armey has tried to get some debate started in that chamber, complaining about "mission creep" as the IMF goes from a lender of last resort to running all the world's economies and even governments. Representative Spencer Bachus promises to explore what the IMF is doing in hearings in a subcommittee he heads.

The amounts involved in asking IMF employees to pay taxes like anyone else may be small relative to Mr. Camdessus's dreams, or even the hundreds of billions the fund has been tossing around these past few years to bail out places like Mexico and East Asia. And the policies these billions leverage out of client nations, such as Indonesia, affect mainly the faraway folks who have to pay for their daily bread in devalued rupiah and render up higher taxes under IMF programs for Djakarta. But a good look at IMF staff taxes could give the average congressperson a good glimpse of the mentality of the place.

Indeed, if only IMF policy shapers had some of their own pocket change at risk, they just might prove a tad more cautious about pushing for things like higher taxes and bigger bailouts. Happily, there may be help on the way. Representative Ed Royce (R., Calif.) tells us he is prepared to add to the IMF funding bill an amendment instructing the U.S. Treasury to demand that the IMF scrap its practice of "compensating IMF employees for taxes paid in their home countries." A modest proposal but one that would remind IMF staffers, as they tinker with tax policies around the globe, that there is such a thing as the real world.

Guess Who Calls the Tune at IMF?

Bob Russell

This letter to the editor of the *Wall Street Journal*, written in response to the preceding selection, "The IMF Wrinkle," appeared on 16 April 1998. Bob Russell is an adviser to the fund's External Relations Department.

How can we IMF staffers have a "wrinkle" ("The IMF Wrinkle," Review & Outlook, 10 April 1998) if we're "faceless bureaucrats" (see almost any previous *WSJ* editorial)? Obviously your editorialists continue to grasp at straws in a vain effort to persuade the public that IMF policy prescriptions are invented by wayward, ignorant, and coddled staff members. How else could they fail to prescribe tax cuts anywhere and everywhere all the time without regard to yawning budget deficits? How else to explain their occasional support for currency devaluations (presumably in lieu of deflation, exchange controls, and unlimited lender of last resort bailouts of currency traders)?

But truth be told, staff views don't matter very much. What you seem to have difficulty accepting is that the country representatives on the IMF board—where the United States and other hard currency countries wield the most votes—call the tune. They, not anonymous staff, decide which tax policy and exchange-rate recommendations are preferable. So long as most national leaders and their IMF directors do not share fully Robert Bartley's [editor of the *Wall Street Journal*] confessional, it's hardly fair to blame IMF staff.

But there must also be a reason why you pretend to believe the proposed IMF quota increase is the personal project of IMF managing director Camdessus rather than the consensus of 182 national governments. Probably it's just too hard to face up to the necessity for backing serious international monetary cooperation with serious lines of credit, just in case global markets don't always work right. That's enough to furrow the editorial brow, indeed.

PART FOUR

RECENT INTERNATIONAL MONETARY FUND FINANCING INITIATIVES

Since 1995, IMF loan commitments have reached unprecedented levels (see table 8). In February 1995, the IMF executive board approved a record-breaking loan of $17.8 billion for Mexico. Two months later, Russia was granted IMF credits of $6.8 billion, followed by an additional $10.1 billion in March 1996. The IMF turned its attention to East Asia in 1997. The Philippines received $1.1 billion in July, Thailand $3.9 billion in August, Indonesia $10.2 billion in November, and South Korea $21 billion in December, smashing the old record. The fund expanded its financing activities in 1998 with its second loan in less than a year to Indonesia and the Philippines and its third loan in a little more than three years to Russia. The Russian loan totaled $11.2 billion. The fund ended 1998 with its second-biggest loan ever—$18.1 billion to Brazil.

The record level of fund assistance has prompted unprecedented scrutiny of fund activities. Anne Krueger, professor of economics at Stanford University and senior fellow at the Hoover Institution, has noted that "the fund and its staff have generally been viewed as doing a satisfactory and competent job of dealing with individual countries' difficulties."[1] This assessment is beginning to change. Although a cadre of fund supporters exists, increasingly journalists and academic analysts are questioning the usefulness of fund programs, given the struggles of recipient countries in the face of record lending.

Part 4 explores the debate over IMF financing programs in Mexico, East Asia, and Russia. The first series of selections examines the 1994–95 Mexican economic crisis. The first article, "On Both Sides of the Border, Peso Ills Were Long Ignored," details the economic policies in Mexico that caused the crisis. Next, Walker Todd argues that IMF loans bailed out foreign—primarily U.S.—investors at the expense of Mexico's poor and middle-class citizens. Bradford De Long, Christopher De Long, and Sherman Robinson defend the IMF support package in "The Case for Mexico's Rescue." They assert that the IMF provided needed liquidity to a solvent country and averted a major depression and the spread of financial

1. Anne O. Krueger, "Whither the World Bank and the IMF?" *Journal of Economic Literature* 36 (December 1998): 2011.

TABLE 8. Major IMF Financing Programs, 1995–98

Member Country	Date Agreement Approved by IMF Executive Board	Amount of IMF Financing (billions of U.S. dollars)	IMF Financing Facility
Mexico	1 February 1995	$17.8	SBA
Russia	11 April 1995	6.8	SBA
Pakistan	13 December 1995	0.6	SBA
Russia	26 March 1996	10.1	EFF
Philippines	18 July 1997	1.1	EFF
Thailand	20 August 1997	3.9	SBA
Pakistan	20 October 1997	1.6	EFF and ESAF
Indonesia	5 November 1997	10.2	SBA but replaced by EFF 25 August 1998
South Korea	4 December 1997	21.0	SBA
Philippines	27 March 1998	1.4	SBA
Indonesia	15 July 1998	1.3	SBA
Russia	20 July 1998	11.2	EFF, SRF, and CCFF
Brazil	2 December 1998	18.1	SBA and SRF

SOURCE: Various IMF press releases available on-line at http://www.imf.org.

problems to other developing countries. Alternatively, Ian Vasquez and L. Jacobo Rodriguez argue that the fund's intervention was unnecessary and a failure. They allege that the bailout postponed necessary reforms, particularly in the banking sector, increased the debt burden on Mexico's taxpayers, and sharply lowered the standard of living for Mexico's citizens. Finally, Robert Barro argues in "The IMF Doesn't Put Out Fires, It Starts Them" that the fund's 1995 Mexico bailout rewarded bad economic policies and imprudent bank lending, thereby fueling future crises.

The second series of selections examines the 1997–98 East Asian financial crises. Jeffrey Sachs in "Power unto Itself" and the *Wall Street Journal* in "The IMF Crisis" contend that Asian economies were fundamentally sound in 1997 and that the financial crises were precipitated by self-fulfilling withdrawals of short-term loans and exacerbated by inappropriate IMF responses. In contrast, Lawrence Lindsey in "The Bad News about Bailouts" and Milton Friedman in "Markets to the Rescue" argue that reckless investment decisions, motivated by moral hazard and crony capitalism, and unsustainable economic policies caused the Asian crises. The next two articles, by journalists Peter Passell and Bob Davis, explore the fund's austere policy prescriptions for Asian borrowers. Finally, David Sanger traces the fund's unrealistic and wrenching policy prescriptions for Indonesia to the fund's lack of expertise in international politics.

The final series of selections examines Russia's persistent economic problems. Jeffrey Sachs in "Rule of the Ruble" and Representative Bernard Sanders in "IMF 'Salvation' in Russia?" assert that IMF assistance to Russia, and other countries, has been counterproductive. George Melloan argues that fund assistance enables the Russian government to postpone politically difficult yet essential institutional reforms. Alternatively, the *New York Times* contends that the July 1998 IMF loan was prudent but notes that Russia is exposed to massive exchange-rate risk that could prove disastrous. This editorial was prophetic since less than one month later Russian president Boris Yeltsin reneged on his commitments to the IMF not to devalue the ruble. This breakdown of the July 1998 accord further damaged Russia's economy. David Sanger details Russian perfidy in "Who Lost Russia? Pushing an Accord That Fell Apart." Finally, Stanley Fischer, first deputy managing director of the IMF, responds to fund critics in "Lessons from a Crisis."

MEXICO

On Both Sides of the Border, Peso Ills Were Long Ignored

David E. Sanger and Anthony DePalma

This selection was originally published in the New York Times on 24 January 1995. David Sanger and Anthony DePalma are staff reporters for the Times.

While the Clinton administration and the Mexican government were saying until late last year [1994] that Mexico was a booming example of an emerging market that would bring wealth to workers in both countries, warnings were running rampant in both capitals that severe economic trouble lay ahead.

According to officials in Washington, the Treasury Department told several Mexican officials beginning last summer [1994] that the country's short-term borrowings had reached a dangerously high level and that the peso was being kept artificially high. But on several occasions, officials said, the Mexicans responded that they were aware of the problem but that nothing could be done during and just after the election that brought Ernesto Zedillo Ponce de León to power.

In Mexico City, officials now acknowledge that they knew the economy was in serious trouble months before Mr. Zedillo's election on 21 August [1994]. But they say that for political reasons, partly related to the elections and partly to the ambitions of President Carlos Salinas de Gortari to head the new World Trade Organization after leaving office, they chose to continue borrowing and spending at a tremendous pace, sustaining the illusion of a thriving economy.

Today, Guillermo Ortiz, the Mexican finance minister, said at a hostile meeting of the legislature in Mexico City that there was "a yellow light" in Mexico's balance sheets that anyone should have seen. He said that while the government was to blame, so was Wall Street, which "endorsed the economic policies and in particular the exchange rate policy of the Mexican Government."

The series of warnings issued from Washington, however, raises a number of questions about what the administration was saying in public about the health of the Mexican economy, signals that were picked up by both American companies and investors. In November [1994], as disaster loomed, President Clinton used the Summit of the Americas in Miami, the first meeting of Latin American leaders in nearly three decades, to celebrate Mexico's economic management as a model for the region's growth. He and his deputies issued no warnings that Mexico was consuming too much too fast or letting its debt grow too rapidly.

Asked today why Mr. Clinton offered no public words of caution, Michael D. McCurry, the White House press secretary, said, "The President's public comments have always stressed the fundamental strength of the Mexican economy and the commitment of the Mexican leadership to economic and political reform."

But a senior White House official added: "There was a great deal of sensitivity, as the Zedillo administration came to office, about not undercutting the very delicate situation they faced as they tried to form a government, so there was a very conscious effort not to be too heavy-handed. All these sovereignty issues are very sensitive."

Mr. Zedillo, an economist, contributed to the atmosphere of unbridled optimism. Visiting Washington on 23 November [1994], just before his inauguration, he talked of economic growth this year [1995] "at 4 percent or better, and soon 5 percent, which we need to generate a million new jobs a year."

Now he will be lucky if his economy posts any growth this year and if the number of jobs do not shrink. At the same time, the Clinton administration is now warning that unless the crisis is resolved, nearly half a million Mexicans seeking higher wages will illegally enter Texas and California during the next year.

In the aftermath of the Mexican debacle, officials in both Washington and Mexico are spinning tales of who knew what and when. The Central

Intelligence Agency, for example, circulated a brief warning in July [1994] that Mexico's foreign currency reserves were being depleted in an effort to keep up the value of the peso. Now it is recirculating the same report, citing it as evidence that top government officials had been warned.

But several leading economic officials say that the original warning was buried in a mountain of economic intelligence issued by the CIA. "There was no headline, and they know how to get your attention when they want to," one official said.

The agency, officials say, provided no warning in December [1994] that Mr. Zedillo was considering a major devaluation of the peso, which precipitated the crisis. Washington was given a half-hour notice of the action.

Other Clinton administration officials said they warned Mexican leaders last year [1994] that the peso was overvalued, especially considering the tremendous pace at which Mexico was printing money.

One senior American official said that while it would be "inappropriate" to discuss private consultations between the Mexican and American governments, "it would also be a big mistake to suppose that we were unaware of the building problem." Mexican officials, he said, acknowledged the problem but did little.

Today, both administration officials and the House Speaker, Newt Gingrich, expressed optimism that Congress would approve $40 billion in loan guarantees—essentially cosigning a loan—in hopes of increasing the confidence of investors in buying Mexican securities again. "It's going to happen," Mr. Gingrich told reporters. Those comments helped reverse slides both on the Mexican stock exchange and on Wall Street.

Mexican officials now acknowledge that they issued far too many short-term bonds—called *tesobonos*—and they say Mr. Salinas's administration passed up several opportunities to devalue the peso slowly, a step that could have averted the huge sell-off in Mexican bonds and other securities.

Mr. Ortiz, the finance minister, said that in September [1994] he argued that the peso should be devalued in an orderly way when a pact with labor and business was renewed. He not only lost that argument but also was originally passed over when Mr. Zedillo picked Jaime Serra Puche as his first finance minister.

Mr. Serra Puche was forced to resign a week after the peso was devalued, and Mr. Ortiz took his place.

Other officials who were carried over from the previous administration say that when Mr. Zedillo took office on 1 December [1994] he knew how seriously overextended the Mexican economy was and that a crash could follow. But he also knew that the economy was addicted to the flood of international capital to keep paying its bills. So they said there was not much he could do except act as if nothing was wrong and encourage investors to keep pouring money into Mexico.

Mexican Handout:
Bailing Out the Creditor Class

Walker F. Todd

This selection was originally published in the *Nation* on 13 February 1995. Walker Todd is an attorney and economic consultant in private practice in Ohio and was assistant general counsel and research officer at the Federal Reserve Bank of Cleveland.

One of the most preposterous financial crimes of the century, the official management of the 1980s developing-countries debt crisis, is being repeated before our very eyes, and by many of the original perpetrators to boot. As this is written, the Clinton administration is pushing, and Congress seems poised to approve, a loan guarantee package for Mexico of up to $40 billion. This is on top of hastily arranged international credit lines worth $18 billion, most of them guaranteed directly or indirectly by the United States and cobbled up since Christmas [1994].

Mexico owes the world about $120 billion (more than $160 billion by some estimates), and about $58 billion of that amount falls due this year [1995]. Hence the need for a total aid package of about $58 billion, although it is not yet certain that most or all of that aid will be drawn upon.

One must be exacting and clear about who the principal beneficiaries of a U.S. guarantee of Mexico's foreign debts would be: Mexico owes foreign—primarily U.S.—investors in stock shares and bonds about $60 billion. Also, about $18.3 billion of the $120 billion total is owed to U.S. banks, led by Citicorp with about $2.9 billion. With the peso down in value by one-third and Mexico's dollar reserves dwindling, it is clear that only a mammoth infusion of funds or forgiveness of its debts can prevent the country from defaulting.

The original crime, now being repeated, was the profligate lending of billions of dollars from the U.S. banking system between 1974 and 1982 to as gaudy a band of tinpot military dictators, kleptocratic presidents, and bon vivant finance ministers as ever graced a Connecticut Avenue diplomatic reception, followed in August 1982 by the discovery that the borrowers either could not or would not repay the money. But it was not practical politics to recognize the stupidity of the situation and call the lenders into account. No, orthodoxy and good form required the ongoing pretense that the loans were still good, with a host of jerry-built solutions from the Treasury, the Federal Reserve, the International Monetary Fund, and the World Bank. So, as an African economist once told me, "One class of people borrowed the money, and a different class of people had to pay it back."

The IMF-policed austerity regimes that were used to keep the loan money flowing (usually only enough to pay the interest; the principal was rarely reduced) became legendary in developing countries during the 1980s. What did governing elites or international financial diplomats care if the vanishing middle classes and teeming poor of the Third World paid the price of "adjustment" while the lifestyles of the rich changed not at all?

In 1982 Mexico owed U.S. banks about $25 billion. The dirty secret of Debt Crisis I was that foreign banks had deposits of flight capital from rich residents of the debtor nations that would have covered much (and in some cases all) of the banks' claims on the debtor countries. But despite the price paid for "adjustment" by the middle classes and the poor of the developing countries, not to mention the price paid in lost export sales to those countries by U.S. manufacturers and farmers in the heartland, the names of the thieves and the amounts they stole were never disclosed.

Now, by devaluing the peso, Mexico has again committed moral (if not technical) default on its dollar-denominated obligations. This is the principal legacy of the administration of former president Carlos Salinas de Gortari and his supporters in the U.S. establishment. It is doubtful that Mexico can meet its external obligations during 1995 without either debt relief (always the right answer in international lending problems involving developing countries) or new loans from First World governments and banks (the establishment's preferred solution). After the lost decade of the 1980s, relieved only briefly in the early 1990s by the North American Free Trade Agreement financial bubble, the Mexican people find themselves once more confronting official demands for renewed austerity, quiet acceptance of further reduced wages (now approximately 60 percent below 1980 levels in inflation-adjusted peso terms), reduced possibilities for immigration to the United States to escape poverty, and diminished prospects for renewed growth of the Mexican economy for the forseeable future.

But here is where the truly intolerable part begins again: The governing elites in both countries who caused, exacerbated, or covered up this mess expect to escape censure, just as happened in 1982.

Secret credit lines for Mexico from the United States, Japan, and European governments amounting to as much as $12 billion were negotiated twice in the past fifteen months or so, ostensibly to defend the peso, but it is now clear that the only possible use of those lines would have been to finance the flight from the peso of Mexico's governing elites and their compatriots in the international financial system. Amusingly, through a tripartite credit line involving Canada as well as Mexico, which was announced publicly in April 1994, the United States essentially has agreed to lend Canada dollars that Canada can then lend to Mexico, which further weakens the U.S. dollar. Our own creditors now understand that we have underwritten the foreign debts of our two neighbors. Federal Reserve chairman Alan Greenspan was an active promoter of those credit lines, as well as the current bailout effort.

The principal purpose to be served by the new Mexican bailout package is to prevent a loss of confidence of foreign investors in a host of other developing nations, such as Argentina. But this is a silly exercise, a true confidence game, because now no rational investor could have faith in Mexico's governing Institutional Revolutionary Party (PRI), which has enjoyed so much official U.S. support in recent decades. The Banco de Mexico, the country's central bank, was still intervening in the Mexico City stock exchange and rigging *tesobono* (treasury bill) auctions in the same week that the bailout package was presented to Congress, a clear indication that stability has not returned to the country's shaky financial markets. Also, if other countries have mismanaged their financial affairs and are courting disaster for their currencies, there is not much that a bailout of Mexico can do to restore investor confidence. Besides, the prospects for repayment from future Mexican oil receipts, for example, are somewhat limited: At current oil production and price levels, the gross export receipts for Pemex, the national petroleum company, are only about $8.5 billion per year, and most of that has already been pledged to other purposes. The time is long since past in Washington for a repetition of the Paul Volcker–directed "lend new money to meet the interest payments and pretend that it is all still good debt" strategy of the 1980s.

Dissent has broken out in both the Republican and Democratic Parties over various aspects of the bailout. A variety of extraneous conditions are being proposed to sweeten the deal: demands that Mexico loosen its ties to Cuba and crack down on illegal immigrants to the United States (red meat for the right) and calls for stronger enforcement of labor and environmental protections (for the liberal left). But at bottom what is needed is a prompt and full disclosure of what the $40 billion will be used for. The names and amounts paid for each disbursement under the credit line should be published. If there are Charles Keatings, Ferdinand Marcoses, and M. Danny Walls lurking, the public is entitled to know who they are and what they intend to do with the money they receive at our expense. And if the names disclosed prove to be those of prominent Mexicans and U.S. banks, securities firms, mutual funds, and pension fund managers, then we should know that, too. Who knows, with enough disclosure, maybe no one would step forward to claim the money. But don't count on it.

Unfortunately, no new U.S. loan guarantees administered by the existing PRI government can foster real stability in Mexico. And support for the side agreements to NAFTA misses the point entirely. Dissenters in Congress should insist on complete institutional and financial reform of the Mexican government, which might then do more to address labor and environmental concerns from an authentic Mexican perspective, not merely as a PRI concession to the United States. The PRI has forfeited all moral authority to govern. President Ernesto Zedillo Ponce de León should invite the two main opposition parties to join his Cabinet on a full power-sharing basis, with all the important Cabinet ministries going to the opposition. The PRI itself should be dissolved.

To combat the PRI's almost unnatural hold on the affections of many of Mexico's uneducated poor, truth commissions independent of the PRI, such as those used in Chile after Pinochet, should be established to investigate matters such as the use of foreign credit lines by the Banco de Mexico, the massacre of student demonstrators in Mexico City in 1968, the manipulation of the 1988 election results, the responsibility for the assassinations of Luis Donaldo Colosio (first presidential candidate of the PRI) and José Francisco Ruiz Massieu (second-ranking PRI official) in 1994, and the murders of journalists and opposition activists under Salinas. Also, a separate inquiry should be mounted into the influence of drug runners and money launderers in Mexican public life, as well as their connections to foreign intelligence services.

As for Washington's pending actions: It once was a federal felony under the Johnson Act for any person subject to U.S. jurisdiction to lend money to a foreign government in default on its loans from the United States. After 1945, however, the act was amended to accommodate the formation of the Bretton Woods institutions. Only international financial "outlaws" like the former Soviet Union and China were excluded. Then, in 1992, during the euphoria over market openings in Russia, the Johnson Act was quietly amended further to exempt from its prohibitions former Soviet-bloc countries that were not yet members of the IMF and World Bank, establishing the principle that even outlaws may now borrow money in international financial markets. This is too bad, for as the crimes of 1982 are repeated, this time we lack a good felony statute with which to punish the miscreants.

The Case for Mexico's Rescue:
The Peso Package Looks Even Better Now

Bradford De Long, Christopher De Long, and Sherman Robinson

This selection was excerpted from an article published in *Foreign Affairs*, May/June 1996. Bradford De Long is a professor of economics at the University of California, Berkeley. Christopher De Long works for a major financial services firm in New York City. Sherman Robinson is the director of the Trade and Macroeconomics Division at the International Food Policy Research Institute.

In the spring of 1994, Mexico seemed to be doing many things right. Since the mid-1980s it had undertaken major reforms. The government budget had shifted from a substantial deficit to a surplus, thus no longer draining Mexicans' savings pool. State enterprises were being privatized and tariffs lowered. Since 1989 the government deficit had fallen from 5 percent of GDP to 0, and the inflow of capital had risen from 0 to 5 percent of GDP.

Some leading economists (e.g., Rudiger Dornbusch, Alejandro Werner, Guillermo Calvo, Leonardo Leiderman, and Carmen Reinhart) forecast trouble, however. Inflation and the relatively fixed peso-dollar exchange rate had left Mexico uncompetitive. While foreign investors still viewed Mexico favorably, Mexicans realized that at current exchange rates new foreign direct investment in Mexico was likely to be unprofitable. Mexicans had been taking foreign investors' money, but they were using it to finance increased consumption rather than increased investment. The solution was to devalue the peso by 20 percent and then, to keep Mexico from losing competitiveness again, maintain the real exchange rate by bringing the peso's rate of inflation down to the U.S. inflation rate—a standard prescription of the International Monetary Fund and the World Bank.

Throughout the spring and summer of 1994, the administration of Carlos Salinas was preoccupied with the Mexican presidential campaign. Although foreign exchange reserves were falling, the government bet that the drawdown was not a permanent change in foreign investors' demand for Mexican assets. Part of the government's strategy for maintaining confidence in the stability of its exchange rate was to replace conventional short-term borrowing with *tesobonos*, short-term securities whose principal was indexed to the dollar, encouraging investors who feared devaluation to keep their capital in the country. In retrospect, this was a double-or-nothing bet. The policy was effective in the short term but risky: It retained some $23 billion of foreign financing but ensured that, if a devaluation came, it would be deeper and more dangerous.

By the end of 1994, it had become public knowledge that the flow of foreign portfolio capital into Mexico had not resumed. From nearly $30 billion, before the assassination of presidential candidate Luis Donaldo Colosio in March 1994, foreign exchange reserves had fallen to perhaps $5 billion. After a tumultuous year that included political assassinations, a tainted presidential election, and a guerrilla uprising in the state of Chiapas, Mexico had nearly reached the bottom of its reserves. Just weeks into his term, the new Mexican president, Ernesto Zedillo Ponce de Léon, announced a devaluation of the peso.

The market reaction was more severe than anticipated. The peso fell 50 percent, far more than the 20 percent economists deemed necessary to restore equilibrium. Each investor in Mexico feared that other investors would pull their money out no matter what the cost and that the last investors to withdraw would lose the most—through hyperinflation, as the Mexican government frantically printed pesos to cover its peso-denominated debts; through capital controls, which would trap money in Mexico indefinitely and eat up its value; or through formal default, a repeat of Mexico's commercial bank crisis of 1982.

With $5 billion in reserves, $23 billion in *tesobono* liabilities, which would be converted into dollars and pulled from Mexico as they matured, and no one willing to lend hard currency, Mexico faced two painful alternatives. The government could push interest rates sky-high to keep capital in the country, in which case the extraordinary cost of money would strangle investment and employment and quickly bring on a great depression. Or it could lose its ability to borrow and start rapidly printing money to meet its obligations, resulting in a spiral of hyperinflation and depreciation, in which case a deep depression would come slowly as hyperinflation eviscerated a productive economy and tore Mexico from the world trade network. To make things worse, the panic began to spread—the so-called tequila effect—raising the possibility that developing countries throughout the world would be forced into strongly contractionary policies leading to deep recessions.

A MEASURE OF SUCCESS

Mexico's predicament was not preordained. At the end of 1994, Mexico's economy was not insolvent but merely illiquid. If investors had been willing to roll over the country's short-term debt, a combination of contractionary policies and a moderate devaluation to reduce imports and encourage exports would have helped pay the government's foreign liabilities as they came due. Such an approach might have caused a recession (although in Britain in late 1992 it did not), but it would have been much shorter and shallower than the one Mexico faced in the absence of funds to roll over its short-term debt. Lack of liquidity was the problem, and liquidity is what the support package provided: some $40 billion in dollar-denominated assets from the United States, the International Monetary Fund, and other donors, put aside for Mexico to draw on.

The peso support package worked: Mexico registered a $7.4 billion trade surplus in 1995. Real exports were more than 30 percent higher in 1995 than in 1994, while imports fell more than 8 percent. The generation of such an export surplus so quickly resulted from the involuntarily large devaluation of the peso and the squeeze the crisis put on the Mexican economy.

Mexico can now export enough to earn the foreign exchange to repay its debts. Indeed, governments and international institutions that contributed to the support package are making money—as is generally the case in a genuine liquidity crisis. So far, $750 million in interest payments has flowed into the U.S. Treasury. The Congressional Budget Office forecasts that the support package will reduce, not increase, the U.S. budget deficit. Moreover, Mexico's foreign exchange reserves at the end of January [1996] were a healthy $16 billion.

The rescue has not been pain free. Mexico's moves during the peso crisis to allay foreign investors' skittishness about lending or refinancing have exacted a high cost: The country's GDP in 1995 was 7 percent below 1994 levels. However, Mexico's unemployment rates have improved since

August [1995], and other data suggest that the worst is over. The severe recession Mexico experienced is much better than the great depression the country might have suffered in the absence of the liquidity support package.

Without an international rescue, a major depression in Mexico seemed almost inevitable, and it would almost surely have led to regional slowdowns in California and Texas and a jump in illegal immigration into the United States. There was a chance — how large, no one knew or was willing to estimate — that the crisis would spread to other developing countries. A sudden end to the $150 billion annual flow of private investment from the industrial core of the world economy to the developing nations would likely have caused severe depressions in Latin America and perhaps in Asia.

FAIR ENOUGH

Initially U.S. congressional barons embraced the rescue. But despite almost daily pilgrimages to Capitol Hill by Treasury secretary Robert Rubin and Federal Reserve chairman Alan Greenspan, legislative support unraveled. A Clinton economic initiative that promised to stem an international liquidity crisis, avoid a great depression in America's neighbor to the south and a large increase in illegal immigration, avert a potential recession in developing countries throughout the world, avoid regional slowdowns in Texas and California, and probably make money for the U.S. Treasury turned out to be impossible to push through Congress in early 1995. The Clinton administration shifted to the joint executive branch–IMF rescue package, which used the Treasury Department's Stabilization Fund to provide liquidity to Mexico.

What seemed to excite rage was that the U.S. government wanted to do something to support Mexico and — even worse — investors in Mexico. Xenophobia confused the debate, but the animus behind the current applause lines of the American left and right appears to be the perception that the U.S. government gave a $50 billion bailout to Secretary Rubin's Wall Street friends.

The current Mexican recession does impose an unfair burden of adjustment, even if it is only a shadow of the potential macroeconomic disaster. From 1994 to 1995, real Mexican GDP fell, and the unemployment rate in late 1995 was some 3 to 6 percentage points above its mark the previous year. Yet investors in *tesobonos*—investors who knew the risks—came out of the crisis whole.

The support package, however, did not make investors richer at others' expense. Stemming financial crises is a positive-sum game: Everyone wins. Workers keep their jobs, and small businesses avoid bankruptcy. These benefits are real, and they add more to the sum of human welfare than the appreciation of a few financial assets on Wall Street. To abandon these benefits to make Wall Street investors suffer would be cutting off one's nose to spite one's face.

A rapid and efficient way to impose the burden of the crisis more fairly, without the legal and economic mess of formal default and without increasing the risk of a wider liquidity crisis, would have been nice. Some political analysts say they would have welcomed a formal default by Mexico, in which case creditors would have had to negotiate with the Mexican government for repayment and bear some of the cost. Default negotiations, however, never end quickly, cast a long shadow over a nation's economy, keeping foreign investment out for up to a decade, and vastly increase the magnitude of the near-term economic losses and depression. Moreover, the default of one developing nation invariably causes investors to perceive more risk in others, causing problems throughout the world. Even with hindsight, however, there was no clear path to a better solution. Alternatives that spread the costs more widely would have amplified them as well.

Part of the problem is that there is no consensus about what constitutes a good economic system. There used to be wide agreement in the United States that the best balance is a "mixed economy," in which government provides key investments and services, a safety net, and social insurance, while most of the risks and rewards from enterprise are left to entrepreneurs and investors. Yet post–cold war Republican rhetoric repudiates this consensus and seeks a retreat to an earlier, less satisfactory form of capitalism, while Democrats fail to defend the mixed economy or put forward a reasoned alternative. The result is a muddle, as in the debate over NAFTA, the Mexican rescue package, and recent U.S. budgets.

Any assessment of what the political firestorm over the peso support package means for future management of the world economy is depressing. Faced with a classic liquidity crisis in which international support would produce huge economic benefits at very little risk, Congress could not step up to the plate. The only positive note is that Congress was equally unwilling to block the rescue package.

Perhaps worse, some of the larger financial powers sounded like the skeptics in Congress, grousing that the Mexican crisis was not a "systemic problem" and that the rescue package helped those who had made imprudent short-term investments in Mexico. Germany and Britain abstained from the IMF executive board vote that authorized the organization's contribution to the support package. Ultimately the IMF did step up to the plate, approved the program, and has announced its willingness to do likewise again. It may have to. The role of the IMF becomes more crucial when the major economic powers are unable to react quickly to dampen liquidity crises.

INCREASING THE ODDS

The long-term benefits from the economic policies instituted in the 1980s by Mexican president Carlos Salinas remain. Mexico's tariffs and nontariff barriers have been slashed. Restrictions on foreign investment have been lifted. Perhaps one thousand state-owned enterprises have been privatized. A central government budget deficit of 13 percent of GDP in 1987 has been transformed into a balanced budget, and inflation is down to 27 percent, from 150 percent in 1987.

Relying on foreign capital inflows to finance industrialization, however, is risky. It can lead not only to rapid growth but to deep recessions, as the United States discovered in the 1800s, when it relied heavily on British financing for its industrial and infrastructure development and was subjected periodically to devastating financial crises. In addition, the Mexican banking sector remains under considerable strain, inflation is a persistent problem, and unemployment and underemployment remain very high.

The Mexican political system may collapse under the weight of economic and political liberalization and the extra burden created by the peso crisis. Noting the assassinations of Cardinal Posadas, Luis Donaldo Colosio, and José Francisco Ruiz Massieu, commentator Jorge Castañeda has concluded that nonviolent dispute resolution mechanisms among Mexican elites are in "a terminal state of dysfunction." Should the Mexican political system collapse, what follows may not be better, economically or politically.

More likely, Mexican politics will muddle along toward greater democracy. And whatever Mexico's destiny, it is surely better off because of the economic engagement the past two U.S. administrations pursued. NAFTA has increased the odds that successive Mexican governments will continue to dismantle the structures of government control and political influence that have been a drag on Mexico's growth. More important, NAFTA has increased the odds that foreign investors will believe Mexico is committed to progrowth policies. It has boosted Mexico's ability to draw on the world's savings to finance further investments directed toward long-term productivity growth.

What to Expect from IMF?
Look at Mexico

Ian Vasquez and L. Jacobo Rodriguez

This selection first appeared in *Investor's Business Daily* on 1 April 1998. Ian Vasquez is director and L. Jacobo Rodriguez is assistant director of the Project on Global Economic Liberty at the Cato Institute in Washington, D.C.

Now that the House has decided to put off a vote on IMF funding until after the spring recess [1998], Congress still has time to consider the wisdom of the White House's $18 billion request.

Lawmakers need only look south of the border. Backers of the International Monetary Fund point to the $52 billion bailout of Mexico in 1995 as a shining example of the fund's success. But three years later, the IMF's failures there are obvious.

The bailout set a bad precedent that could cost U.S. taxpayers dearly. Mexico has already repaid the money it borrowed from the U.S. Treasury, mostly by borrowing from other sources. But it has yet to repay the IMF—and 18 percent of IMF funds are donated by the United States.

Clinton claims that the bailout forced Mexico to "put in place a tough adjustment program to get its economic house in order." That's wrong. In fact, IMF credit actually let the Mexican government put off necessary reforms.

Take the state-owned oil monopoly, Pemex. It has not been privatized or even deregulated. Today, the price of gasoline at the pump is much higher in Mexico than in the United States.

Without the bailout crutch, Mexico would have been forced to renegotiate an extension of its debt's maturity with its creditors and sell its assets to pay them off. Such measures would have restored market confidence in Mexico. They also would have meant a fairly quick resumption of private capital inflows. Instead, the Mexican government was let off the hook, and Mexico's debt holders got their money back.

Truth is, the risk of a global crisis was never credible, even if the Mexican economy—about one-twentieth the size of the U.S. economy—had collapsed completely.

And Mexico's citizens surely didn't benefit. In fact, they suffered a sharp decline in their standard of living. Real per capita income has fallen back to its 1974 level, and the people of Mexico still have to bear the greater debt burden.

From the end of 1994 to the end of 1996, Mexico added $60 billion to its total external debt, which now tops $160 billion. Instead of fully opening up banking to foreign investment, the government has bailed out commercial banks to the tune of $45 billion by buying all their bad or shaky loans.

The result? Mexico's weak banking sector, a major cause of the crisis, is still in urgent need of restructuring.

Regardless of whether or when Mexico repays the IMF, America's contributions to the fund add to the U.S. national debt and affect the borrowing costs of the federal government.

IMF loans waste taxpayers' money because the IMF lends at rates of interest that do not reflect the true risk of the loans, and rates of return the U.S. receives are lower than interest rates for U.S. Treasury bills. The fact that the fund keeps asking for more money is not a good indication that the money it has already received has been spent wisely.

In any event, whether or not Mexico repaid all of its loans to the United States misses the point. The problem, according to economist Allan Meltzer, is that the "IMF's programs drive a large wedge between the social risk—the risk borne by the troubled country—and the private risk borne by bankers."

The legacy of the Mexican bailout of 1995 is the Asian crisis of today—or at least its severity. The bailout sent a signal to the world that if anything went wrong in emerging economies, the IMF would come to investors' rescue. What else can explain the near doubling of private capital inflows to East Asian countries in 1995 alone?

To end the crisis-generating system in which neither governments nor investors bear the full cost of their reckless behavior, Congress should "just say no" to Clinton and the IMF.

The IMF Doesn't Put Out Fires, It Starts Them

Robert J. Barro

This selection was originally published in *BusinessWeek* on 7 December 1998. Robert Barro is a professor of economics at Harvard University and a senior fellow of the Hoover Institution at Stanford University.

Congressional Republicans disgraced themselves before the recent elections by acting like Democrats. They approved far too much new federal spending, the worst of which was the $18 billion for the International Monetary Fund. No doubt some in Congress were convinced by President Clinton's argument that the IMF was the world's fire department, which ought not to be deprived of water while the fire was burning. But a better analogy would be to Ray Bradbury's *Fahrenheit 451,* in which the fire department's mission is to start fires.

The politics of IMF funding is as clear as it is insidious. If Congress does not provide money for the fund to bail out, say, Brazil, and Brazil collapses, then Congress gets blamed. But no one is willing to blame Congress if the IMF actually works to encourage Brazilian-type financial crises time and again. Some economists believe that bailouts increase "moral hazard" by rewarding and encouraging bad policies by governments and excessive risk taking by banks. Aware that they can be bailed out in the crunch, banks will often lend at interest rates that do not reflect fundamental risks. This, in turn, generates new financial crises and reduces world economic growth.

In Asia, a flood of low-cost capital from Europe, Japan, and the United States wound up financing real estate speculation and overcapacity, thanks in part to an assumed IMF "guarantee." But nobody will ever be able to prove that the IMF effectively starts new fires in this way. Hence, the political forces favor IMF funding and limitless bailouts.

CRUTCHES

IMF economists like to argue that these moral hazard problems are minimal. But consider the case of the recent $42 billion package for Brazil. How did the Brazilians qualify for this support? They did so mostly by not exercising sound fiscal policies. If their policies had been better, they would not be in their current difficulties and would not qualify for IMF money.

Russia is another example. In most respects, effective reforms in Russia ceased by 1993. Since then, the availability of IMF and other foreign money provided an excuse to avoid making tough political decisions. Instead of cutting public outlays or increasing tax collections, undertaking efficient privatizations or enacting legal reforms, the government counted on foreign bailouts to hold things together.

An interesting question is what the IMF will do now in Russia. The current government will never formulate a sensible economic plan, and the fund therefore cannot demand that new lending be conditioned on sound policies. But if no money is forthcoming, then Russia will default on past IMF obligations and the IMF will no longer be able to pretend that it always gets repaid. My prediction is that the IMF will come up with a way to keep up the chain-letter game in which it provides Russia, Ukraine, and Indonesia with enough money to keep payments "current."

MEXICAN MESS

The sequence of unrestrained global bailouts began with Mexico in 1995. In this case, the IMF-U.S. lending package was effectively a reward for corrupt and risky bank lending and poor macroeconomic policies. Particularly striking were the massive interventions of the Mexican central bank in an attempt to support the peso. The bank failed and lost billions of dollars in international reserves but did not allow the money supply to contract. Not surprisingly, this policy failed to prevent a sharp devaluation of the currency.

The Mexican bailout kept foreign lenders whole. The mountain of bad bank loans, about 16 percent of gross domestic product, became a liability of Mexican taxpayers. The bailout also did not avoid sharp economic contraction and high inflation—both much worse than in Argentina, which ties its money supply directly to its international reserves.

The real shame of the Mexican bailout is that it was judged by many observers to be a success, mainly because the U.S. Treasury got repaid. If, instead, it had properly been labeled as a massive policy blunder, then subsequent unrestrained global bailouts might not have occurred. Countries such as Brazil and Russia would have had the appropriate incentives to implement good policies, instead of knowing that the IMF or the United States would respond to bad policies with showers of money.

One healthy consequence of the recent global financial crisis is the emphasis on increased transparency in financial transactions. In this spirit, the IMF might consider changing its name to the IMH—the Institute for Moral Hazard. Better yet, the IMF could admit that it was insolvent and go out of business.

EAST ASIA

Power unto Itself

This selection first appeared in the *Financial Times* on 11 December 1997. Jeffrey Sachs is the director of the Harvard Institute for International Development.

It is time that the world take a serious look at the International Monetary Fund. In the past three months, this small, secretive institution has dictated economic conditions to 350 million people in Indonesia, South Korea, the Philippines, and Thailand. It has put on the line more than $100 billion of taxpayers' money in loans.

These bailout operations, if handled incorrectly, could end up helping a few dozen international banks to escape losses for risky loans by forcing Asian governments to cover the losses on private transactions that have gone bad. Yet the IMF decisions have been taken without any public debate, comment, or scrutiny.

While it pays lip service to "transparency," the IMF offers virtually no substantive public documentation of its decisions, except for a few pages in press releases that are shorn of the technical details needed for a serious professional evaluation of its programs. Remarkably, the international community accepts this state of affairs as normal.

The world waits to see what the fund will demand of country X, assuming that the IMF has chosen the best course of action. The world accepts as normal the idea that crucial details of IMF programs should remain confidential, even though these "details" affect the well-being of millions. Staff at the fund, meanwhile, are unaccountable for their decisions.

The people most affected by these policies have little knowledge or input. In Korea, the IMF insisted that all presidential candidates immediately "endorse" an agreement they had no part in drafting or negotiating—and no time to understand.

The situation is out of hand. However useful the IMF may be to the world community, it defies logic to believe that the small group of a thousand economists on Nineteenth Street in Washington should dictate the economic conditions of life to seventy-five developing countries with around 1.4 billion people. These people constitute 57 percent of the developing world outside China and India (which are not under IMF programs). Since perhaps half of the IMF's professional time is devoted to these countries—with the rest tied up in surveillance of advanced countries, management, research, and other tasks—about five hundred staff cover the seventy-five countries. That is an average of about seven economists per country.

One might suspect that seven staffers would not be enough to get a sophisticated view of what is happening. That suspicion would be right. The IMF threw together a draconian program for Korea in just a few days, without deep knowledge of the country's financial system and without any subtlety as to how to approach the problems.

Consider what the fund said about Korea just three months ago [September 1997] in its 1997 annual report. "Directors welcomed Korea's continued impressive macroeconomic performance [and] praised the authorities for their enviable fiscal record." Three months ago there was not a hint of alarm, only a call for further financial sector reform—incidentally without mentioning the *chaebols* (conglomerates) or the issue of foreign ownership of banks or banking supervision that now figure so prominently in the IMF's Korea program.

In the same report, the IMF had this to say about Thailand, at that moment on the edge of the financial abyss. "Directors strongly praised Thailand's remarkable economic performance and the authorities' consistent record of sound macroeconomic policies."

With a straight face, Michel Camdessus, the IMF managing director, now blames Asian governments for the deep failures of macroeconomic and financial policies that the IMF has discovered. It would have been more useful, instead, for the IMF to ponder why the situation looked so much better three months ago, for therein lies a basic truth about the situation in Asia.

There is no "fundamental" reason for Asia's financial calamity except financial panic itself. Asia's need for significant financial sector reform is real but not a sufficient cause for the panic, and not a justification for harsh macroeconomic policy adjustments. Asia's fundamentals are adequate to forestall an economic contraction: Budgets are in balance or surplus, inflation is low, private saving rates are high, economies are poised for export growth.

Asia is reeling not from a crisis of fundamentals but from a self-fulfilling withdrawal of short-term loans, one that is fueled by each investor's recognition that all other investors are withdrawing their claims. Since short-term debts exceed foreign exchange reserves, it is "rational" for each investor to join in the panic.

Without wider professional debate, the IMF has decided to impose a severe macroeconomic contraction on top of the market panic that is already roiling these economies. Consider the Korea program (or at least those parts that have been announced to the public). The won has depreciated by around 80 percent in the past twelve months, from around 840 a dollar to a record low of 1,565 yesterday; this currency depreciation will force up the prices of traded goods. Yet despite that, the IMF insists that Korea aim for an essentially unchanged inflation rate (5.2 percent in 1998, in comparison with 4.2 percent in 1997). To achieve unchanged low inflation in the face of a huge currency depreciation, Korea will need a brutal monetary squeeze. And indeed this is just what the fund has ordered. Short-term interest rates jumped from 12.5 percent to 21.0 percent upon the signing of the program and have since risen further.

The fund argues that these draconian monetary measures are "to restore and sustain calm in the markets" and "[to] demonstrate to markets the government's resolve to confront the present crisis." It is hard to see how recessionary monetary policy will restore calm. Indeed the panic has so intensified since the signing of the agreement that Korean banks may now be on the verge of outright default. Just one day after the measures were unveiled, the eleventh-largest conglomerate declared bankruptcy when Korean banks abruptly refused to roll over its short-term debts. In recent days more well-known local companies have gone under.

In addition to the rise in interest rates, the IMF is insisting that fiscal policy be tightened by 1.0 to 1.5 percent of GDP. On top of this, the IMF required that nine out of thirty merchant banks suspend operations. The IMF is aiming for Korean growth to fall to 2.5 percent in 1998 from 6.0 percent in 1997. But the projected slowdown may turn out to be the least of Korea's worries by next year [1998] since the underlying macroeconomic measures could easily push the economy into outright contraction. None of this overkill makes sense for an economy that was (rightly) judged to be pursuing sound macroeconomic policies just months earlier.

A better approach would have been for the IMF to stress the strengths rather than the weaknesses of the Korean economy, thereby calming the markets rather than further convincing them of the need to flee the country. Months ago, when the financial crisis began, the fund could have quietly encouraged Japan, the United States, and Europe to provide some credit support to the Bank of Korea. It might well have worked with the major banks to encourage them to roll over their short-term debts without inflaming the panic. With appropriate confidence-building measures, Korea could probably have got by with a modest slowdown in growth, no credit crunch, and a realistic time horizon of a few years to complete its needed financial reforms.

In more than six dozen developing countries, the IMF is in a position to choose make-or-break financial policies. While its instincts are often correct, they can sometimes be wrong, with serious consequences.

In recent years, the IMF mishandled the Russian reforms (for example, by insisting for more than a year that all fifteen successor states to the Soviet Union share a common currency, thereby delaying stabilization and undermining the political support for reforms). In Bulgaria, the IMF signed a program in July 1996 based on 2.5 percent growth and 20 percent inflation in 1997. Instead, Bulgaria has suffered an outright collapse of gross domestic product of more than 10 percent and inflation in the hundreds of percent. The IMF (in common with others) failed to foresee the Mexico crisis in 1994 and the Asian crises in 1997.

Three general conclusions can be reached. First, the IMF is invested with too much power: No single agency should have responsibility for economic policy in half the developing world.

Second, the IMF's executive board should do its job of overseeing the staff, rather than simply rubber-stamp the staffs' proposals. It is high time the board consult outside expertise in the exploratory stages of IMF operations; it should also canvass international opinion about the origins and policy implications of the Asian crisis.

Third, IMF operations should be made public, so that professional debate and review can help ensure the highest possible professionalism of the institution, especially since (for all its faults) the fund will surely continue to play an important role for many years in the future.

The IMF Crisis

Wall Street Journal Editorial

This selection was originally published in the *Wall Street Journal* on 15 April 1998.

What caused the Asia crisis? That's the big question, or ought to be, as the world's economic rule makers converge on Washington this week for the spring meetings of the International Monetary Fund, World Bank, and industrialized nations' Group of Seven. The future management of the world economy surely depends on some understanding of what made the Asian miracle implode so quickly.

While seeking another $18 billion from the United States and total resources of $285 billion to handle this and future crises, the IMF has been puzzling for months over the question of causes. In a speech last November [1997], IMF managing director Michel Camdessus wondered why what began as a local problem in Thailand last summer [1997] spilled into crisis for Malaysia, Indonesia, and South Korea—economies that had been growing at a famous clip until "contagion" sent their currencies into free fall. Mr. Camdessus noted that the currency slides in the Far East "acquired an almost self-perpetuating character" and asked "how could it happen?"

We suggest Mr. Camdessus consult the mirror on the wall. The IMF tripped this crisis by urging the Thais to devalue, then promoted contagion by urging everyone else to do likewise. Now Mr. Camdessus and Treasury secretary Robert Rubin want fresh billions to deal with the train wreck.

Recall the events that sent Asia reeling. By early last year [1997], Thailand was running into problems, borrowing abroad in dollars for projects at home that were not paying off. Clearly this put downward pressure on the baht, which was roughly tied to the dollar. But the Thais had a choice. They could curtail baht creation to defend the exchange rate, which would force a reckoning with the bad banks and finance companies. Or they could try to paper over the problem by devaluing.

The IMF began urging Bangkok to devalue the baht. In an interview last December [1997] with *BusinessWeek*, Mr. Camdessus recounted: "I visited Thailand four times from July 1996 to July 1997, for the exclusive purpose of telling them: 'You are going to make a mess. You must get rid of this very dangerous peg to the dollar.'" Mr. Camdessus said the IMF gave the same advice to "Indonesia, Korea, and the Philippines."

On 2 July [1997] Thailand cut loose the baht—which immediately began its downhill run. That day the IMF hailed Thailand's "managed float," saying "the IMF welcomes today's important steps aimed at addressing Thailand's present economic difficulties and adopting a comprehensive strategy to ensure macroeconomic adjustment and financial stability."

What followed was anything but stable. To compete with Thailand, Malaysia devalued the ringgit. Indonesia—pressured by the IMF to devalue the rupiah—followed suit. In line with IMF prescription, the Philippines devalued. South Korea let slide the won. By late October [1997] what began as an IMF program for "stability" had turned into round after round of competitive devaluation. Taiwan had jumped into the act, needlessly debasing the Taiwan dollar. The Hong Kong and Singapore dollars had come under speculative attack. Brazil, linchpin of South American commerce, was fighting off attacks on the real. The world stared briefly at the possibility of a global currency crisis, in which competitive devaluations could jar normal business so far out of alignment that even relatively healthy economies might face collapse.

Fortunately, some of the most threatened economies stood fast. They let interest rates rise to whatever heights were necessary to persuade speculators it wasn't worthwhile to bet against their currencies. Hong Kong and Singapore defended their dollars. Brazil stuck up for its real. Argentina, as in the 1995 crisis—when the IMF actually helped—stood by its currency board peg to the dollar. The threat of widespread monetary collapse ebbed.

Fund officials, and their backers at the U.S. Treasury, protest that the countries hard hit by devaluations had other problems that now need IMF help to fix. Asia by this account has been a welter of bad banking practices, reckless borrowing, poor governance, corruption, and speculative attacks by George Soros. There is some truth to all that, but none of it was exactly news and none of it was cause for what became Asia's sudden pileup of damaged economies.

Corruption and presidential nepotism in Indonesia, for example, is a wretched problem but has been an unhappy part of the landscape for decades. The market knew about it years ago. The urgent question is why almost overnight Indonesia lost more than half its value—with the rupiah plunging to 15,000 to the dollar before rebounding to roughly 7,750, still less than half what it was before Mr. Camdessus got his wish for Asian devaluation.

Asia's crisis has been primarily a currency crisis, not an explosion of economic fundamentals. Devaluations made it much harder to service foreign, dollar-denominated debt. That, in turn, caused lenders to run for the exits, fearing the last one out would be stuck with any defaults. And that stampede caused a series of genuine dislocations, which chopped value off what might otherwise be profitable ventures.

Even for countries like the United States, where Mr. Camdessus and his Treasury supporters—Secretary Rubin and Deputy Secretary Larry Summers—take a back seat to the Fed in charting monetary policy, this is no minor matter. Asia's crisis has by the IMF's own estimates lopped some 1 percent off global economic growth this year [1998], cutting it to 3.1 percent for 1998 from 4.1 percent in 1997. That's trillions of dollars' worth of wealth lost. The brunt falls not on rich lenders, or on the officials at the IMF and treasury departments, but on ordinary folks in places like

South Korea and Indonesia—who have seen their jobs, savings, and hopes wiped out in one swift swat.

Debate on IMF funding is finally taking shape in Congress—where last fall [1997] what killed the bill was less a genuine understanding of the IMF's mistakes than an unrelated abortion amendment. House majority leader Dick Armey, in a recent memo to his colleagues, focused on the moral hazard that has been growing with each new IMF bailout. Fund bailouts invite lenders to go on taking excessive risks—because the market expects the IMF will cushion the downside. This expectation leads naturally to fresh crises. Mr. Armey noted that the IMF, instead of acting as lender of last resort to basically sound enterprises, has begun "bailing out the bankrupt" and added, "I am far from convinced we should provide any new resources for the IMF."

In a letter this week, former vice presidential contender Jack Kemp congratulates Mr. Armey on his stand and enlarges on the IMF's currency problem. Writes Mr. Kemp: "By all indications, it was the IMF that nudged Southeast Asia over the cliff by enticing them to float their currencies last year [1997]." Adds Mr. Kemp, "The Mexican experience of four years ago should have taught us that these currencies do not float when they come under pressure. In Mexico, what the IMF anticipated would be a 10 percent devaluation turned into a 50 percent free fall of the peso."

To the IMF, this issue seems to remain a source of mystery, requiring much study and much money in the IMF till, lest it happen again. Somehow, fund experts just don't seem able to work out why their careful formulas for devaluation don't work as planned. Folks who actually have to wrestle with the real world are starting to see the crux of the problem. For example, in a visit to this newspaper's offices Monday, Brazilian finance minister Pedro Malan talked about the dangers of abrupt devaluation. He has fought to keep his country's currency on a steady track because "nobody believes it is possible—especially with the current conditions—to have controlled devaluation."

Well, nobody but Messrs. Camdessus, Rubin, and Summers. As long as the IMF prowls the central banks of the planet, fanning moral hazard and urging currency debasement, there will be plenty of self-made problems to employ the IMF. There's a case for world markets needing a lender of last resort—one of the few roles that IMF officials say the fund actually does not aim to play. But putting more money into today's IMF is not likely to solve any crisis. It is more likely to cause new ones.

The Bad News about Bailouts

Lawrence B. Lindsey

This selection was originally published in the *New York Times* on 6 January 1998. Lawrence Lindsey, a resident scholar at the American Enterprise Institute in Washington, D.C., is a former governor of the Federal Reserve System.

Suppose your brother-in-law announced to the whole family at Christmas that he had lost a bundle on Wall Street, couldn't meet his margin calls, and didn't have the money to meet either his credit card bills or his mortgage. Would you bail him out?

Your answer would probably be, "It depends." While the issues involved in the international bailout of South Korea (and other countries) are complex, some of the questions you would ask yourself about your brother-in-law aren't much different from the ones we should be asking ourselves about South Korea.

First, how did the debt burden get so large? In South Korea's case it was a web of sham accounting standards. The reported size of South Korea's exposure has mushroomed over the last several months. Last month [December 1997] the Korean government gave a "final" estimate of $160 billion, and that is just international debt; it doesn't include what Korean companies owe domestically. It is as if your brother-in-law lied to his broker about his assets, cheated on his mortgage application by misrepresenting his income, and then used one credit card to pay off the other.

Second, was the money used for a good purpose? In South Korea's case the loans were used to finance economic development and build an industrial infrastructure. There is no question that this is worthy. Unlike other countries we have bailed out, South Korea did not go on a consumption binge. In 1995, only about 10 percent of its total imports were consumer goods. The rest were capital goods to build productive capacity and raw materials and energy to drive those factories. Furthermore, Koreans work very hard. The great majority work six-day weeks, and it is easy to be impressed with their dedication and sacrifice.

Those investments, however, were made without much thought about the risks involved. The job of the Korean banking system was to say yes if one of the giant *chaebols* [corporate conglomerates] that run the economy asked for money. Under a web of protectionism and cozy relations with the bureaucracy, none of these companies ever got into trouble, even though their profit performance was poor. The national purpose was rapid industrialization and growth; gaining market share was the objective.

Assume your brother-in-law did not buy fancy consumer goods with his money. He used the proceeds from his home refinancing and his credit cards to build a position on Wall Street, which he leveraged further by using his margin account. Like South Korea, he was trying to get rich quickly, but he ran into trouble.

Third, what signals are sent if you finance the bailout? The Korean bailout is all being done very publicly. The United States Treasury and the International Monetary Fund are telling the other nations of the world *and their creditors* that they will be the lenders of last resort. Consider Mexico, which is being touted as a success. The money that flooded into the countries now in trouble really started flowing after our bailout of Mexico. The interest-rate markups were unusually low for the supposed risk on these loans, and the greatest financing binge in world history quickly followed.

Remember, it is not South Korea that pockets the bailout money but the large multinational financial institutions that get paid back. They presumably lent this money in the expectation of making a profit. Their job was to make sure of the creditworthiness of the people they lent to. They could have insisted that the accounting standards of their customers be cleaned up. They didn't and lost.

Interestingly, American banks that were forced by the Federal Reserve and other regulators to accept more careful risk assessment standards and build their capital base were much less exposed to South Korea than European or Japanese banks. When lenders are burned on bad loans, they become much more cautious the next time around.

Back to your brother-in-law. Since everyone will know that you bailed him out, what will be the effect on your siblings, aunts, uncles, and cousins? Will they borrow more and assume that they can count on you? For that matter, will your brother-in-law have learned his lesson? And, if all of the lenders in the country know that there is someone in every family just like you, will they supervise the loans they make as closely?

Finally, what happens if there is no bailout? Unable to get their money, the creditors take possession of the companies, factories, and machinery that their loans financed and look for a new owner. The new buyers aren't necessarily part of the same bankrupt crony system; they are the ones who will pay the highest price. They may be American entrepreneurs or Koreans who have been on the outside in the past.

If the creditors can't get all their money back, they will take the loss and be forced to be much more cautious the next time. In some cases these losses may be quite large, and the regulators of these banks may be forced to take some remedial action (though these same regulators let their wards get overextended in the first place).

However, this route is far preferable to a bailout; both the South Korean and the world economies will be much better off. In South Korea, there will be much more competition and a greater focus on the bottom line. New credit will flow to the new owners much more easily than it would ever flow to the old deadbeats. All the "conditions" supposedly negotiated by the IMF will be forced on South Korea by the market.

The parallel to our home-front analogy is this: Not wanting to see your relations on the street, you might consider your brother-in-law's house a good asset, assume the mortgage from the bank, and allow him to pay you back. Let the other creditors get burned.

Rest assured, though, that you will have a lot more control over your in-law's behavior when you hold the mortgage on his house than if you

simply bail him out. Not to mention the chances that Aunt Sally will need
a bailout next Christmas will be substantially reduced.

Markets to the Rescue

Milton Friedman

This selection first appeared in the *Wall Street Journal* on 13 October 1998. Milton Friedman
is a senior research fellow of the Hoover Institution at Stanford University and a recipient
of the Nobel Prize in economics.

The air is rife with proposals to reform the International Monetary Fund,
increase its funds, and create new international agencies to help guide
global financial markets. Indeed, Congress and the Clinton administration
spent much of the last week's budget negotiations fine-tuning the details
of the United States' latest $18 billion IMF subvention package. Such talk
is on a par with the advice to the inebriate that the cure for a hangover is
the hair of the dog that bit him. As George Shultz, William Simon, and
Walter Wriston wrote on this page in February: "The IMF is ineffective,
unnecessary, and obsolete. We do not need another IMF. . . . Once the
Asian crisis is over, we should abolish the one we have." Centralized
planning works no better on the global than on the national level.

The IMF was established at Bretton Woods in 1944 to serve one
purpose and one purpose only: to supervise the operation of the system of
fixed exchange rates also established at Bretton Woods. That system collapsed on 15 August 1971, when President Nixon, as part of a package of
economic changes including wage and price ceilings, "closed the gold
window"—that is, refused to continue the commitment the United States
had undertaken at Bretton Woods to buy and sell gold at $35 an ounce.
The IMF lost its only function and should have closed shop.

But few things are so permanent as government agencies, including international agencies. The IMF, sitting on a pile of funds, sought and found a new function: serving as an economic consulting agency to countries in trouble—an agency that was unusual in that it offered money instead of charging fees. It found plenty of clients, even though its advice was not always good and, even when good, was not always followed. However, its availability, and the funds it brought, encouraged country after country to continue with unwise and unsustainable policies longer than they otherwise would have or could have. Russia is the latest example. The end result has been more rather than less financial instability.

The Mexican crisis in 1994–95 produced a quantum jump in the scale of the IMF's activity. Mexico, it is said, was "bailed out" by a $50 billion financial aid package from a consortium including the IMF, the United States, other countries, and other international agencies. In reality Mexico was not bailed out. Foreign entities—banks and other financial institutions—that had made dollar loans to Mexico that Mexico could not repay were bailed out. The internal recession that followed the bailout was deep and long; it left the ordinary Mexican citizen facing higher prices for goods and services with a sharply reduced income. That remains true today.

The Mexican bailout helped fuel the East Asian crisis that erupted two years later. It encouraged individuals and financial institutions to lend to and invest in the East Asian countries, drawn by high domestic interest rates and returns on investment, and reassured about currency risk by the belief that the IMF would bail them out if the unexpected happened and the exchange pegs broke. This effect has come to be called "moral hazard," though I regard that as something of a libel. If someone offers you a gift, is it immoral for you to accept it? Similarly, it's hard to blame private lenders for accepting the IMF's implicit offer of insurance against currency risk. However, I do blame the IMF for offering the gift. And I blame the United States and other countries that are members of the IMF for allowing taxpayer money to be used to subsidize private banks and other financial institutions.

Seventy-five years ago, John Maynard Keynes pointed out that, "if the external price level is unstable, we cannot keep both our own price level and our exchanges stable. And we are compelled to choose." When Keynes wrote, he could take free capital movement for granted. The introduction of exchange controls by Hjalmar Schacht in the 1930s converted Keynes's dilemma into a trilemma. Of the three objectives—free capital movement, a fixed exchange rate, independent domestic monetary policy—any two, but not all three, are viable. We are compelled to choose.

The attempt by South Korea, Thailand, Malaysia, and Indonesia to have all three—with the encouragement of the IMF—has produced the external financial crisis that has pummeled those countries and spread concern around the world, just as similar attempts produced financial crises in Britain in 1967, in Chile in the early 1980s, in Mexico in 1995, and in many other cases.

Some economists, notably Paul Krugman and Joseph Stiglitz, have suggested resolving the trilemma by abandoning free capital movement, and Malaysia has followed that course. In my view, that is the worst possible choice. Emerging countries need external capital, and particularly the discipline and knowledge that comes with it, to make the best use of their capacities. Moreover, there is a long history demonstrating that exchange controls are porous and that the attempt to enforce them invariably leads to corruption and an extension of government controls, hardly the way to generate healthy growth.

Either of the other alternatives seems to me far superior. One is to fix the exchange rate by adopting a common or unified currency, as the states of the United States and Panama (whose economy is dollarized) have done and as the participants in the euro propose to do, or by establishing a currency board, as Hong Kong and Argentina have done. The key element of this alternative is that there is only one central bank for the countries using the same currency: the European Central Bank for the euro countries; the Federal Reserve for the other countries.

Hong Kong and Argentina have retained the option of terminating their currency boards, changing the fixed rate, or introducing central bank features, as the Hong Kong Monetary Authority has done in a limited way. As a result, they are not immune to infection from foreign exchange crises originating elsewhere. Nonetheless, currency boards have a good record of surviving such crises intact. Those options have not been retained by

California or Panama and will not be retained by the countries that adopt the euro as their sole currency.

Proponents of fixed exchange rates often fail to recognize that a truly fixed rate is fundamentally different from a pegged one. If Argentina has a balance of payments deficit—if dollar receipts from abroad are less than payments due abroad—the quantity of currency (high-powered or base money) automatically goes down. That brings pressure on the economy to reduce foreign payments and increase foreign receipts. The economy cannot evade the discipline of external transactions; it must adjust. Under the pegged system, by contrast, when Thailand had a balance of payments deficit, the Bank of Thailand did not have to reduce the quantity of high-powered money. It could evade the discipline of external transactions, at least for a time, by drawing on its dollar reserves or borrowing dollars from abroad to finance the deficit.

Such a pegged exchange-rate regime is a ticking bomb. It is never easy to know whether a deficit is transitory and will soon be reversed or is a precursor to further deficits. The temptation is always to hope for the best and avoid any action that would tend to depress the domestic economy. Such a policy can smooth over minor and temporary problems, but it lets minor problems that are not transitory accumulate. When that happens, the minor adjustments in exchange rates that would have cleared up the initial problem will no longer suffice. It now takes a major change. Moreover, at this stage, the direction of any likely change is clear to everyone— in the case of Thailand, a devaluation. A speculator who sold the Thai baht short could at worst lose commissions and interest on his capital since the peg meant that he could cover his short at the same price at which he sold it if the baht was not devalued. In contrast, a devaluation would bring large profits.

Many of those responsible for the East Asia crises have been unable to resist the temptation to blame speculators for their problems. In fact, their policies gave speculators a nearly one-way bet, and by taking that bet, the speculators conferred not harm but benefits. Would Thailand have benefited from being able to continue its unsustainable policies longer?

Capital controls and unified currencies are two ways out of the tri-lemma. The remaining option is to let exchange rates be determined in the market predominantly on the basis of private transactions. In a pure form, clean floating, the central bank does not intervene in the market to affect the exchange rate, though it or the government may engage in exchange transactions in the course of its other activities. In practice, dirty floating is more common: The central bank intervenes from time to time to affect the exchange rate but does not announce in advance any specific value that it will seek to maintain. That is the regime currently followed by the United States, Britain, Japan, and many other countries.

FLOATING RATE

Under a floating rate, there cannot be and never has been a foreign exchange crisis, though there may well be internal crises, as in Japan. The reason is simple: Changes in exchange rates absorb the pressures that would otherwise lead to crises in a regime that tried to peg the exchange rate while maintaining domestic monetary independence. The foreign exchange crisis that affected South Korea, Thailand, Malaysia, and Indonesia did not spill over to New Zealand or Australia because those countries had floating exchange rates.

As between the alternatives of a truly fixed exchange rate and a floating exchange rate, which one is preferable depends on the specific characteristics of the country involved. In particular, much depends on whether a given country has a major trading partner with a good record for stable monetary policy, thus providing a desirable currency with which to be linked. However, so long as a country chooses and adheres to one of the two regimes, it will be spared foreign exchange crises and there will be no role for an international agency to supplement the market. Perhaps that is the reason why the IMF has implicitly favored pegged exchange rates.

The present crisis is not the result of market failure. Rather, it is the result of governments intervening in or seeking to supersede the market, both internally via loans, subsidies, or taxes and other handicaps and externally via the IMF, the World Bank, and other international agencies. We do not need more powerful government agencies spending still more of the taxpayers' money, with limited or nonexistent accountability. That would simply be throwing good money after bad. We need government, both within the nations and internationally, to get out of the way and let the market work. The more that people spend or lend their own money, and the less they spend or lend taxpayer money, the better.

Critics: The IMF Is Misguided.
Skeptics: Too Much Rot in Asia.

Peter Passell

This selection first appeared in the *New York Times* on 15 January 1998. Peter Passell is a columnist at the *Times*.

Who lost Asia? No, the vandals aren't at the gates of Bangkok, Seoul, or Djakarta. But with Thailand on the brink of depression, South Korea in shock over the rude end to its economic miracle, and Indonesia in a succession crisis, finger-pointing seems irresistible.

On one side stand liberals including Joseph E. Stiglitz, the World Bank's chief economist, who are critical of the International Monetary Fund's failure to distinguish between Asia's problems and the more fundamental failings of Latin American and African economies. The fund's demands for austerity, Stiglitz suggests, will prolong Asia's agony.

On the other side are skeptics including Rudi Dornbusch, an economist at MIT, who see this currency crisis—along with resistance to austerity—as symptoms of deeper rot. "The Asian economies aren't the same as Latin America's," Dornbusch agrees, "they're even more corrupt and have wasted even more capital."

Governments that end up on the IMF's doorstep typically spend far more than they take in through taxes—and typically spend it on palaces or highways to nowhere that siphon savings from private investment. So when these governments run out of dollars or when foreign investors scramble for the exits, the fund's conditions for loans are invariably these:

Step One. Balance the budget, put strict limits on the supply of money, and allow interest rates to rise. The idea is to restore price stability and convince investors, domestic and foreign, that it is safe to hold the local currency.

Step Two. Rebuild economic institutions using the template of modern free market capitalism. That involves everything from privatizing public enterprises to eliminating consumer subsidies to nourishing competitive banking.

Mexico, the fund's highest-profile patient before the Asian emergency, suffered from austerity imposed by outsiders. Yet by most accounts the economy emerged on a much sounder footing.

The IMF's hastily drawn plans for Thailand, Indonesia, and Korea were cut from the same sackcloth. While the emphasis in each is on Step Two—particularly in reforming banking systems at the fulcrum of Asia's notorious "crony capitalism"—Asians now out of work might be excused for missing the nuance.

Tight credit is the order of the day. Most businesses simply cannot borrow, while others pay punishingly high interest rates. Indeed, an internal IMF report on Indonesia admits to missteps in a wave of forced bank closings in November [1997]. Moreover, to find money to reimburse depositors, the fund is insisting that governments slash spending.

That galls Mr. Stiglitz, who argues that Asia, with its high savings rate, strong work ethic, and high productivity, should not be lumped with the classically mismanaged undeveloped economies. "You don't want to push these countries into severe recession," he told the *Wall Street Journal.* "One ought to focus on the things that caused the crisis, not on things that make it more difficult to deal with."

Why demand balanced budgets from countries that are already in recession due to lack of demand? these critics ask. "Nobody dreamed of a pay-as-you-go bailout of America's saving and loans in the 1980s," says Robert Z. Lawrence of the Kennedy School of Government at Harvard.

And while the IMF's critics acknowledge that high interest rates may help to coax back capital, they say that tight money will still prove counterproductive. "How does it help Thailand to deprive apparel manufacturers of the working capital needed for exports?" asked Steven Radelet, an economist at the Institute for International Development at Harvard.

Fund officials and their allies within the Clinton administration are not budging. Indeed, this week both Stanley Fischer, first deputy managing director of the IMF, and Deputy Treasury Secretary Lawrence H. Summers journeyed to Indonesia to read the riot act to President Suharto.

The public rationale for the tough talk is the need to contain the currency panic. But less diplomatic supporters of austerity also want to cut off any backlash to sweeping reforms. They see opposition to stern measures as the last gasp of failing "Asian-style" capitalism that produced rapid growth by wastefully mobilizing domestic savings. "Somehow Suharto's kid's pet projects will survive the budget cuts," Mr. Dornbusch predicted.

Albert Fishlow, a senior fellow at the Council on Foreign Relations, worries that the schism is making pragmatic problem solving more difficult. "None of the current IMF programs in Asia are currently valid," he argues, because they all assumed currency depreciation would be checked with the first infusion of dollars.

Most important, Mr. Fishlow adds, the policy squabble is distracting attention from what appears to be a systemic failure of global capitalism. "The old rules didn't work and the new ones haven't been invented," he said.

Rubin Prescribes Tight Money for Asia

Bob Davis

This selection was originally published in the *Wall Street Journal* on 30 June 1998. Bob Davis is a staff reporter for the *Journal*.

Treasury secretary Robert Rubin is spreading the gospel of high interest rates to troubled Asian nations that don't want to hear it.

After a one-hour meeting with Malaysia's feisty prime minister, Mahathir Mohamad, an apostle of lower rates, Mr. Rubin defended the International Monetary Fund's tight monetary policy.

"If you had looser monetary policy, you'd run the risk of substantial depreciation of the currency," Mr. Rubin said at a news conference [in Kuala Lumpur, Malaysia]. That "generates additional inflation, discourages capital investment, encourages capital flight, and greatly increases the problem of repaying debt" denominated in dollars.

Monetary policy has become the great debate topic of the Asian crisis. IMF critics such as Harvard economist Jeffrey Sachs and World Bank chief economist Joseph Stiglitz argue that boosting interest rates to defend weak currencies worsens Asia's problems. High rates haven't stemmed Asian currency crashes, they argue, but have stifled economic activity.

When countries run high interest rates for months, companies and banks get buried under bad debt, Mr. Sachs said.

In recent months, that view has gained adherents as Asian economies deteriorated despite IMF programs. "These countries didn't get into trouble because of profligate monetary policy," said Alan Blinder, former vice chairman of the Federal Reserve and once a Clinton administration economist. "The IMF probably made the problems worse."

At a symposium [in Kuala Lumpur] yesterday attended by Mr. Rubin, Malaysian finance minister Anwar Ibrahim, who earlier resisted calls to loosen monetary policy, now complains that "interest rates are already prohibitively high." Mr. Rubin expects to hear the complaint again today in Bangkok and tomorrow in Seoul.

Bank lending rates are about 13 percent in Malaysia, 25 percent in Thailand, 18 percent in South Korea, and 50 percent in Indonesia. "There's considerable discussion about the proper stance of monetary policy," says David Lipton, U.S. Treasury's undersecretary for international affairs.

Treasury officials haven't been sure how to handle the criticism. At times, they have blamed the IMF for the tight monetary policy — and the Germans for insisting that it apply such conditions. Sometimes they've ducked the question in public. And at other times, they support the tough IMF stance and help guide it.

Mr. Rubin made a spirited defense of IMF policy yesterday. Speaking after Mr. Anwar at the symposium, he said, "The cause (of the Asian crisis) isn't the reform programs; reform is the answer."

The Treasury secretary says the Asian crisis is essentially one of confidence. The best way to restore investor confidence, he argues, is to reform financial institutions, restructure corporations overburdened by debt, and prohibit governments' telling banks to lend to favored companies. Healthier banks could begin lending again to power an economic revival.

THE TROUBLE WITH EASY MONEY

Easy money would hinder such changes, Mr. Rubin argues, leading to further declines in local currency values and making repayment of dollar-denominated debt even harder. That would worsen banking problems and cause investors to shun economies that try such a strategy, he says.

Mr. Rubin tested his theories yesterday on U.S. business officials who gathered at the residence of the U.S. ambassador to Malaysia. Peter Woicke, managing director of J. P. Morgan & Company's Asia-Pacific subsidiary, said he advises the Malaysian government to boost rates even higher to defend the currency and push companies to reform. "With artificially low rates, you postpone problems," Mr. Woicke said.

The argument intrigued Mr. Rubin, a former cochairman of Goldman, Sachs & Company. "In a way," he responded, lower rates "are a device for delaying and not facing what needs to be done."

But then he asked the group, What about the potential for high rates to "strangle business"? Mr. Woicke cited Japan, where interest rates are below 1 percent and banks still aren't lending. That clinched it for Mr. Rubin, who criticizes Japan at every Asian stop for failing to solve its economic problems.

Pressed at the news conference later, Mr. Rubin said, "What the IMF has done is about right." Raising rates further "could strangle the economy," but lowering them would wreck things too. "It's a question of reaching the right balance," he explained before heading off in an air force jet to spread the word in Thailand.

The Miscalculations:
Ignoring Politics and Safety Nets

David E. Sanger

This selection was excerpted from an article by New York Times staff reporter David Sanger, "As Economies Fail, the IMF Is Rife with Recriminations," published in the Times on 2 October 1998.

On a steaming January [1998] day, Michel Camdessus, the IMF's top official, slipped into Djakarta to the private residence of President Suharto and sat down for a four-hour meeting to tick off, line by line, the huge reforms Indonesia would have to implement in return for tens of billions of dollars in emergency aid. Two previous deals had collapsed when Mr. Suharto ignored the fund's conditions, so Mr. Camdessus insisted that he strike a deal directly with Mr. Suharto, then Asia's longest-serving leader. It was a meeting of men who knew different worlds of power politics: Mr. Suharto rose as a general in central Java and Mr. Camdessus went up through the bureaucratic ranks of the French Treasury on his way to becoming head of France's central bank.

"It was all there," a senior IMF official recalled. "He was told he had to dismantle the national airplane project, the clove monopoly, all the distribution monopolies."

At one point, Mr. Camdessus looked at the impassive Mr. Suharto and said, "You see what this means for your family," a reference to their vast investments in the country's key industries.

"He said, 'I called in my children and they all understand.'"

But within months, that exchange in Djakarta came to symbolize the IMF's twin troubles: its inability to understand and reckon with the national politics of countries in need of radical reform and its focus on economic stabilization rather than the social costs of its actions.

Mr. Suharto had no intention of fulfilling the agreement. It was, one of his former Cabinet members said, "a delaying move that was obvious to everyone except Camdessus."

Perhaps one reason why the fund sometimes appears tone-deaf is that its senior staff is almost entirely composed of Ph.D. economists. There are few officials with deep experience in international politics, much less the complexities of Javanese culture that were at work in Indonesia. Historically, experts in politics and security have gravitated to the United Nations, development experts to the World Bank, and economists to the IMF—creating dangerous gaps in a crisis like this one.

As a result, the fund had only a rudimentary understanding of what would happen if its demands were met and all Indonesia's state monopolies were quickly dissolved. While that system lined the pockets of the Suhartos and their friends, it also distributed food, gasoline, and other staples to a country that stretches for three thousand miles over thousands of islands. To help balance the budget, the fund demanded a quick end to expensive subsidies that keep the price of food and gasoline artificially low. But that, combined with the huge currency devaluation that sparked the crisis, resulted in high prices and shortages that fueled riots that continue to this day [killing more than 1,200 people], as millions of Indonesians lose their jobs.

The fund—unintentionally, its officials insist—also sped Mr. Suharto's resignation, insisting on the elimination of "crony capitalism," code words for removing the Suharto family from the center of the economy. Ultimately, that may prove to be Indonesia's salvation, if the new government can contain the rioting against the ethnic Chinese minority—whose money is desperately needed to save the country's fast-shrinking economy.

"It is worth noting," Stanley Fischer [first deputy managing director of the IMF] said this week, "that our programs in Asia—in Indonesia, Korea, and Thailand—only took hold after there was a change in government."

Nonetheless, the Indonesia experience has revived the argument that the fund is so focused on stabilizing banks and currencies, on preventing capital flight and freeing up markets, that it is blind to the social costs of its actions.

[Editors' Note: Indonesian president Suharto resigned on 21 May 1998 after thirty-two years in power and was succeeded by Vice President B. J. Habibie.]

RUSSIA

Rule of the Ruble

Jeffrey D. Sachs

This selection was originally published in the *New York Times* on 4 June 1998. Jeffrey Sachs is the director of the Harvard Institute for International Development. From December 1991 to January 1994, he was an economic adviser to the Russian government.

Here we go again. In its seventh straight year of ministering to the Russian economy, the International Monetary Fund is about to begin another "emergency bailout." Just five months ago [January 1998], the IMF pronounced the Russian economy on its way to recovery, declaring that "Russian economic reform is entering a less dramatic phase."

Now the Russian stock market is collapsing and the currency is under attack, despite a temporary lull in trading on Tuesday and Wednesday. The IMF has promised to speed another $670 million in loans and is being called on by the Clinton administration and the markets to provide much more. The administration has also renewed its call to Congress to allocate more money for the IMF itself.

The fund continues to fail in its economic advice. The bailout loans are unfair and ineffective. If we need a new global financial architecture, as Treasury secretary Robert Rubin has urged, then we need a new architect as well, a thoroughly revamped IMF.

Understand the logic of the bailouts first. In the past three years, under IMF auspices, Russia has been borrowing short-term funds from abroad to keep a corrupt and mismanaged government afloat. The fund stood by as the government squandered tens of billions of dollars by transferring state-owned oil and gas companies to cronies at cut-rate prices.

At the same time, the Russian government borrowed from foreign speculators at interest rates of 20 percent or more, and often much higher. The sky-high interest rates compensated the investors for the risk that the ruble might lose value against the dollar or that the government might default.

Suddenly, foreign investors have called in these loans. They are spooked by several things, including the Asian crisis, the fall in the price of oil (a principal Russian export), and labor unrest. Suddenly, the ruble is about to lose value. In short, the risk that was long implicit in Russia's high interest rates is about to be realized.

The financial community in Moscow is understandably in a panic. The IMF and the United States have been called in to save the ruble. This would ensure that the earlier loans are repaid and that the ruble keeps its value long enough for speculators to get their money out without large losses.

Therefore, the name of the game is to defend the exchange rate at any cost. Predictably, the IMF has cheered as Russia raised short-term interest rates to a crippling 150 percent a year to try to keep the investors from running.

But the ruble probably can't be saved at this point—too much short-term money is fleeing the scene. True, the crisis that could follow a steep ruble devaluation might indeed be severe. But an IMF-led bailout will likely do Russia more harm than good.

The problem is that the IMF has become the Typhoid Mary of emerging markets, spreading recessions in country after country. The IMF lends its client governments money to repay foreign investors, with the condition that the government also jack up interest rates, cut the flow of credits to the banking system, and close weak banks. The measures are intended to restore investors' confidence. Instead, they kill the economies and further undermine confidence.

It would be much more sensible to keep interest rates moderate and let the economies continue to grow. True, currencies would lose value and speculators would lose their bets. But both borrowers and lenders would be more cautious in the future. The rare case for exceptional monetary tightness occurs when economies are suffering from exceedingly high inflation.

The IMF orthodoxy has been put to the test in Asia in the past nine months. The fund gave us specific predictions about what would happen when it attempted its Asian rescue. It told us in its August 1997 rescue plan for Thailand that the economy would grow by 3.5 percent in 1998. It told us in October [1997] that Indonesia would grow by 3 percent. In December [1997], it predicted Korean 1998 growth of 2.5 percent.

The IMF's own bad advice destroyed its own forecasts. Every few weeks it has had to renegotiate its Asian programs, sharply downgrading the growth forecasts. It now predicts that Korea will shrink by 1 percent or more, Thailand by 5.5 percent or more, and Indonesia by a staggering 10 percent or more.

In emerging markets all over the world, the drama is repeated. Investors who chased high short-term interest rates with short-term loans in recent years are calling in their loans. In just about every case, the IMF is urging a heroic defense of the currency through draconian interest rate increases, sometimes backed by bailouts, sometimes not. The monetary medicine is now being applied with IMF moral support in Brazil and South Africa and with IMF financial support in other parts of Africa, in Russia, and throughout Asia.

The administration and other financial observers should ask why the IMF can't come close to its own targets. They should ask why many economies under its care continue to stagnate or collapse for years. And they should insist that the IMF's free run of the international financial system be brought to an end.

IMF "Salvation" in Russia?

Bernard Sanders

This selection first appeared in the *Christian Science Monitor* on 25 June 1998. Representative Bernard Sanders (I.-Vt.) has regularly dealt with IMF reform issues in the U.S. House of Representatives.

For the seven years since the fall of communism, the IMF has been guiding the Russian economy—to disaster. Now the IMF, with President Clinton's blessing, is considering a proposed $10 billion bailout for Russia. Should they be allowed to "save" Russia again?

As in Mexico, Indonesia, Korea, and Thailand, the IMF has prescribed that Russia run its economy for the benefit of foreign investors and a few wealthy Russians at the expense of the Russian people. The results are clear: a few world-class billionaires, combined with economic collapse, soaring debt, mass unemployment, grinding poverty, and unpaid wages and pensions.

When communism fell, the IMF prescribed "shock therapy," essentially a Russian translation of the devastating "structural adjustment" the fund imposed on Mexico, Africa, Southeast Asia, and much of the rest of the Third World. It insisted that Russia cut government spending, sell off public assets, and raise interest rates to attract foreign investment. But as early as 1992 it was clear that this was a road to disaster: Even the World Bank, normally an IMF ally, warned that Russia's first priority should be to revive domestic production.

The result of the IMF's shock therapy? Between 1992 and 1995, Russia's GDP fell 42 percent and industrial production fell 46 percent— far worse than the contraction of the U.S. economy during the Great Depression.

The effect on the Russian people has been devastating. According to Russian officials, real income has plummeted 40 percent since the Soviet Union collapsed in 1991. A quarter of all Russians are living below the subsistence level. Nearly one-third live below the poverty level. Three-quarters barely survive on an average income of $100 a month. The Red Cross calls conditions in Russia "a silent disaster," reporting, "We saw babies who were being fed powdered animal fodder because of lack of baby food." The average life expectancy for men has declined by seven years, to fifty-nine, since 1990. One-quarter of Russia's labor force receives its wages late, in kind, or not at all.

Meanwhile, privatization has concentrated wealth in a few hands. For example, privatization has created two energy companies, Gazprom and United Energy System, that are largely privately owned and together worth more than 30 percent of Russia's GNP.

What will more IMF remedies do to address the root causes of Russia's economic collapse? Will the proposed bailout help provide baby food for children or put people back to work? One doubts it. According to Jeffrey D. Sachs, director of the Harvard Institute for International Development and a former adviser to the Russian government, the reason for such new loans is to "ensure that the earlier loans are repaid and that the ruble keeps its value long enough for speculators to get their money out without large losses." Indeed, interest rates that recently reached 150 percent will almost certainly be paid out of funds currently earmarked for retired pensioners and unpaid workers.

Russia desperately needs economic reform. The goal should be re-building the economy from the ground up, not bailing out foreign inves-tors. We're told that the crises in Asia and now Russia threaten to spread to other countries and even to become a global economic meltdown. We are told that we must expand the funding of the IMF to combat this and future crises. But there is no evidence that IMF intervention does anything to prevent economic crisis in the long run. Instead, as Mr. Sachs points out, the IMF's track record indicates that it has become a veritable Typhoid Mary, spreading economic austerity and collapse to one country after another.

If the threat of a spreading global economic collapse is real—and I fear that it is—the evidence of the past year indicates that current IMF policies are only helping spread the collapse. We'd better stop it.

But we need to do more than that. It's time to establish a moratorium on happy talk about the benefits of the global economy while we take a hard look at its problems and seriously debate what to do about them. After all, the future of the world economy may be at stake.

Russia's Latest Bailout: How High the Moon?

George Melloan

This selection first appeared in the *Wall Street Journal* on 14 July 1998. George Melloan is a columnist at the *Journal*.

Boris Yeltsin warned the world of his dark fears of an impending military coup and got the desired results: The International Monetary Fund over the weekend arranged a new bailout of the Russian financial system, this time totaling $17.1 billion. For the edification of the U.S. Congress, the German Bundestag, the Japanese Diet, and other legislatures that are asked to commit public resources to these exercises, the IMF has once again asserted that its largesse preserves peace and stability in the world. Send more money, please.

But as Congress ponders whether it should approve the further $18 billion U.S. commitment to the IMF that Bill Clinton is urging, it might want to look closely at whether the IMF money is in fact likely to banish the goblins that haunt Russia. Even the IMF emissary to Moscow, John Odling-Smee, seemed to have doubts initially. But they quickly vanished when Mr. Clinton and Germany's Helmut Kohl made it quite clear that they didn't want to hear any quibbling from some IMF bureaucrat. That Mr. Odling-Smee probably knows better than anyone else how past IMF transfusions have been squandered was clearly irrelevant to the political calculations of the Clinton-Kohl axis.

But legislators often are more concerned than heads of state with the interests of taxpayers and might want to ask a simple question—one that would occur, for example, to a reasonably bright high school student: What do we get for the money? If there is going to be a military coup in Russia, how will parceling out $17.1 billion between now and the end of next year [1999] prevent it?

Such questions have not lacked for answers from bailout proponents, of course. The hype that always precedes IMF "rescue" efforts has been particularly intense this time around. We have been reminded that Russia is a potentially dangerous nuclear power and that the fate of Mr. Yeltsin's new reformist government, headed by thirty-five-year-old Prime Minister Sergei Kiriyenko, is at stake. Unrest throughout the federation, with strikes or disruptions by miners and railroad workers, is cited. So is the collapse of the Russian stock market this year [1998]. And 80 percent interest rates, as the central bank struggles to avoid devaluation of the ruble, are pushing up government borrowing costs and the federal debt at a frightening pace.

All these things are true. Russia remains a dangerous country seven years after the end of the cold war, and the Yeltsin government clearly is in trouble. A flight from the ruble into dollars or marks, conducted particularly by Russian tycoons who prefer to ship their ill-gotten gains to some safe haven abroad, has diminished the government's hard currency reserves. A ruble devaluation would hit ordinary Russians, who have no Swiss bank accounts, further heightening their annoyance over the low yield on what has passed for economic reform these last seven years.

But how will the IMF bailout help? It will shore up the government's hard currency reserves and, perhaps, give the financial markets greater confidence in the ruble, which might allow interest rates to fall and attract some money back into the stock market. Please note that the IMF now is trying to stave off devaluation, whereas in Asia it encouraged same. A learning curve, perhaps?

Saving the ruble is a worthwhile goal, but an old question arises. Does an IMF bailout really aid economic reform or does it instead, in most cases, postpone it?

Economic reform hasn't failed in Russia. The failure has been an insufficiency of economic reform, which if properly undertaken would have a very broad scope. It would include not only privatization of state industry, which has made progress mainly because it has been in the interest of that small class of tycoons who have been busily appropriating state property, but judicial reform, particularly directed at enforcement of contract law. It would include the privatization of land to the extent of allowing land to be bought and sold freely. It would include real tax reform, not the cobbled-up plan now before the Duma. It would include a set of enforceable banking regulations that would provide a legal framework for reliable banks that would serve the needs of local businesses and farmers.

These measures, plus extensive deregulation, are needed to permit real entrepreneurship, the starting and development of new businesses at the grassroots level. So far, Russia's privatization has consisted mostly of former communist managers cannibalizing state assets for their own profit. Given the extent of crime and corruption, there is not yet a climate suitable for the development of honest business.

These things can only be accomplished politically. Boris Yeltsin is not really addressing them in any serious way. He has not yet created a well-organized political party to explain the country's reform needs to the Russian people. If he had such an organization, it could easily defeat the old communist hangers-on who control the Duma and could put forth a credible successor to Mr. Yeltsin, who is barred by present constitutional law from running for a third term. In a properly functioning political system, Mr. Yeltsin would have political backers in every region railing at the obstructionist, do-nothing Duma. That would be far more effective than the technique he once used of firing a few cannon shells through the windows of the White House, where representatives to the Duma have their offices. It would be a lot more legal, too.

With a true commitment to the politics of change, Mr. Yeltsin could safely disband the Duma and call for new elections with a great deal of confidence of electing a reformist legislature. But the longer that is postponed, the stronger radical elements, such as neo-fascists or politically ambitious generals, will become.

The problem with IMF bailouts is that they allow political solutions to be postponed. The government might be able to use the respite to pay some back salaries of government employees and to funnel money to losing enterprises. But that is like a corporation issuing bonds just to meet its arrearages, with no clue as to how to make more money and repay the debt. An ordinary lender or bond buyer wouldn't risk much on that kind of borrower. But that, in the final analysis, is what the IMF is doing, under heavy political pressure. Look for another crisis before Christmas [1998].

A Needed, but Risky, Bailout

New York Times **Editorial**

This selection was originally published in the *New York Times* on 22 July 1998.

The collapse of the Russian economy is an unnerving prospect, so it was prudent of the International Monetary Fund to release $4.8 billion from its new $11.2 billion Russian bailout package. But it is far from clear that the Kremlin can carry out the reforms needed to make the Russian economy more stable.

This is not the first time the fund has leaned on Boris Yeltsin to deal with financial deformities. The Russian government has been unable to come up with the money it needs to operate. That is because the tax system is dysfunctional. Rates are inordinately high, and few corporations or people bother to file tax returns. The government has been forced to pay extraordinarily high interest rates—sometimes above 50 percent—to borrow rubles, but it still cannot meet its obligations.

The government once again promised comprehensive changes in the tax system. Much of its package was approved by parliament, but parts of it were defeated. That left the IMF with a tough choice: Refuse to pay the money, and risk collapse, or give in on some of the demands it made during negotiations for the bailout. It wisely chose to trim the first payment by $800 million to send a message that it was unhappy but still willing to provide needed money.

President Yeltsin has imposed by decree some parts of the tax package that did not win parliamentary approval. That is an encouraging sign of his determination to make the needed changes, but governance by decree is undemocratic and ultimately self-defeating. It would be better if the communist-dominated Duma and Mr. Yeltsin could agree on a package that both secures the needed money and has democratic legitimacy.

Russia also bought itself time by persuading investors to exchange $4.4 billion in ruble-denominated treasury bills for new dollar-denominated bonds that will not mature for as long as twenty years. That will save the country as much as $1 billion in interest payments over the next year. But the risk is that the cost of the dollar borrowing will soar if the government is eventually forced to devalue the ruble. It may be a necessary gamble, but it is also one that could backfire, particularly if the price of oil—Russia's major export—remains depressed.

The IMF is gambling in another way. With its latest commitment to Russia, its own lending reserves are dangerously low if another crisis develops suddenly. Alan Greenspan, the chairman of the Federal Reserve, advised Congress yesterday that the need for congressional action to provide the requested $18 billion in additional IMF funding is critical. The House, which has delayed too long, should promptly follow his advice.

■ Moscow, 30 September 1998—The IMF should learn a lesson from the past five years. The IMF was pretending that it was seeing a lot of reforms in Russia. Russia was pretending to conduct reforms. The Western taxpayer was paying for it.
—Boris G. Fyodorov, Russia's former tax chief

Who Lost Russia?
Pushing an Accord That Fell Apart

David E. Sanger

This selection was excerpted from an article by *New York Times* staff reporter David Sanger, "As Economies Fail, the IMF Is Rife with Recriminations," published in the *Times* on 2 October 1998.

The pattern [of Washington influencing the lending decisions of the fund when major American strategic interests are involved] was repeated this summer [1998], when the United States raced to put together a $17 billion package for Russia. The fund's staff in Moscow declared that Russia needed no money at all—it just needed to enact policies that would restore confidence in investors. The Americans and Germans came to a different conclusion.

Soon after, American officials gathered in the White House situation room to consider what might happen to Russia if the ruble was devalued and market reforms collapsed and to push the IMF to come up with emergency money. So the fund began assembling a last-ditch program to prop up a country that had resisted its reform plans for seven years.

IMF officials say Michel Camdessus [managing director of the IMF] was still hesitant, questioning whether the fund should risk its scarce resources in Russia. "We had to pull Michel along," a United States official recalled, though Lawrence Summers [deputy secretary of the U.S. Treasury] denied it.

As it turned out, Mr. Camdessus's instincts were right while the bet made by Robert Rubin [secretary of the U.S. Treasury] and Mr. Summers quickly went sour. The first installment of that payment—$4.8 billion— was wasted, propping up the currency long enough, in the words of one fund official, "to let the oligarchs get their money out of the country." Then [on 17 August 1998] Boris Yeltsin reversed his commitments, let the ruble devalue anyway, began printing money with abandon, [effectively defaulted on the government debt], and fired virtually every reformer in his government—resulting in a collapse of the IMF agreements and the indefinite suspension of its aid program.

Now, inside the fund and on Capitol Hill, there are recriminations over "who lost Russia."

Stanley Fischer [first deputy managing director of the IMF] argues that "there are no apologies owed for what we attempted in Russia." But some fund officials complain privately that they let Mr. Rubin and Mr. Summers run roughshod over them, striking a deal that fell apart within weeks as the Russian parliament rebelled and Mr. Yeltsin backed away from his commitments.

Mr. Summers responds that the United States "took a calculated risk" because "it was vastly better that Russia succeed than not succeed."

The Russian collapse touched off new rounds of economic contagion, with investors fleeing Latin America, and setting off huge losses in hedge funds like Long Term Capital, the Greenwich, Connecticut, investment firm that needed to be rescued by Wall Street powerhouses whose money it had invested.

"Russia was a turning point," said Robert D. Hormats, the vice chairman of Goldman, Sachs & Company. "It made the world realize that some countries can fail, even if the IMF and the Treasury intercede. And that changed the perception of risk."

Response

Lessons from a Crisis

This selection was originally published in *The Economist*, 3–9 October 1998. Stanley Fischer is first deputy managing director of the IMF.

When finance ministers and central bank governors gather in Washington this weekend for the [1998] annual meetings of the IMF and the World Bank, the global economic crisis will dominate the agenda. The role of the IMF will come in for close examination. Three issues will feature prominently: the design of IMF-supported programs in Asia and Russia, the international financial architecture, and how to respond to the immediate crisis without doing further damage to the international system. I consider these in turn.

The IMF programs in Thailand, Indonesia, and South Korea were designed to restore macroeconomic stability and growth and to remedy structural weaknesses in each country. Early in each program interest rates had to be raised temporarily to stabilize currencies. That was achieved in South Korea and Thailand, whose currencies are now stable in ranges about 35 to 40 percent below precrisis levels, with short-term interest rates of around 8 to 9 percent, also below precrisis levels.

Those who criticized temporary high interest rates fail to see that further depreciation caused by lower rates would have raised the burden of dollar-denominated debts. And while the burdens imposed by higher interest rates were temporary, those created by deeper devaluations would have been permanent.

Thailand embarked on its IMF program with a current account deficit of 8 percent of GDP. To shrink that, the program included an increase in the budget surplus of 3 percent of GDP. Fiscal contractions suggested for Indonesia and South Korea were smaller, designed to cover only the expected interest costs of financial restructuring. Had we known, when the Thai program was signed in August 1997, that Asia, including Japan, was heading for major economic slowdown, less fiscal contraction would have been recommended. As growth in South Korea, Thailand, and Indonesia has slowed, the agreed fiscal deficit has increased; each country is running a sizable deficit. More fiscal expansion, including additional social spending for the poor, would now make sense.

The inclusion of structural measures in these programs has been criticized. But financial and corporate inefficiencies were at the epicenter of the economic crisis and have to be dealt with to restore durable growth. Indeed, the priority now should be to accelerate restructuring. Some argue that because this will take a long time to have its effects, it was a mistake to try to move so rapidly. But delay does not make banking problems go away: As seen in Japan, it makes them worse.

PROGRAM PROBLEMS

If their design was right, why have the IMF programs worked less well than hoped? There are two answers. First, governments were initially reluctant to implement them. In each of the three countries the program began to take hold and the currency to stabilize only after a new government took office. And second, the external economic environment has worsened, due especially to the Japanese recession.

The consequences have been most visible in the three countries' exports. Rapid export growth to the United States helped bring Mexico out of its 1994–95 crisis. This time, the value of exports from Thailand, Indonesia, and South Korea to both Europe and America did indeed rise in the year to the second quarter, but the value of their exports to Japan has declined sharply, by about 25 percent. So exports have not, so far, served as a source of growth.

Where do these countries stand today, a year after the start of their IMF programs? Remember that the average American recession lasts about a year and that a year into the Mexican crisis, there was a period of severe jitters. There are important signs of progress in both South Korea and Thailand, in the stabilization of their currencies, the fall in interest rates, and the start of bank and corporate-debt restructuring (see figure 5). Growth could still resume this year [1998], though much depends on the external environment. A year from now each country is likely to be growing again and to have made more progress in structural reform than most of its neighbors—a good basis for sustainable recovery.

The problems in Indonesia are deeper, for the civil unrest that accompanied the end of the Suharto regime led to massive capital flight and a loss of investor confidence that will take time and careful political and economic management to repair. Critics blame the closing of sixteen banks at the start of Indonesia's IMF program for the collapse of the rupiah and investor confidence. But a careful look at the timing suggests the main culprits were President Suharto's illness in December [1997], perceptions that the government would not carry out the program, and excessive creation of liquidity by the central bank.

Indonesia has made some progress in recent months. The rupiah has strengthened, as foreign assistance has started flowing in. But attempts to keep food prices below world levels have failed and rice prices have risen. So the government, with the assistance of the World Bank, is removing general subsidies on food and switching to the provision of subsidized rice and other essentials for the poor. A start has been made in dealing with the linked problems of internal and external corporate debt and the banking sector, though more needs to be done.

RUSSIA'S DANCE

Ever since 1992 the IMF has been the world's main vehicle for assisting Russia and promoting economic reform. This was difficult from the start, for reformers never had full control over economic policy. Nevertheless, the world's stake in Russian reform was too critical not to make the effort.

Some progress was made: The ruble was stabilized, inflation was cut to single figures, and positive growth was recorded in 1997 (see figure 6). On the structural side, privatization took off. But little was done to restructure the military-industrial complex. And the government, unable to collect enough revenue, was often in arrears on wage and pension payments. The banking system was ill-regulated and heavily exposed to the risks of devaluation. And corruption was a huge problem for the economy and for foreign investors.

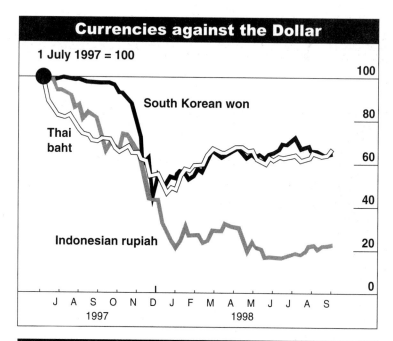

Currencies against the Dollar

1 July 1997 = 100

South Korean won

Thai baht

Indonesian rupiah

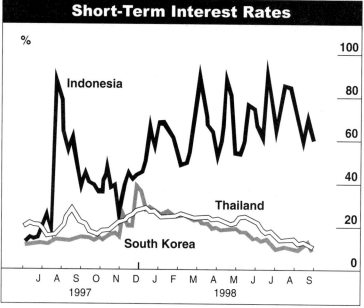

Short-Term Interest Rates

%

Indonesia

Thailand

South Korea

J A S O N D J F M A M J J A S
1997 1998

Source: Datastream/ICV

FIGURE 5. East Asian Exchange and Interest Rates

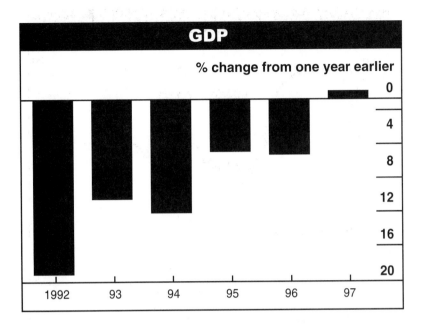

GDP

% change from one year earlier

0

4

8

12

16

20

1992   93   94   95   96   97

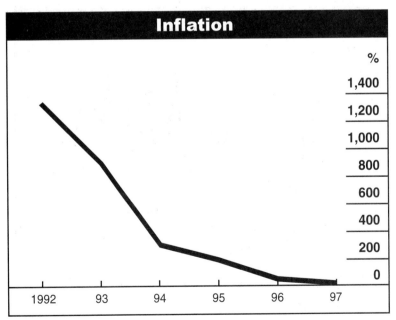

Inflation

%

1,400

1,200

1,000

800

600

400

200

0

1992   93   94   95   96   97

Sources: Russian authorities; IMF staff estimates

FIGURE 6. Russia's Growth and Inflation Rates

The extent of Russia's fiscal problem is hard to overstate. In 1997, federal tax receipts amounted to 9.7 percent of GDP, less than $4 billion a month. The budget deficit was 6.9 percent of GDP. Since 1996 the Russian government has been in a race between its need to collect more taxes and a rising interest bill on its growing debt. This year [1998] tax collection improved. In the second quarter, for the first time, federal revenues covered noninterest spending. But falling oil and commodity prices reduced export revenues, interest rates rose, and the government had to roll over $1 billion a week of GKOs, or short-term ruble-denominated debt.

In July [1998] the international community faced a hard choice: whether to help Russia try to prevent devaluation. The adverse effects of a devaluation were clear, and the reformist Kiriyenko government was making progress on taxes and in other areas. So the decision was made to help, recognizing that this was a calculated risk. An official package of $22 billion was assembled, on condition that the Russians undertake major tax reforms; and a voluntary debt restructuring scheme for GKO holders to switch to longer-term dollar obligations was introduced.

The takeup of this offer was, however, small. The program could still have been viable if GKO holders had been ready to roll over their maturing holdings. But after the Duma rejected two tax measures (though it passed most of the legislation submitted to it), and with doubts about the ability of the government to deliver on policy commitments growing, this did not happen. So the government was faced with an unenviable choice between devaluation, debt restructuring, or both. It chose both: The ruble was devalued, the GKO restructuring was imposed unilaterally, and a temporary moratorium was put on private debt payments.

The contagion following Russia's actions has been serious. The realization that Russia was, after all, not too big to fail shook investor confidence—although it is hard to credit that sophisticated investors who had earned an average of 50 percent a year on GKOs since 1994 really believed these investments were safe. Investors were concerned that other countries might follow suit and unilaterally restructure their debts, although almost all have rejected this.

Much of the contagion was caused by technical factors. Highly leveraged investors have had to realize assets to meet margin calls; investors seeking to move out of emerging markets have sold in the most liquid markets to raise cash. The shocks are now reaching rich-country markets too.

The new Russian government is in an extremely difficult situation. In the short run it may employ a mixture of money printing and more controls. But these approaches will not work; sooner or later a Russian government will have to return to the tasks of stabilizing and reforming the economy. At that point the world may be able to reengage financially. In the meantime we should encourage the authorities to try to agree with creditors how to restructure the GKOs and how to lift the ninety-day moratorium on private debt payments.

What went wrong in Russia? Fundamentally, although progress was made over the years, successive governments have been too weak to implement their desired policies. The international community, through the IMF, was right to try to support reform in Russia. And the IMF was right from early on to stress the need to sort out the fiscal mess. Eventually, as a weak internal situation combined with external shocks, the crisis came. Its effects will take time to overcome, but the story of Russian reform is not yet over.

There is no shortage of suggestions for reshaping the international financial system. Among the main ones are plans to strengthen national banking and financial systems; mechanisms to reduce contagion; capital controls; the need to minimize moral hazard; new exchange-rate regimes; and reform of the IMF itself.

Banking weaknesses have either caused or aggravated all the recent crises. Most of these weaknesses were identified in advance by the IMF, but efforts to get countries to take preemptive action were not successful. The development of international banking standards, the Basle core principles, is an advance. But although we are starting to strengthen surveillance of banking systems, enforcement mechanisms are lacking. One option among others might be to impose differential provisioning requirements against loans to different countries, depending on the standards met by their banking systems.

CONTAINING CONTAGION

The virulence of the recent contagion raises troubling questions about financial markets. Admittedly, contagion is rarely baseless: The markets treat countries in better shape more kindly than those in worse shape. Nonetheless, the technical factors contributing to contagion suggest it has been excessive—and that a way should be found to moderate it. That task will fall mainly to financial regulators, who should ensure greater transparency of positions being taken by investors and consider when leverage can be excessive.

Fuller information should increase the efficiency of international capital flows. Through its special data dissemination standard, the IMF is prodding countries toward greater transparency. The standard needs strengthening, for instance, by providing more timely data on foreign exchange reserves and complete data on forward transactions by central banks. We also need better information on short-term debt, on which the Bank for International Settlements and others are working.

Malaysia's decision to impose controls on capital outflows—and support for the idea among some academics—raises the question of whether such controls will once again become widespread. The IMF's position has long been that capital-account liberalization should proceed in an orderly way: Countries should lift controls on outflows only gradually as the balance of payments strengthens; liberalization of inflows should start at the long end and move to the short end only as banking and financial systems are strengthened. We have not opposed Chilean-style, market-based measures to regulate capital inflows at the short end, but they must be considered case by case (Chile has recently eased its controls).

Yet long experience shows that any short-term benefits that controls on outflows produce will be outweighed by their long-term disadvantages, as they encourage domestic evasion and capital flight and discourage foreign investors. After Malaysia's imposition of controls, other Asian countries have firmly rejected them, as has Latin America. We should, even so, recognize that the lure of isolation from the international system will increase unless market turbulence settles.

Next is the issue of moral hazard. It is hard to see evidence of this on the part of policymakers. Most countries do their utmost to avoid going to the IMF. The thornier issues arise on the side of investors. Some point to investors who take excessively risky positions on the back of an IMF safety net. Others are concerned that investors who should have paid a penalty may be bailed out by IMF lending.

These worries should now be mitigated as most investors in Asian countries, and especially investors in Russia who bet on the "moral hazard play," have taken very heavy losses. We need to balance concerns over moral hazard against the costs for the system of exacerbating instability by failing to assist countries in need. This issue is closely tied to the question of how to "bail in" the private sector (i.e., get it to roll over its debts or provide new money rather than rushing for the exit). The IMF and other groups, including the G22, are working on this high-priority problem.

We also again need to appraise exchange-rate regimes for emerging market countries. The recent crises have all taken place in countries with fixed or semifixed exchange rates. Yet several countries, including Argentina, have benefited from a fixed rate; and currency crises also affect countries with flexible rates. The argument has been made that there are really only two stable exchange-rate systems: a freely floating rate or the adoption (perhaps via a currency board) of another country's currency. With the expected success of the European Monetary Union, more currency blocs may develop. But for now, we are in an uncomfortable in-between world in which floating rates are sometimes too volatile and fixed rates sometimes too vulnerable to attack.

Lastly there is the question of reforming the IMF. Many of the changes discussed above will affect its role. There is also general support—including from the management of the IMF—for greater transparency in IMF operations. There has been much progress in recent years, as a visit to our web site (www.imf.org) can show. More can be done but only with the full support of the membership.

It is sometimes argued that the IMF is not accountable. That is not true. It is fully accountable to its membership, through the twenty-four-member executive board that represents the 182 member countries. No loan or other big decision is taken without the board's approval. Overall IMF policies are set by the twenty-four-member interim committee, made up of finance ministers and central bank governors, which meets twice a year. Most complaints about accountability are really about transparency. If more details of IMF operations were published, there would be more room for appraisal by outsiders—which would be to the good.

WHAT TO DO NOW

While work on the international financial architecture moves ahead to prevent the next crisis, we need urgently to contain the present one. Four steps are needed.

First, as the balance of risks in the international economy has shifted, so should the stance of monetary policy in America and Europe. This week's cut in American interest rates is welcome news. It is also good that European central bankers have suggested that European rates should converge to the low levels in France and Germany rather than meet in the middle.

Second, Japan's continuing recession is a major problem, both for Japan and for the rest of the world. Rapid action to sort out its banks, and further fiscal stimulus, would go a long way to help Japan and the rest of Asia recover.

Third, the key to stopping the spread of the crisis is Latin America; and in Latin America it is Brazil. Latin American countries have made genuine progress in structural reforms this decade. They have reacted courageously to recent financial pressures by tightening monetary and fiscal policies. Brazil's president Cardoso has left no doubt that he will take more fiscal action after the election.

The international financial system, which has sustained the world economy through fifty years of growth and prosperity, needs reform to ensure that this continues—and that the mistakes of the 1930s are not repeated. For the IMF, which has had a central role in the system, to continue to play its part, it needs the support of its membership as it adapts to a changing world economy—and it urgently needs the quota increase.

PART FIVE

MISSION CREEP

In July 1997, the IMF executive board approved new lending guidelines that instruct the fund to withhold financial assistance to member countries with "poor governance." Meanwhile, the IMF refuses to withhold assistance to countries with poor human rights records, citing the "political noninterference" provisions of its Articles of Agreement. This interpretation of the noninterference provisions has created a state of affairs where IMF assistance is withheld for government bribery and corruption but not torture and murder. Brutality is excused, mismanagement is not. Furthermore, critics charge that the IMF disregards the noninterference provisions to promote its own brand of international security. Part 5 explores "mission creep" at the IMF, specifically, the extent to which financing decisions are, or should be, influenced by considerations of human rights, government corruption, and geopolitics and international security.

The first series of selections discusses human rights. David Sanger examines the congressional debate over IMF loans to human rights violators. Jim Hoagland and Jerome Levinson call for the cessation of IMF assistance to Indonesia based on its denial of democracy and human rights. Finally, John Williamson presents an opposing view, arguing that the IMF cannot devise a workable human rights membership standard that would also allow it to combat global economic crises.

The second series of articles explores the fund's recent decision to require "good governance" as a condition for IMF support. Articles by Chidanand Rajghatta, Robert Shaw, and Paul Deveney detail the 1997 suspension of IMF assistance to Kenya because of government corruption and mismanagement.

The third series of selections discusses the extent to which IMF financing decisions are influenced by considerations of geopolitics and international security. Sebastian Edwards argues that the United States and other industrialized countries influence the IMF to approve loans for geopolitical reasons—loans that the fund knows will fail economically. Next, an *Economist* editorial alleges that the IMF gave preferential treatment to Russia before its 1996 presidential election to ensure an uninterrupted flow of fund assistance and a Yeltsin victory. IMF official John Odling-Smee denies the allegations in a letter to the editor. He contends that the IMF closely monitored Russia and it complied with fiscal and monetary targets. Next, J. Michael Waller argues that IMF loans to Russia help finance its military buildup, which threatens U.S. and international security. Finally, in "What's an IMF For?" the *Wall Street Journal* questions the expanding role of the IMF and encourages the fund to return to its basic mission of "lender of last resort."

CRITICISMS OF THE EXPANDING ROLE OF THE INTERNATIONAL MONETARY FUND

Human Rights

The fund's broad interpretation of the "political noninterference" provisions of the Articles of Agreement permits it to underwrite venal and brutal governments around the world.

Government Corruption

New conditionality guidelines, approved by the executive board on 25 July 1997, instruct the IMF to suspend or delay financial assistance to any member country with "governance" so poor that it threatens the success of an IMF financing program. This rule allows the fund to meddle in the administration of member governments.

Geopolitics and International Security

Strategically important member countries receive preferential treatment in IMF financing programs, thereby involving the fund in geopolitics.

HUMAN RIGHTS

IMF Loans to Rights Violators Are Attacked in Congress

David E. Sanger

This selection first appeared in the *New York Times* on 22 April 1998. David Sanger is a staff reporter for the *Times*.

Every year, the State Department's human rights report dwells at length on Indonesia's many forms of political repression, from its use of torture and killings to silence dissenters to its widespread military control of East Timor.

So Indonesia's record might appear, at first glance, to require the use of a law compelling the United States to vote against lending billions of dollars through the International Monetary Fund to gross violators of human rights. But the United States favored a $40 billion IMF bailout of Indonesia and even offered to throw in $3 billion of back-up American financing if Indonesia needs more.

Defending that decision during two hours of hostile questioning by a congressional committee, Treasury Department officials asserted that in the pantheon of human rights violators the government of President Suharto did not rank among the worst of the worst.

"The State Department makes these judgments, and Indonesia did not meet the standard to be on the list they send us," Timothy F. Geithner, an assistant secretary of the Treasury, said in testimony, as he urged Congress to approve an additional $18 billion for the monetary fund.

The debate over providing additional funding has turned into one of the hottest foreign policy issues on Capitol Hill. It has become a magnet for human rights activists, abortion opponents, and critics of the monetary fund's role as the world's lender of last resort.

The testimony called into question whether the administration, in its race to contain the Asian financial crisis, skirted a law that requires the United States to use its "voice and vote" to deny assistance to countries that "engage in a pattern of gross violations of internationally recognized human rights."

The State Department insists that it keeps no official list of human rights violators that should be denied such loans. But, responding to questions, Mr. Geithner said there were five countries that the United States would likely oppose for such aid: China, Sudan, Equatorial Guinea, Iran, and Mauritania.

"I concede," one senior administration official said, "that to the uninitiated it is a bit of a strange list."

Clearly, it has a number of gaping holes. For example, Nigeria, a country that has seen widespread violence and political repression since a 1993 coup, would not be automatically denied American support. Nor would Iraq, which is barred from borrowing money from the IMF because it has not repaid loans for the last eight years.

At the hearing before the House banking subcommittee on general oversight and investigations, Representative Bernie Sanders, the Vermont independent who ranks among the fiercest critics of the monetary fund in the House, charged that the administration violated the law. "You are funding a vicious dictator who jails his opponents," he said. "It seems to me you very clearly disobeyed the law."

Mr. Geithner and Karin Lissakers, the United States representative to the monetary fund, insisted that the administration, working behind the scenes, has used its influence to promote both human rights and labor rights. It has blocked the IMF from considering loans to Iran and the Sudan, they said, and held up money for Croatia while it was harboring war criminals.

The human rights argument is part of a broader examination of the workings of the fund that has never before taken place in Congress. The fund is known for its secretiveness, in large part because it offers confidential advice to its 182 member countries, many of which turn over sensitive economic data to the fund.

But that secretiveness has also made it difficult for the United States to defend its support of the fund or discuss specific decisions. Now, increasingly fearful that the funding it seeks could be denied, Washington has begun to turn over thousands of pages of data about its interactions with the fund.

Each disclosure, though, has raised new objections. Some Republicans argue that the IMF should not provide below-market-rate loans to recipient countries; Mr. Sanders argued the opposite, maintaining that the fund has turned into a "loan shark" burdening deeply indebted countries with even more interest payments.

So Much Aid for Suharto

Jim Hoagland

This selection was originally published in the *Washington Post* on 17 May 1998. Jim Hoagland is a columnist at the *Post*.

Indonesia's peaceful student revolt against President Suharto has ignited bloody repression by the government and then a wave of rioting and looting. The smoke rising from burning buildings in Djakarta should not obscure the roots of a crisis that is draining Suharto's government of control and credibility.

This is a struggle over power and the true nature of Asia's political values. The spasm of violence was a disastrous side effect of that struggle, which must now be quickly brought to a head.

This explosive conflict drives a final nail into the coffin of the "Asian values" theories advanced by some Asian politicians to justify authoritarian rule and the denial of the concept of universal human rights and freedoms.

Indonesia confirms the obvious: No one set of values controls the region or even individual countries within it. There is not a single, all-embracing paternalistic social code that will determine Asia's destiny, despite theories to that effect elaborated by Singapore's Lee Kwan Yu, China's communist gerontocracy, and other regional chauvinists.

The democratic values of the students who took to the streets three months ago [February 1998]—Asians all—are in collision with the self-centered values of their rulers. That is a divide seen before, on a much more massive scale in the Philippines in 1986, in China in the spring of 1989, and in a different form in South Korea in the late 1980s.

Once again, the Asians in the streets are demanding that the Asians in power treat them with respect and decency, rather than order them to fulfill their duties to the central authority in the name of collective discipline and social conformity.

The student demonstrators' display of courage, the quest for individual freedoms, the desire for less conformity in society and more honesty in government that surfaced in Djakarta's streets, as they did in Tiananmen Square and in Cory Aquino's People Power movement—these are Asian values too.

This is not to be naive. The looting, ethnic violence, and wanton destruction in Djakarta last week rode on the coattails of the calls for political change. But Asian democrats want change precisely to be able to preserve order. The longer the conflict around Suharto's reign lasts, the more violent the conflict is likely to become and the more radical its outcome is likely to be.

Suharto, seventy-six years old and thirty-two years in power, allocated himself a new five-year term in March [1998]. His callous handling of the economic hardships caused by the collapse of Indonesia's currency and stock markets the previous summer sparked the first protests. The revolt has become more political, and more subversive, as he has stubbornly refused to consider any political reform. Indonesia is in flames; he must now choose to step aside or hang on by brute force.

And the Clinton administration must now choose to continue to support ill-advised financial bailouts for Suharto's regime or side with the values of a new Asian generation that challenges the aging autocrat. You would think the choice would be automatic; you would be wrong.

A few months ago I listened to Henry Kissinger scold those who had the arrogance to try to impose so-called Western political values on the ancient societies of Asia, and particularly on China. In a speech at the University of Oklahoma, the former secretary of state, who is often brilliant when it comes to balance of power politics and diplomatic analysis, explained that China needed no lessons from outsiders about organizing its society.

As I listened, I realized that for Kissinger, "China" seemed to be China's rulers. The values of the million people who took to the streets of Beijing night after night to support the students in Tiananmen Square in May 1989 and to call for democracy and an end to corruption did not seem to count as Asian, or authentic, in this kind of calculus.

President Clinton's decision to visit Tiananmen Square on his China trip in June [1998] reflects that same ruler-centered sensibility. Visiting the blood-stained square to honor the Chinese leadership places Clinton on the wrong side of the Asian values conflict. Tiananmen is Clinton's Bitburg, except that Ronald Reagan and his handlers did not know of the Waffen SS connection to that small German town when they put it on a presidential tour of Europe.

Visiting Tiananmen Square seems now to be the price of admission for a state visit to China. Without apparent hesitation, Clinton agreed to offer visible support for Jiang Zemin's version of Asian values. And it is important to remember that there was no rioting or looting in the extended Chinese protests.

Clinton should not repeat the same error in Indonesia, where Suharto seems tempted to follow the Chinese model of repression. The United States and the International Monetary Fund should halt financial support for a regime that is digging its own grave.

Repressive Regimes Shouldn't Get a Loan

Jerome I. Levinson

This selection first appeared in the *Washington Post* on 15 June 1998. Jerome Levinson is a professor of international law at American University and a research associate at the Economic Policy Institute in Washington, D.C.

When dealing with crises such as the one in Indonesia, the traditional U.S. preference is for stability, even if it results in repression and the denial of democracy and human rights. Jim Hoagland took note of this problem last month [op-ed, 17 May 1998] when he called on the United States and the International Monetary Fund, in the case of Indonesia, to "halt financial support for a regime that is digging its own grave."

What Hoagland implies is a revolution in the way we think about development finance and the rules governing it: the Articles of Agreement of the World Bank and the International Monetary Fund. These are the two Bretton Woods institutions that set the conditions for financial aid of borrowing member countries. And at the center of those conditions is a "Chinese wall" between "economic" and "political" considerations. Unfortunately, it is, as Indonesia so graphically demonstrates, an artificial construct.

Nevertheless, it has an institutional expression in the Articles of Agreement of the two institutions. Both include provisions directing that the officers of these institutions shall neither interfere "in the political affairs of any member; nor shall they be influenced in their decisions by the political character of the member or members concerned. Only economic considerations shall be relevant to their decisions."

It is these strictures that have provided the shield behind which the World Bank and the IMF have continued to provide financing to countries that engage in egregious abuses of human rights, so long as they are diligent in carrying out the economic policy recommendations agreed upon—above all, those creating the conditions for attracting foreign direct investment.

But this interpretation of the "political" sections of the articles is unnecessarily restrictive. There is no definitive statement as to what the authors intended, more than fifty years ago, by their use of the term *political*. Congressional hearings at the time simply indicated a concern that decisions on particular loans not be influenced by "political" favoritism.

If we understand the political sections of the articles in the context of the time, a more reasonable interpretation emerges. In 1944 the cold war had not yet begun. World War II had not yet ended. The Bretton Woods institutions were conceived as universal institutions that would include the Soviet Union. Postwar political competition in individual countries would exist between conservative, liberal, and socialist parties. It certainly was reasonable to ensure that the Bretton Woods institutions not take sides in this political competition. And that is what the political sections of the Articles of Agreement should be understood to prohibit.

But that limited and reasonable objective has been expanded to justify financing by the World Bank and the IMF of governments that have been some of the worst abusers of human rights. Such an interpretation almost certainly distorts the intentions of the men who drafted the articles: Harry Dexter White, on behalf of the U.S. Treasury, and Lord John Maynard Keynes, for the United Kingdom, both of whose democratic credentials were impeccable.

In order to accept such an expanded interpretation of the political provisions, we have to believe that Keynes and White, at the time that the war against Nazi Germany was still going on, intended to provide a cover that would permit the Bretton Woods institutions to provide financing in the future for governments that, like the Nazis if on a lesser scale, were egregious abusers of human rights. Such an interpretation defies reason and common sense.

It is precisely that expanded interpretation, however, that has provided the legal justification for constructing the wall between economic and political considerations. That is why Indonesia, before the current crisis, could be represented by both the World Bank and IMF as their star performer in Asia.

Indonesia did accomplish much; it was a leader in reducing absolute poverty. But it also suppressed trade unions, a free press, an independent judiciary, and opposition political parties. This was considered irrelevant by the Bretton Woods institutions in assessing Indonesia's development "performance."

This constricted view of development performance has found support in successive U.S. administrations, including Clinton's. This view has been exploded in Indonesia. For it must now be clear that, even on their own terms — that is, even when the primary goal is fostering a secure investment climate — the IMF and World Bank cannot ignore the absence of institutions that ensure an orderly transition in government and can provide effective checks against abuse of power. In other words, democratic institutions are as relevant to development "performance" as traditional considerations such as fiscal probity.

The Chinese wall has come down and it is neither possible nor desirable to reconstruct it. Accepting that conclusion involves a revolution in thinking inside the Bretton Woods institutions and our own Treasury, which is the dominant force in U.S. policy with respect to these institutions.

[Editors' Note: The IMF suspended a $1 billion disbursement from a $10.2 billion loan to Indonesia from 4 June 1998 to 15 July 1998 because, according to Stanley Fischer, first deputy managing director of the IMF, Indonesia did not have a reasonable political system with which to work and economic reforms could not succeed without political stability. Human rights violations were not mentioned as a cause for the loan suspension.]

Radical Proposals for Change in the Fund's Objectives

John Williamson

This selection was excerpted from "Reforming the IMF: Different or Better?" published in *The Political Morality of the International Monetary Fund*, edited by Robert Myers (1987). John Williamson is a senior fellow at the Institute for International Economics in Washington, D.C.

The IMF is a coalition of countries that see mutual gain in cooperating for limited monetary purposes. Some propose that the IMF's objectives be broadened beyond that limited area, to include political objectives like promoting democracy, human rights, and racial equality.

An attempt to convert the fund into an instrument for overtly advancing the cause of democracy or human rights would seem to be misconceived. Not only would many of the fund's current members clearly be disqualified, but there would be potentially endless disputes as to whether particular countries did or did not qualify for membership. Once the offending members had been identified, they would presumably either be expelled or would withdraw voluntarily once they realized that they were to be denied the benefits of membership. There is even the possibility that some Third World countries would withdraw from the fund in sympathy (even some that do respect human rights) on the ground that the ethical principles being imposed are those for which the West's record is good, while other ethical concerns on which the West's record is appalling—such as a willingness to redistribute income to the poorest—are ignored.

When the size of the fund had shrunk to include only the righteous, its ability to fulfill its present monetary objectives would inevitably be circumscribed. For example, with membership limited by such criteria, the IMF would have been unable to deal with the debt crisis. A decision would also have to be made whether to help excluded countries (which may actually serve to reward countries for being undemocratic or abusing human rights) or whether to abandon such countries to their fate. The position of the technocrats in the excluded countries, who are generally the element most sympathetic to liberal values, would be compromised by their inability to invoke the support of the fund, and the reduction in working contacts with the West would weaken one of the long-term forces for liberalization. The only possible gain to be set against these losses would be that some countries may be bribed into democratic forms of government or the termination of human rights abuses by the possibility of drawing on the fund's resources.

The other broad political issue that has been raised in discussion of IMF reform is whether the fund should be neutral on the issue of capitalism versus socialism. Neutrality should be favored for all of the reasons cited above. These reasons are supplemented by the ethical consideration that the choice between capitalism and socialism is on an order of magnitude less important than that between democracy and authoritarianism, between respect for human rights and suspension of the rule of law, or between racial equality and apartheid.

The argument that membership in the fund or the right to borrow from it should not be conditioned on a country's performance with regard to democracy, human rights, apartheid, or free enterprise raises the question of whether the fund has exhibited such neutrality in the past. While the fund has very rarely, if ever, been accused of positively favoring regimes that suppress human rights or practice apartheid, it certainly has been accused of favoring authoritarian regimes and of being hostile to socialism. There have indeed been instances when the fund showed indecent haste in sending a mission to negotiate with the authoritarian successor to a democratic regime, but the last instance of this was in Chile in 1973; one hopes that the fund has now learned its lesson. The accusation of anti-socialism does not seem to be supported by the scale of fund lending to socialist governments in recent years, although Cheryl Payer has suggested that the fund gives "special introductory offers" to entice countries to enter its "trap" (1985, 6).

GOVERNMENT CORRUPTION

IMF Crackdown on Corruption in Projects

Chidanand Rajghatta

This selection was originally published in the *Indian Express* (Bombay, India) on 9 August 1997. Chidanand Rajghatta is a staff reporter for the *Express*.

In a stunning move that should send a jolt through India's venal political class and corrupt bureaucracy, the International Monetary Fund has actually acted upon its recent threats to move against graft in developing countries.

In an unprecedented move, the IMF this week suspended a $216 million loan to Kenya because of that country's refusal to clean up pervasive bribery and self-enrichment. The action came just before the IMF adopted new guidelines on Monday allowing it to withhold aid to countries where it believes corruption is so endemic and corrosive as to endanger the IMF's goals of economic recovery.

Kenya's currency plunged by as much as 20 percent as a result of the move, reports from Nairobi said. Kenyan president Daniel Arap Moi reacted with outrage at the move, describing it as "purely political."

The IMF move follows the repeated assertions in recent days by both IMF managing director Michel Camdessus and World Bank president James Wolfensohn against the pervasive graft in developing countries. They had promised to act against it.

According to the new guidelines, "financial assistance from the IMF . . . could be suspended or delayed on account of poor governance . . . if there is reason to believe it could have significant macroeconomic implications that threaten the successful implementation of the program, or puts in doubt the purpose of the use of IMF resources."

India was recently ranked fifth in a list of corrupt nations by Transparency International, an anticorruption advocacy group. In the 1980s, then Prime Minister Rajiv Gandhi had estimated that only about 15 percent of the money marked for development actually reached the end user in India. New Delhi is one of the biggest clients of the multilateral institutions, having borrowed close to $50 billion over the years.

Transparency International vice president Frank Vogl welcomed the IMF move, saying it's long overdue that multilateral organizations involved in financing developing countries place on par with macropolicies the basic soundness of government institutions with which they are dealing.

"The cut off (to Kenya) sends a signal because the guidelines are being issued at the same time," Vogl said.

Although the new guidelines say the IMF should not "interfere in domestic or foreign politics," the IMF and World Bank's increasing assertiveness is bound to be seen in some quarters as intrusiveness that may directly interfere in governance. For instance, the guidelines call for IMF employees handling particular countries to point out the economic consequences of corruption.

IMF Unlikely to Resume Loans to Kenya Soon

Robert Shaw

This selection first appeared in *The Nation* (Nairobi, Kenya) on 7 September 1997. Robert Shaw is a businessman and commentator on the Kenyan economy.

There is a popular perception that since the IMF sent a team to Kenya to talk to the government the turning on of its money tap is at best imminent, or, at worst, a matter of time. This is a serious misconception.

But to be fair to Kenyans, it is understandable that many jump to such conclusions. First of all, the suspension of the IMF's $216 million enhanced structural adjustment facility loan has been such bad news, especially in terms of the increasing cost of living, that any straw of possible good news is worth clutching.

Second, both the IMF and the government have often not helped in dispelling the notion that all will be okay. The statement by the IMF managing director, Mr. Michel Camdessus, on 21 August [1997] confirming that a mission will "leave immediately for Nairobi" wittingly or unwittingly sent signals that some accommodation was possible. Given the IMF's record, the assumption was that some form of deal would be patched together that would result in some money flowing in.

As regards the government, several of its members have most wittingly encouraged the notion that the talks have progressed well and that all will be okay soon. The implication is that the IMF will resume funding in the forseeable future.

But the likelihood that there will be an agreement that will result in a resumption of IMF money within six months is next to zero. Even if one lengthens that horizon to the next twelve months, the chances remain slim.

The reasons for this are twofold. One is to do with the actual lengthy practicalities of negotiating and putting together a package that in turn has to be presented to the IMF board and passed. But the more important one is to do with the fact that the IMF and its sister organization, the World Bank, are undergoing some very fundamental changes. This will make it almost impossible for them to agree to the type of deals struck in the past because of their embracing of new governance guidelines.

Before going any further it is worth giving some background to this fundamental shift. Corruption, particularly in countries such as Kenya, has become a sore issue with many electorates in the bilateral donor countries. In turn the governments of many bilateral nations, who are ultimately the shareholders of the IMF, feel that tackling corruption should be an integral part of the IMF's mandate, especially as it is seen as a major impediment to economic growth.

Bearing in mind many of the larger shareholders are trying to cut their contributions, the IMF has little choice but to take on board this subject.

[In July 1997], the IMF executive board adopted "guidelines covering the issues of governance" that will be added to its core operations to do with correcting macroeconomic imbalances, reducing inflation, and undertaking key economic reforms.

These guidelines are a detailed, almost legalistic, hands-on approach on how to apply its governance policy. Guideline 16 is very specific and relevant to Kenya.

> Weak governance should be addressed early in the reform effort. Financial assistance from the IMF in the context of completion of a review under a programme or approval of a new IMF arrangement could be suspended or delayed on account of poor governance, if there is reason to believe it could have significant macroeconomic implications that threaten successful implementation of the programme or if it puts in doubt the purpose of the IMF resources.
>
> Corrective measures that at least begin to address the governance issue should be prior actions for resumption of IMF support, and, if necessary, certain key measures could be structural benchmarks or performance criteria.

This statement is specific in what should be done if there is corruption or governance obstacles and also how to judge whether enough progress has been made. Progress will be ascertained by "prior actions" and not by statements of intent as has often been the case with Kenya in the past.

Hence the pledges by the government to the IMF to strengthen management of the energy sector and renegotiate the two stop-gap power projects, more thorough tax collection "on all imports, including sugar imports," establish an independent anticorruption authority, and to ensure accountability and transparency in the management of public finances are not only monumental but have to be delivered before there is any talk of money.

Two obvious questions arise out of this. One is that, given the government's long and ballooning association with corruption and the fact that it is such a vital part of running its affairs, it is exceedingly difficult to see how it is going to deliver sufficiently to satisfy the IMF. It is akin to insisting that someone chop his or her fingers off.

The second question is to do with how much or little will need to be done to satisfy the IMF. Going by the tone of some of its board members about there being no room for "slippages" or "nonadherence" anymore, it is unlikely that there is much latitude for arbitrary flexibility by its staffers.

Going by the answers to the above questions it is difficult to see how there can be much progress with the IMF until there are some fundamental changes here that remove corruption from the center stage of government.

Moreover these governance conditions are becoming more and more widespread. Many bilaterals already have them. Last Tuesday [2 September 1997], the board of the World Bank reviewed some tentative proposals on its own governance code. The likely outcome is that they will be made more thorough and will complement those of the IMF.

Kenya is seen as a very corrupt country, and, with the goalposts being changed by the donors, the only solution will have to be a significant reduction in corruption if it is to become a recipient of significant chunks of donor money.

Kenya's Mismanagement Is Detailed

Paul J. Deveney

This selection was originally published in the *Wall Street Journal* on 14 April 1998. Paul Deveney is a staff reporter for the *Journal*.

Kenya may be viewed by some as one of the more sophisticated nations in Africa, but the way it keeps its books is raising eyebrows. An auditor-general's report details unauthorized or excessive spending throughout the government, adding credence to the International Monetary Fund's halting of a $216 million loan package last summer. At the time, the IMF cited mismanagement and government corruption in the East African nation. But the auditor-general's office delves into the nitty-gritty. It says it still hasn't received supporting documents from the president for the purchase of a $46 million jet and that part of the payment for land for a new international airport included the transfer of a much-desired site near Nairobi, land the government apparently doesn't even own.

GEOPOLITICS AND INTERNATIONAL SECURITY

The Fund and the Debt Crisis: Some Political Angles

Sebastian Edwards

This selection was excerpted from "The International Monetary Fund and the Developing Countries: A Critical Evaluation," published in *IMF Policy Advice, Market Volatility, Commodity Price Rules, and Other Essays,* edited by Karl Brunner and Allan Meltzer (1989). Sebastian Edwards, formerly World Bank chief economist for Latin America and the Caribbean, is the Henry Ford II Professor of International Economics at the Anderson Graduate School of Management, University of California at Los Angeles.

In many cases, by approving standby programs whose targets everyone knows will not be met, the IMF is participating in a big charade; it is implicitly saying that, according to the Articles of Agreement, the resources have been provided on a *temporary* basis, and that there is a high probability that the country will attain balance of payment viability in the near future. For many countries this is not the case, and everybody knows it. The issue, of course, is not whether these countries should undertake reforms and prudent macroeconomic policies—they certainly should—but whether these policies will suffice for solving the crisis.

The fund has not participated in this delusion willingly. In many cases its participation was the result of *political* decisions made by the largest members, in particular by the United States. For political reasons—dictated by geopolitical or other considerations—and many times against the judgment of the staff, the United States and other industrialized countries saw fit to request (force?) the fund to approve unrealistic programs for Egypt, the Sudan, Nicaragua, Argentina, and Brazil. What has happened

is that concessionary development funds have been given through the
IMF. Of course, there is per se nothing wrong with providing aid. Quite
the contrary, given these countries' positions, aid is a good step. What is
questionable is the wisdom of using a financial institution such as the fund
for this purpose. David Finch, the former director of the Exchange and
Trade Restrictions Department at the fund, has strongly argued against
the use of the fund for political purposes. He rightly points out that the
fund, by approving programs that everyone knows are destined to fail, will
not only lose credibility but also will see its own resources imperiled, in
the not so unlikely event that some of these countries default on the fund.
He asks politicians that they "let the IMF be the IMF."

Of course, it is naive to ask that the large members do not try to
influence IMF policy in ways that favor their global interests, as it would
be naive to ask the staff not to oppose measures that reduce its own power.
It is not clear, however, whether long-term interests of the major countries
are indeed enhanced by these policies. Why do they risk damaging the
fund in this process?

Mr. Yeltsin's Flexible Friend

The Economist Editorial

This selection first appeared in *The Economist*, 13–19 July 1996.

The International Monetary Fund likes to say that it lends against economic policies, not against governments. But policies and governments
do not always fit neatly into separate categories. As this year's Russian
presidential election approached, hopes for reform and free enterprise
rested on the reelection of Boris Yeltsin. Had voters plumped for Gennady
Zyuganov, his communist rival, the country's economy would probably
now be heading back into the dark ages.

The election is over and to almost universal relief Mr. Yeltsin is still in office. Now, though, there arises a ticklish question. Did the IMF, in effect, cast a vote for him? In principle, the fund is apolitical. It is supposed to be bound by strong internal rules and to be a strict enforcer of conditions attached to its loans. But some of its big shareholders, especially America and Germany, clearly cared more about Mr.Yeltsin's survival than about a percentage point here and there in Russia's national accounts. Did the fund take the hint and treat Russia with special leniency?

One reason to suspect that it did was the fund's readiness in the first place to grant a three-year loan of just over $10 billion — after Mexico's, the second-biggest ever — to Russia in March [1996]. This was a clear signal that nobody at the fund wanted to "lose Russia." And although the loan was supposedly tied to Russia's meeting a number of strict economic targets, there is a good deal of evidence that lender and borrower colluded to interpret these as flexibly as possible, at least until the election.

Certainly, nobody at the fund wanted to risk helping the Communists back to power by undermining the core of Mr.Yeltsin's campaign: promises of jam today and jam tomorrow. When, after the loan was promised, Russia's budget deficit began to exceed agreed levels and structural reforms languished, the IMF behaved as if it was happy to view many such terms as mere details to sort out once the vote was over.

To judge by its actions, the Russian government took this view as well. Having signed its deal with the fund, it issued no overall decree to make the package binding on its spending ministries. And, according to one minister, "bookkeeping tricks were pulled on both sides."

When Mr.Yeltsin dished out campaign promises to spend an unplanned $10 billion, and wrested $1 billion from a furious central bank in June [1996], the fund did not blench. Its boss, Michel Camdessus, said in June that Russia was "up to date on performance criteria." Thomas Wolf, head of the IMF's Moscow office, said [at the beginning of July], "In light of the presidential campaign, the authorities seem to have done well."

Perhaps. Officially the fund publishes neither its monthly targets for Russia nor its calculations of Russia's performance. It has declined to comment publicly in any detail. But the evidence is that Russia broke through the ceiling originally agreed for the budget deficit almost immediately, in March (see table 9). By April it would have been doing so even

TABLE 9.   Russia's Budget Deficit (as percentage of GDP)

	IMF target	Outcome (IMF basis)*	Outcome (Russian basis)*
March 1996	5.7	7.9	4.6
April 1996	4.8	7.5	7.0

* Outcomes are calculated before crediting loans from Germany and France; the Russian calculation excludes interest on treasury bills.

SOURCES: *Russian Economic Trends*; Russian government data

on the narrower calculation preferred by Russia's finance ministry, which, unlike the IMF, excludes interest paid out on high-yielding treasury bills.

The IMF and Russia were let off this hook by France's and Germany's decisions to lend Russia $400 million and $2.7 billion, respectively, in April, and by the fund's willingness to let Russia treat this as spending money, instead of insisting, as it could have done, that it was used to finance the agreed deficit in place of costly treasury bills.

However, for all Mr. Yeltsin's extravagant spending promises, the root cause of the deficit overrun was a collapse in tax collection (a defect that the government said this week it would correct in the second half of the year). Having expected to collect the equivalent of 11.5 percent of GDP in taxes this year, the government managed to collect only at a rate of 8 percent of GDP in the first half. And in the weeks before the election, receipts fell to less than half that rate.

TAX, BUT NO BRASS

This was not entirely the government's fault. The IMF itself made Russia abandon counterproductive excise and wages taxes. In addition, some big companies chose to withhold taxes until they knew who had won the election. But the government made a bad situation worse by granting tax exemptions to some firms, thereby breaching undertakings to the IMF. Some exemptions were, in effect, a surrogate for public spending: Firms received tax breaks in exchange for giving goods free to other firms to which the state owed money.

Although Russia had promised to keep this in-kind taxation below a ceiling of $1.8 billion this year, it already stood at $3.2 billion by June. The government's lame excuse was that many of the offsets covered debts incurred in 1995 and so should not be reckoned into the current IMF program.

Russia's record on IMF-agreed monetary targets appears to have been at least as questionable as its record on fiscal targets. The former were fixed in terms of "net domestic assets," defined as the amount by which the monetary base (roughly, notes and coins in circulation) exceeded the net hard currency reserves held by the central bank. This formula allowed the money supply to grow so long as official reserves grew too. In the spring of 1995, when the ruble was rising, the central bank printed rubles and used them to buy dollars. Money supply rose by 27 percent in two months, reserves doubled to $6 billion, and the IMF"s targets—set with respect to a preceding, one-year loan—were undisturbed.

This spring the picture was different. Base money grew by 7 percent in March and at the same rate in April, but this money was spent buying votes, not dollars. Worried by Mr. Yeltsin's extravagance, central bank officials revealed in June that almost $3 billion of reserves had been spent during April and May to prop up the ruble. Official numbers have not been published, but the combination of a rising money supply and falling reserves must have pushed up net domestic assets sharply.

If, as the IMF has insisted, monetary targets were met until at least the end of May (June figures have yet to be calculated), it is hard to see how. The IMF's Moscow office worried privately about the effect on the ruble. "The immediate challenge," said a preelection memorandum, "is to steer the exchange rate clear of a crisis."

Some on the Russian side made the same assessment, but thought it an acceptable risk. "A victory would be worth a Black Tuesday," said one minister in an unguarded moment, referring to the day in October 1994 when the ruble crashed 22 percent. With the election over, the currency looks much less vulnerable. Although official reserves are down from their peak, the central bank has about $7 billion in hand, adjusted for short-term liabilities. The government says it is confident that inflows of foreign investment and repatriated capital will support the ruble, so pushing interest rates down and making the budget deficit cheaper to finance. Annualized treasury bill yields have fallen below 90 percent, from a peak of 215 percent before the election.

Does it matter if the IMF bent over backward to help Mr. Yeltsin? Arguably, saving Russia from communism matters more than the niceties of monthly bookkeeping. And it would not be the first time the fund has been influenced by the political calculations of its chief shareholders. In 1987, for example, the Germans and Americans urged the IMF to lend to Egypt, a cornerstone of America's Middle East diplomacy, on terms that some fund officials considered too generous (one resigned over the issue). Some officials also resented America's hustling the fund to the rescue of Mexico after the peso collapsed in 1994.

Against such precedents, Russia, newly emerged from communism and still bristling with nuclear weapons, was arguably an even more suitable case for rule-bending treatment. But the fund has been left in a weaker position than it was to extract reforms from Russia. And in its dealings with other countries, the hint of double standards may come to haunt it.

A Watchful IMF

John Odling-Smee

This letter to the editor was written in response to the preceding selection, "Mr. Yeltsin's Flexible Friend." It was originally published in The Economist, 27 July–2 August 1996. John Odling-Smee is the director of the fund's European II Department.

Sir—In your 13 July [1996] issue you suggest that, in the run-up to the Russian presidential election, the IMF "turned a blind eye" to financial overruns, and granted Russia special treatment.

Let me start with a basic point: Despite the election campaign, the macroeconomic performance of the Russian economy during the past six months has been truly remarkable. Monthly inflation has been brought down to about 1 percent from around 4 percent at the beginning of this year. Moreover, during the first half of this year the ruble exchange rate displayed extraordinary stability, staying well within its preannounced band. This performance is a result of Russia's following policies agreed with the IMF under the 1995 standby arrangement and the 1996 extended fund facility.

Unfortunately, your article insinuates otherwise and asserts that Russia "broke through the ceiling originally agreed for the budget deficit almost immediately, in March." This is simply untrue, as are a number of other assertions in the article. Despite your inviting the reader to infer otherwise, virtually every monetary target under the program was met during this period.

Your article demonstrates a lack of full appreciation of how programs supported by the IMF are designed and assessed. It is quite common, particularly under a tight and ambitious program of the kind designed with the Russian authorities, to modify certain parameters to reflect exogenous developments that may be difficult to quantify fully at the outset of the program year. For example, when much higher-than-foreseen treasury bill interest rates emerged, reflecting in part the political uncertainties in the run-up to the election, adjustments were made to the monthly fiscal deficit ceilings. However, the primary deficit (i.e., excluding interest expenditures) was kept roughly equivalent to that foreseen for the first half of 1996.

Rather than turn a "blind eye" to Russian economic policy, the IMF has continued to work very closely with Russian policymakers as they pursued the difficult course of stabilization. Indeed, the intensity of the IMF's involvement with Russia may be unprecedented. There is certainly no question of its having applied a lesser standard to that country.

The Economist Editors' note: We wrote: "The evidence is that Russia broke through the ceiling originally agreed for the budget deficit almost immediately, in March." It remains our view that a comparison of official data on Russia's public finances with the monthly targets set in the March [1996] agreement between Russia and the IMF points to that conclusion. Unfortunately, the IMF's data and calculations remain confidential.

IMF and the Russian Missiles

J. Michael Waller

This selection first appeared in the *Washington Times* on 23 January 1998. J. Michael Waller is vice president of the American Foreign Policy Council in Washington, D.C.

American national security depends on Congress providing more money for the International Monetary Fund. That's what Defense secretary William Cohen is telling fellow Republicans on Capitol Hill, in a last-ditch administration effort to bail out troubled economies in Asia and elsewhere.

For those unmoved by economic arguments, national security concerns are often persuasive. But before accepting the Pentagon chief's pleas, Congress should look at how the IMF has helped secure U.S. national security goals in one of the fund's largest recipient states: Russia.

Since 1992, the IMF has approved more than $20 billion in loans to the Russian government. Currently, the IMF is paying out a three-year, $10.2 billion loan, and IMF managing director Michel Camdessus recently said he's open to sending more. These monies are transferred directly to the Russian central bank to be spent as the Kremlin chooses. Even though American tax dollars serve as collateral for one-fifth of the loans, the United States has demanded no accountability for any of it. As a result, as Mr. Camdessus acknowledged to reporters during the height of the Chechnya war, Moscow used IMF loans to fund the carnage.

No sooner did the IMF agree earlier this month [January 1998] to release its latest tranche of $667.5 million to Moscow than the finance ministry, which lobbied hard for the release, announced the money would be poured into military industry. Citing First Deputy Finance Minister Aleksei Kudrin, Russia's Interfax news agency reported 9 January [1998] that most of the cash will be spent mainly to pay up what the government owes for defense industry orders.

This runs against U.S. interests for four reasons. The IMF loan props up companies owned or controlled by the state. Second, the loan subsidizes a virulently anti-Western political constituency. Third, the money fuels the very sector most responsible for weapons proliferation to rogue regimes. And fourth, the IMF loan is financing the modernization of Russia's submarines and weapons of mass destruction.

Soldiers have been reduced to begging, fighter pilots are grounded for lack of spare aircraft parts and fuel, surface ships rust away at their berths, and the defense ministry is happy to accept Western aid to dismantle obsolete weapons systems already slated for the scrap heap anyway. Since the Soviet collapse, Moscow has neglected obsolete systems—and the men who operate them—as it focuses scarce financial resources on research and development in high-tech and strategic weapons. According to Richard F. Staar of the Hoover Institution, research and development funding in this area ballooned from $2.1 billion in 1994 to an estimated $12.8 billion in 1997.

With these priorities, what kind of military industry orders might the IMF—and by extension, the American taxpayer—be funding?

It might be paying for one of First Deputy Prime Minister Anatoly Chubais's pet projects: the *Yuri Dolgoruki*. Mr. Chubais doesn't mention the military when he asks Washington for more money for economic reform, but the *Yuri Dolgoruki* is the first in a series of Russia's fourth-generation nuclear-powered ballistic missile submarines.

In October 1996, Mr. Chubais hailed the *Yuri Dolgoruki* as a submarine for the next century. To spur the stalled project along, he announced that he had arranged for the finance ministry to free up funds in time for the official keel-laying ceremony at Shipyard No. 402 of the Russian State Center for Nuclear Shipbuilding in Severodvinsk. But the same day, the IMF announced it was postponing its monthly tranches of the $10.2 billion loan, citing Moscow's inadequate economic policies. In a curious coincidence, the keel-laying ceremony was hastily postponed, supposedly due to inclement weather. Finally, on 7 February 1997, the IMF released the money. That very day, the finance ministry announced that it had come up with cash to pay the Russian State Center for Nuclear Shipbuilding, averting a strike. Construction of the *Yuri Dolgoruki* continued. Once in service, the main targets of the submarine's nuclear missile complement will be American cities. (In the same port, the new Severodvinsk class of attack submarines has also begun production. Its advanced features are forcing the U.S. Navy to revise its strategy.)

Perhaps the IMF loan will pay to perfect the SS-NX-28, the next-generation submarine-launched ballistic missile with a range of nearly 5,000 miles. The missile will be deployed aboard the *Yuri Dolgoruki*. The SS-NX-28 underwent its most recent trial last November [1997] at a test range near Arkhangelsk, but malfunctions require more testing and, therefore, more money.

Or the IMF cash might help the strategic rocket forces speed up production of the new Topol-M2 intercontinental ballistic missile (ICBM), known in the West as the SS-27. Late last fall [1997], senior Republican congressional staffers heard a Pentagon briefer pooh-pooh the missile as inconsequential because Russia's strapped military didn't have the funds to begin serial production. But on 27 December [1997], the strategic rocket forces deployed the first Topol-M2s at the Tatishchevo missile base in the Saratov region and announced that the missiles would soon be stationed in Valdai, the southern Urals, and the Altai region.

Speaking of the Urals, we are reminded of Yamantau Mountain, site of one of the largest underground construction projects in human history. A nuclear blast–proof subterranean city sprawling across an area the size of the greater Washington, D.C., area inside the beltway, the complex is described in one Russian newspaper as a new strategic missile command center. Top Russian military leaders refuse to comment on it, and the Clinton administration hasn't pushed the issue. Construction work continues unabated. The money has to come from somewhere, and the IMF is just as good a source as any.

Troubling, too, are persistent reports that Russia maintains a clandestine binary chemical weapons program in violation of its international commitments. While concealing binary weapons production, it appeals to the West for aid to destroy obsolete chemical weapons stocks. And even President Clinton has been unable to certify to Congress that Moscow has terminated its germ warfare development and production. Might the IMF money be channeled to these sensitive programs?

We don't know because Washington has never wanted to embarrass Moscow by asking. And until it does, Congress should treat the defense secretary's national security talk with a bit of skepticism before approving any more money for the IMF.

THOUGHTS ON MISSION CREEP

What's an IMF For?

Wall Street Journal Editorial

This selection was originally published in the *Wall Street Journal* on 6 April 1998.

To listen to President Clinton and Treasury secretary Rubin, the safety of world markets hangs these days on whether the United States provides $18 billion in fresh money to the International Monetary Fund. "We need this money as quickly as possible, because right now the IMF does not have sufficient funds to deal with a truly major crisis," Mr. Rubin testified last month [March 1998].

Congress, unimpressed, listened to a couple of weeks of this kind of stuff and then recessed for Easter. Before lawmakers left, they had in various versions freighted Mr. Clinton's IMF funding request with such extraneous issues as abortion policy, dolphin conservation, and ways of preventing South Korea from plying U.S. consumers with cheap ladies' apparel.

Such casual reaction should surprise no one, least of all Messrs. Clinton and Rubin or even the IMF. This is what happens when institutions created to discharge serious responsibilities—like the IMF—depart from their basic missions and start using taxpayer money to restructure the known universe. House majority leader Dick Armey, in a memorandum Friday protesting any more money for the IMF, called the syndrome "mission creep."

Spelling out the precise mission of the IMF is a project that by now badly needs doing. We'd like to suggest that buried somewhere under all the frills and turf grabs, there might be one valid reason for the IMF to exist: that is, to act as genuine lender of last resort. By this we mean a fund that would step in only when a mismatch between short-term liabilities and long-run value of assets might threaten to wreck some sizable piece of the world's financial machinery. An example would be the fund's backing for the Argentine banking system during the 1995 crisis in which interest rates briefly skyrocketed while Argentina held fast its peso link to the dollar. It is on the role of lender of last resort that the IMF debate needs to focus.

Paring back the fund's goal to that point will take some doing—though Mr. Armey's memo may help spur debate. To see just how far the IMF's mission has crept, it helps to recall that the IMF was founded at the end of World War II solely to help defend the Bretton Woods system of fixed exchange rates. The fund's role was to step in only as needed to adjust temporary payment imbalances that threatened the overall fixed-rate system. It worked fine.

Then the United States in 1971 took the dollar off the gold standard. Bretton Woods collapsed. The IMF lived on and began devising new reasons for its existence. So inventive did the fund become that it now deploys a capital base of some $205 billion—some $37 billion of that already supplied by the United States. The fund's managing director, Michel Camdessus, is now asking the IMF's 182 member nations for a 45 percent increase, subject of the current Clinton request.

Increasingly the fund has drawn on these billions to reorganize and often subsidize growing chunks of economic life, lending to member governments at below market rates, with conditions attached. Along with deciding which banks should be shut down here, or intimating which dictator deposed there, the fund these days likes to "fine-tune" exchange rates not according to some clear, fixed system—as with Bretton Woods—but according to some incantation which Mr. Camdessus keeps to himself.

One result of this micromanagement is that the fund has by now crept into direct contravention of its own Articles of Agreement. These state that among the IMF's purposes is "To promote exchange stability, to maintain orderly exchange arrangements among members, and to avoid competitive exchange depreciation." That's a far cry from the IMF's backing last year [1997] for what turned into the damaging spiral of competitive devaluations in East Asia. These still threaten the larger world economy. To cope with the Asian wreckage caused at least in solid part by its own love of depreciating currencies, the IMF then employed itself putting together bailouts totaling some $120 billion for Thailand, Indonesia, and South Korea.

Treasury deputy secretary Larry Summers has further been urging that the IMF work harder on things like health care and "needs of the poor." Because the IMF operates as one of the world's most secretive multilateral institutions, the issue of who decides just what gets cared for, or at what cost, is left to the confidential debates of folks like Mr. Summers and the IMF staff. The only thing clear is that, whatever they're planning, they think it needs $18 billion in U.S. funding—which Mr. Rubin says could be leveraged by the IMF into some $90 billion in "usable resources." This policy enlarges the risk that some day the IMF will be hit with a very large default.

The hazard of IMF bailouts goes beyond the problem that bad IMF conditions such as higher taxes harm client countries. Worse, bailouts don't actually bail out troubled nations or their poorest citizens. Rather, bailouts tend chiefly to reduce losses to large investors who made bad bets. And the scope of bailing has been expanding fast.

Time was when IMF bailouts dealt with creditors holding sovereign debt, as in the 1994 Mexico crisis. With the fast growth of global markets, the IMF in Asia has found itself a new, much bigger niche, bailing out loans in which both lender and borrower are from the private sector. All this invites fresh, overly risky lending, which will lead to new bankruptcies and bigger bailouts—until the world finds itself facing that "truly major crisis" Mr. Rubin so fears.

For now, IMF funding has devolved into another of those issues—like global warming, or that budget surplus Mr. Clinton wants to spend before he's even got it—where any genuine policy needs have been lost to the government craving to spend and grow. The beginning of a solution lies in refocusing the debate on what it would mean for the IMF to act not as a creature of infinite resources but solely as a lender of last resort.

PART SIX

ABOLISH THE INTERNATIONAL MONETARY FUND?

During the fiftieth-anniversary celebrations for the IMF, a reporter asked a top fund official what the public should expect from the IMF in the future. He paused for a moment and said, "the fifty-first anniversary." This reply epitomizes what many critics see as a lack of creativity and initiative at the fund, not unlike the inertia afflicting many bureaucratic organizations. This exchange also reinforces the view, correct in most cases, that bureaucratic organizations live forever. As noted by Milton Friedman, Nobel laureate and Hoover Institution senior research fellow, "There is nothing so permanent as a government agency, especially if it is international."[1] But does the IMF still serve a useful purpose or does it cause more harm than good? Should the IMF be strengthened or abolished? Part 6 explores these fundamental questions.

In "Who Needs the IMF?" George Shultz, William Simon, and Walter Wriston argue that the fund is "ineffective, unnecessary, and obsolete." This assessment motivates rebuttals by Paul Krugman and Jim Hoagland. In "Why America Needs the IMF," Lawrence Summers, deputy secretary of the U.S. Treasury, makes his case for strengthening and expanding the fund. Jack Kemp answers Summers in a *Wall Street Journal* letter to the editor. In "Who Needs the IMF?" James Glassman asserts that the fund does more harm than good. William Lassetter, Shailendra Anjaria of the IMF, and Robert Solomon oppose Glassman in a series of *Washington Post* letters to the editor. Part 6 concludes with four independent essays written by Robert Samuelson, Anna Schwartz, David Rockefeller, and Doug Bandow.

1. Gene Epstein, "Mr. Market: An Interview with Milton Friedman," *Barron's*, 24 August 1998, p. 32.

OVERVIEW OF THE PROS AND CONS OF
INTERNATIONAL MONETARY FUND INTERVENTION

Pros	Cons
The IMF acts as an international "lender of last resort" to guarantee international liquidity in order to prevent self-reinforcing collapses of confidence and the spread of financial crises.	The IMF is not a true "lender of last resort," and its bailouts of privileged investors and politicians encourage excessive risk taking, delay necessary reforms, and discourage the voluntary restructuring of debt and the reorganization of insolvent companies through bankruptcy proceedings. These effects promote future global crises.
The IMF prevents competitive currency devaluations and exchange restrictions and lessens the frequency and severity of balance of payments problems and global demand contractions.	The IMF too often encourages currency devaluations, and its loans discourage fiscal responsibility, fundamental reform, and economic growth, thus deepening and prolonging demand contractions.
The IMF promotes strong export markets, stable financial markets, reductions in military spending and government corruption, and the spread of market-based democracy, which is central to U.S. national security.	Austere IMF loan conditions reduce growth rates, prolong recessions, and affect most severely the poorest people in the borrowing countries, thus producing a backlash against the West rather than a backlash against their corrupt, brutal, and kleptocratic governments.
The IMF achieves more trade liberalization than bilateral or multilateral negotiations.	Given the volume of today's global capital and currency flows, IMF resources are insufficient to truly "rescue" member countries but are large enough to bail out privileged investors and thus distort incentives in international capital markets.
The IMF entices member countries to undertake reforms that are necessary but politically difficult to implement.	The fund's one-size-fits-all reforms, which are rarely appropriate or sufficient, are imposed by an outside agent on sovereign governments, thus weakening the governments' domestic legitimacy.

Who Needs the IMF?

George P. Shultz, William E. Simon, and Walter B. Wriston

This selection first appeared in the *Wall Street Journal* on 3 February 1998. George Shultz, a distinguished fellow of the Hoover Institution at Stanford University, was secretary of state under President Ronald Reagan. William Simon, president of the John M. Olin Foundation, was secretary of the Treasury under Presidents Richard Nixon and Gerald Ford. Walter Wriston is a former chairman and CEO of Citicorp/Citibank.

Last winter President Clinton and the International Monetary Fund shifted into overdrive in their effort to save the economies of Indonesia, the Philippines, South Korea, and Thailand—or, to be more accurate, to save the pocketbooks of international investors who could face a tide of defaults if these markets were not shored up. But that must be the last time that the IMF acts in this capacity. If it is not, further bailouts, unprecedented in scope, will follow. Therefore, Congress should allocate no further funds to the IMF.

It is the IMF's promise of massive intervention that has spurred a global meltdown of financial markets. When such hysteria sweeps world markets, it becomes more difficult to do what should have been done earlier—namely, to let the private parties most involved share the pain and resolve their difficulties, perhaps with the help of a modest program of public financial support and policy guidance. With the IMF standing in the background ready to bail them out, the parties at interest have little incentive to take these painful, though necessary, steps.

LARGEST BAILOUT EVER

The $118 billion Asian bailout, which may rise to as much as $160 billion, is by far the largest ever undertaken by the IMF. A distant second was the 1995 Mexican bailout, which involved some $30 billion in loans, mostly from the IMF and the U.S. Treasury. The IMF's defenders often tout the Mexican bailout as a success because the Mexican government repaid the loans on schedule. But the Mexican people suffered a massive decline in their standard of living as a result of that crisis. As is typical when the IMF intervenes, the governments and the lenders were rescued but not the people.

The promise of an IMF bailout insulates financiers and politicians from the consequences of bad economic and financial practices and encourages investments that would not otherwise have been made. Recall how the Asian crisis came about. Asia's "tiger" economies were performing well, with strong growth, moderate price inflation, fiscal discipline, and high rates of saving. But these countries encountered a currency crisis because their governments attempted to maintain an exchange rate pegged to the U.S. dollar, while conducting monetary policies that diverged from that of the United States. Capital inflows covered up this disparity for a time. But when the Thai currency wobbled on rumors of exchange controls and devaluation, the currency markets quickly swept aside increasingly unrealistic currency values.

This led quickly to a solvency crisis. It became difficult, if not impossible, to repay loans made in foreign currency on time. The devaluations shrank the values of local assets, which were often the product of speculative excesses, unwise ventures directed by government, and crony capitalism. The private lenders and borrowers involved were in deep trouble. They were more than ready for money from the IMF.

The world financial system has changed fundamentally since 1945, when the Bretton Woods agreement was approved. The gold standard has been replaced by the information standard, an iron discipline that no government can evade. Foreign exchange rates are now set by tens of thousands of traders at computer terminals around the globe. Their judgments about monetary and economic policies are instantly translated into the cross rates of currencies.

No country can hide from the new global information standard—but the IMF can lull nations into complacency by acting as the self-appointed lender of last resort, a function never contemplated by its founders. When the day of reckoning finally does arrive, the needed financial reforms are extremely difficult politically because they are imposed by the IMF under duress, rather than undertaken by the countries themselves. The photograph, widely published throughout Asia, of Indonesian president Suharto signing on to IMF conditions with IMF managing director Michel Camdessus standing over him imperiously reinforces the perception of an outside institution dictating policy to a sovereign government.

Even though the IMF recognizes the causes of the crises, and conditions its loans on remedial measures, many observers believe that these remedies often make the situation worse. In any event they are rarely carried out in a timely fashion. There are already indications that several Asian countries have violated the terms of their agreements. Furthermore, IMF-prescribed tax increases and austerity will cause pain for the people of these nations, producing a backlash against the West. There is already talk of a conspiracy to beat down Asian asset values in order to provide bargains and control for Western investors.

And yet, because these countries are able to avoid fundamental economic reforms, their currencies continue to collapse. Indonesia, South Korea, and Thailand have each seen their currencies lose more than half their value against the U.S. dollar, despite the promised IMF bailouts. The loans from the IMF are, in fact, trivial when compared to the size of the international currency market, in which some $2 trillion is traded daily. These markets' instant verdicts on unsound economic and financial policies overwhelm the feeble efforts of politicians and bureaucrats.

The IMF's efforts are, however, effective in distorting the international investment market. Every investment has an associated risk, and investors seeking higher returns must accept higher risks. The IMF interferes with this fundamental market mechanism by encouraging investors to seek out risky markets on the assumption that if their investments turn sour, they still stand a good chance of getting their money back through IMF bailouts. This kind of interference will only encourage more crises.

Asian nations are facing financial difficulties not because outside forces have imposed bad economic policies on them but because they have imposed these policies on themselves. The issue is not whether the IMF can move from country to country dispensing financial and economic medicine. The issue is whether the governments in these countries have the political will to fix problems of their own making.

What should we do about the problem? We certainly shouldn't follow the advice of George Soros, a well-known figure in the international currency markets, who has called for the creation of a new international credit insurance corporation to be underwritten by taxpayers of the member countries. The new institution, which would operate in tandem with the IMF, would guarantee international loans up to a point deemed safe by the bureaucrats running the organization. "The private sector is ill-suited to allocate international credit," Mr. Soros writes in the *Financial Times*. "It provides either too little or too much. It does not have the information with which to form a balanced judgment."

APPALLING COMMENT

When will we ever learn? This appalling comment is exactly the opposite of the truth. The protected markets, not the open ones, are in trouble. Only the market, with its millions of interested participants, is capable of generating the information needed to make sound financial decisions and to allocate credit (or any other resource) efficiently and rationally. Governments and politically directed institutions like the IMF have shown time and again that they are incapable of making these kinds of decisions without creating the kinds of crises we are now facing in Asia.

The IMF is ineffective, unnecessary, and obsolete. We do not need another IMF, as Mr. Soros recommends. Once the Asian crisis is over, we should abolish the one we have.

REBUTTAL

The Indispensable IMF

Paul Krugman

This selection was originally published in the *New York Times* on 15 May 1998. Paul Krugman is a professor of economics at the Massachusetts Institute of Technology.

Suppose a group of prominent experts declared that the Federal Reserve should no longer be allowed to lend money during bank runs. Far from helping prevent financial panics, they say, such lending actually fosters them by encouraging the public to be careless; if we returned to the good old days when banks were free to fail, depositors would make sure that a bank was sound before placing money in its care.

Most sensible people would reject this view as irresponsible, no matter how eminent the authors. As Charles Kindleberger showed in his classic study *Manias, Panics and Crashes,* those good old days were marked by frequent and often devastating panics, in which even people who thought their money was in safe hands could be wiped out.

Both theory and evidence suggest that no matter how much due diligence individual investors may exercise, financial markets are vulnerable to self-reinforcing collapses of confidence unless there is a "lender of last resort": some institution like the Fed that can provide emergency cash to threatened banks and companies. The Fed makes mistakes, sometimes grievous ones; nonetheless, we all sleep better knowing that Alan Greenspan has the power and resources to help fight whatever crises may arise.

Some people who should know better have waged a campaign to prevent the International Monetary Fund from fulfilling that same role in an international crisis. Congress has effectively blocked consideration of a potentially crucial $18 billion increase in the IMF's financing, motivated in large part by the antifund views of people like George Shultz, the former secretary of state.

Mr. Shultz has argued that the fund should withdraw from its role as the "self-appointed lender of last resort." When faced with a crisis, he says, the "private parties most involved" should share the pain and resolve the problems themselves. To see how irresponsible that view is, try the same argument on a purely domestic crisis.

Suppose that, worried by tales of bad management, depositors began trying en masse to withdraw money from Citibank—and that the bank, unable to raise that much cash on short notice, was about to be forced to close. Would you really want the Fed to stand on principle and refuse to supply the needed cash, leaving it instead for the "private parties most involved"—the bank and its depositors—to work it out themselves? Not likely. Even those who do not have money at Citibank would be concerned that a bank run would spread, perhaps engulfing many banks and companies that would otherwise have been perfectly sound.

If we need a domestic lender of last resort to deal with domestic financial crises, doesn't the globalization of financial markets mean that now, more than ever, we need a lender of last resort to cope with inter-national crises?

You can argue that the IMF is not ideally suited to be that backstop. Unlike the Fed, which can regulate banks on a continuing basis, the IMF has little power until a country plunges into crisis. That means that some-times its efforts to save a country from financial collapse also end up providing a safety net for the undeserving—careless international bankers, even corrupt local politicians. The IMF also makes mistakes; its programs in Asia have been bitterly criticized (although the critics seem to disagree as much with each other as with the IMF).

But the International Monetary Fund is all that we have, and it is a lot better than nothing at all. To hobble the IMF in the belief that world financial markets will take care of themselves is to gamble the stability of those markets on a speculative theory—a theory that even most of the theorists think is refuted by the lessons of history.

REBUTTAL

Which Way for the IMF?

Jim Hoagland

This selection first appeared in the *Washington Post* on 10 May 1998. Jim Hoagland is a columnist at the *Post.*

George Shultz would dismantle the International Monetary Fund, yes-terday if he could. Paul Volcker would strengthen the fund to iron out the spreading wrinkles of global capitalism.

Indonesia's rulers defy, plot with, or ignore the fund, according to the moods and needs of the day. Their citizens riot against economic pain inflicted by the fund's rules.

In Birmingham, England, next weekend [16–17 May 1998], French and American leaders are likely to lock horns during the Group of Seven industrial nations summit over French ideas on giving the fund some supervision of private international investment flows.

After a half century of quiet labor on balance of payments problems, the secretive and staid IMF finds itself embroiled in controversy around the globe. Its critics come from virtually every point on the political spectrum, agreeing on only one thing:

The fund and the international financial system it heads have been woefully inadequate in dealing with the continuing Asian financial crisis.

Shultz and others even fear that the IMF and its ally in Asia, the U.S. Treasury, are actually contributing to Asia's problems and to more devastating capital crunches to come.

He voiced that fear in testimony to a congressional committee last week. The fund encourages investors and bankers to take imprudent risks by providing taxpayers' money to bail them out, he said. The man who was Richard Nixon's Treasury secretary and Ronald Reagan's secretary of state urged Congress to turn back "a pattern of escalation of ambitions of the IMF" so unhindered markets could resolve these problems.

Shultz goes too far. The IMF is a lightning rod for the financial storms kicked up in the reshaping of the world economy by the forces of technology, expanding capital markets, education, and democracy. Pushed by the United States, the fund stepped into the Asian crisis not because of ambition but because there was no one else to deal with the problem.

That—Shultz's demonstrated wisdom on other topics notwithstanding—is the real problem.

Asia's troubles show that in the four years since Mexico's currency debacle the world's most powerful political and financial leaders have taken no effective action to prepare the fund, or other international institutions, to deal with the financial consequences and vulnerabilities of globalization.

This is not even an Asian crisis, Volcker, former chairman of the Federal Reserve, said in a speech at Johns Hopkins University. The collapse of Indonesian, Thai, South Korean and other currencies and markets is "only the latest, and most dramatic, episode in a series of events that raise some basic questions about global finance and its implications for economic development."

Volcker then put those questions in considerable depth and breadth, endorsing the IMF as "the only vehicle we have to bring consensus and legitimacy to reform of the financial system on a global scale."

But that goes too far for the Clinton administration, which opposes broad reform of the world's financial system, led by the IMF or by anybody else.

Treasury secretary Robert E. Rubin argues that moments of crisis are the wrong time for monkeying with basic architecture. He favors incremental action—such as upping the U.S. contribution to the IMF by $18 billion, which will encourage other countries to add $65 billion to the fund's reserves—and opposes anything that would change a global status quo that America dominates.

But the incremental approach is in trouble here and abroad, as Asia's economies show signs of sinking once again.

Following Shultz's testimony, House Speaker Newt Gingrich was said to be leaning toward not scheduling a vote on the $18 billion request this year [1998]. Democratic leaders in Congress would use this retreat as ammunition for November, when they will run against an isolationist, do-nothing Republican Congress that imperils America's standing in the world.

But in their different ways Shultz and Volcker establish that a historic conflict of big ideas about market efficiency and economic justice in the era of globalization is under way, with the IMF serving as a catalyst. Rubin's voice is missing in that debate as he concentrates on technical fixes and warding off pressures to change a system created fifty years ago for different purposes.

That strategic absence, more than Republican isolationism, is the problem with Rubin's $18 billion request. It may now fail, both as legislation and as an election issue, unless the administration can quickly show that this new money is part of a new strategy for dealing with international financial problems that America's success in penetrating other markets has helped create.

Or, as Bill Clinton might have once put it, it's the global economy, stupid.

Why America Needs the IMF

Lawrence Summers

This selection first appeared in the *Wall Street Journal* on 27 March 1998. Lawrence Summers is deputy secretary of the U.S. Treasury.

Congress is currently engaged in a high-stakes debate about whether the United States will continue our long-standing commitment to the International Monetary Fund. This issue takes on special urgency in the wake of the Asian financial crisis, which has depleted the IMF's resources. And it is crucial to the future of this country. Congress needs to support the IMF because a well-funded IMF is critical to promoting American workers' interest in strong export markets, American savers' interest in stable financial markets, and all Americans' interest in the spread of market-based democracy, which is central to our national security. Meeting U.S. obligations to the IMF also maximizes our ability to bring about much-needed changes in the way it and the international monetary system operate.

Economists and historians will be debating the causes of the Asian financial crisis for a long time. What is clear now is that a central element in spurring the crisis was a loss of confidence on the part of both these countries' own citizens and foreign investors. Confidence eroded for many reasons, including the belated recognition of severe policy errors, the accumulation of large debts, and the changing global economic environment. The approach the IMF has taken on behalf of the international community—conditioning financial support on strong domestic policy measures to restore confidence—is the right one. And it has had important successes. A potentially catastrophic default in South Korea has been avoided, Thailand has seen its currency appreciate nearly 30 percent since its low in mid-January [1998], and a crisis that once seemed likely to go global has so far been contained.

CHALLENGES REMAIN

To be sure, important policy challenges remain, particularly in the uncertain environment of Indonesia. But without the support the IMF provides in these situations, we would probably now be dealing with a great deal worse: debt moratoriums in some countries, a generalized withdrawal of capital from the developing world, and potentially large consequences for our export industries and our financial markets. The history of the 1930s is instructive. There is little debate among economic historians that the international system's failure to respond to the spreading financial problems that occurred in the wake of the Austrian Credit Anstalt failure did far more to perpetuate the economic misery of the 1930s than the Smoot-Hawley tariff did.

Insurance against the spread of the Asian financial crisis would be reason enough for the United States to support the IMF. But there are others reasons:

- IMF and sister World Bank programs, not just in East Asia but in India, Latin America, Central Europe, and Africa, have led to more systematic trade liberalization than our bilateral or multilateral negotiations have ever achieved.

- IMF financing and conditions have been the primary external mode of support for the dramatic changes in Russia's economy over the past five years, changes that have seen it move from a state-dominated hyperinflating economy to an economy with stable money and a lower share of public employment than in much of Europe.

- The IMF has further promoted U.S. interests by supporting stabilization in Poland and other Central European nations, preventing the spread of the Mexican financial crisis through strong support for Argentina, and supporting economic reform in the states of the former Soviet Union.

- U.S. security has surely been enhanced by the IMF's success in inducing program countries to reduce military spending, to around 2 percent of gross domestic product by 1996 from an average of more than 5 percent in 1990.

Looking back a few years, it was IMF financial support that played the central role in containing the threat to the American banking system posed by the Latin American debt crisis of the 1980s. Then, as now, every dollar the United States put into the IMF leveraged four of five dollars from the rest of the world.

Providing funding for the benefits the IMF provides does not cost taxpayers anything. And it does not add to the federal deficit. That is because the United States supports the IMF by providing a line of credit in return for which we receive a rate of return that roughly matches our borrowing cost. The IMF's credit is good: It has not had a major default in fifty years, and its loans are substantially backed by gold.

So the IMF is indispensable and without expense. Yet its critics have raised important and legitimate issues—issues that the administration and the Federal Reserve believe are best addressed by funding and changing the IMF rather than abandoning it. The IMF should be more transparent and accountable to its member countries and more open in its reaching of agreements with countries. It should allow for external evaluation of its procedures and the results they bring. And it should develop ways of sharing the information it has with those in the markets. It has come a considerable distance here, but it is not yet at the finish line.

Transparency is necessary but not sufficient for preventing crises. There is also a need for improved surveillance techniques to focus more on capital flows and the health of key financial institutions. There is a need for better regulation of banking systems around the world and more rigorous monitoring of implicit government subsidies for risks taken by financial intermediaries. And there is a need for better dialogue with countries that—like Mexico in 1994 and Thailand in 1997—are heading for serious difficulty. Without a strong IMF or something very much like it, it is hard to see how the United States could go about fulfilling any of these needs.

There is also the moral hazard concern: that too-ready IMF financial support may encourage imprudent lending and borrowing. This is why the IMF has, at U.S. behest, begun charging penalty interest rates on extraordinary loans. It is why we sought in late December [1997] to condition further IMF support for South Korea on actions by its creditors to roll over and extend their loans and why IMF programs in Asia have included conditions requiring the adoption of bankruptcy statutes and preventing government bailouts of private corporations or their creditors.

There is no question that, as Treasury secretary Robert Rubin and Fed chairman Alan Greenspan have often said, the international community has to devise new procedures to reduce the likelihood that policymakers will again have to face the kind of choice they faced last fall [1997]— between large-scale financial support on the one hand and contagion and possible chaos on the other. Again, it is difficult to see how any such procedures could operate without an international institution very similar to the IMF we have today.

IMPORTANT LESSONS

The content of IMF programs will be a matter of continuing debate and evolution. The past few years have taught important lessons: that mismanaged devaluations can have catastrophic consequences; that the quality of deficit reduction matters as much as the quantity; that macroeconomic reforms can be ineffective unless economies are liberalized and trade barriers and corruption are reduced; and that the success of reforms depends on their being carried out in a way that protects a country's workers rather than a privileged elite, to name just a few. In part because of the efforts of U.S. representatives, these lessons are increasingly being reflected in the advice the IMF gives and the conditionality it imposes. But there is more to be done.

If the United States does not contribute to the IMF, we risk losing the opportunity to help shape its approach to economic policy around the world. Like a decision not to take out insurance, the decision to delay funding for the IMF could work out just fine. But at a time when markets in many countries are fragile and looking for confidence from the world's only superpower, it is a gamble that's not worth taking.

REBUTTAL

Who Needs the IMF?

Jack Kemp

This letter to the editor of the *Wall Street Journal*, written in response to the preceding selection, "Why America Needs the IMF," appeared on 3 April 1998. Jack Kemp is codirector of Empower America.

Virtually nothing Lawrence Summers cites in his 27 March [1998] editorial page piece, "Why America Needs the IMF," to demonstrate why America needs the IMF is true, and everything in the article that is true demonstrates how the IMF hurts our country and the rest of the world. It is no exaggeration to say that the IMF has over the decades since it was founded in 1944 gathered up its own kind of Evil Empire. Mr. Summers's sky-is-falling hyperbole about how important the IMF is to mankind sounds more like an applicant to succeed Managing Director Michel Camdessus than a sitting deputy secretary of the Treasury.

I'm sure that the IMF boss, Michel Camdessus, is a fine man, but his record is the worst record of a financial institution in the history of the world. People in countries that have come under the IMF's sway despise it, and they see it as an agent of the United States. For example, throughout the 1970s and 1980s, the IMF impoverished Latin America by constantly urging higher tax rates. Despite promises of reform, the IMF still urges higher tax rates rather than lower rates. Specifically, in recent months, IMF bureaucrats have been urging government officials in Bulgaria, Albania, and Russia to increase rather than decrease tax rates.

Three years ago, anyone with one eye open in Washington could see that the IMF helped engineer the peso devaluation in Mexico so its friendly supporters at the banks could cash in. The people of Mexico looked up to the United States and hoped through the NAFTA agreement that we could finally protect them from the periodic monetary devaluations that decimate entire economies and wipe out the savings of ordinary people.

But open trade without a sound international monetary arrangement can easily be destabilized by an international bureaucracy like the IMF, willing to use extortion to foster beggar-thy-neighbor currency devaluations as it has recently in Indonesia. How tragic that it takes so little effort by so few international bureaucrats to cause so much pain and suffering. No one with a firm grip on reality can doubt that the Asian currency crisis that has hit the Pacific rim so hard was at least encouraged by Michel Camdessus and his associates at the IMF.

This is why, if it were up to me, I would not give one dime, one nickel, one cent to the IMF, which is asking our taxpayers for $18 billion—until it changes its policies and top personnel, without Mr. Summers in the running to lead it.

Clearly, we have to figure out a way to improve the performance of the IMF, totally reform it, or abolish it altogether—because the people of the world do see it as our agent. What the world needs is a stable monetary regime that would prevent currency meltdowns in the first place. The greatest threat to worldwide economic stability today is the international monetary arrangement of floating currencies in which no currency is linked to a stable anchor and all countries are being encouraged to use currency devaluation as an economic policy instrument during times of economic duress. Rather than shilling for the IMF, our Treasury Department should be hard at work figuring out how to reconstitute a stable international monetary system.

Who Needs the IMF?

James K. Glassman

This selection first appeared in the *Washington Post* on 9 December 1997. James Glassman is a business columnist at the *Post* and the DeWitt Wallace–Reader's Digest Fellow at the American Enterprise Institute in Washington, D.C.

The International Monetary Fund, or IMF, was set up in 1945 to help guard the world's currencies under the Bretton Woods monetary agreement. But that deal was ditched long ago, and the IMF became something else entirely—a lender of last resort to countries that get into financial trouble.

In that role, it's doing far more harm than good. A free market economy has a very efficient way of dealing with misjudgment, excess, and failure. It's called bankruptcy. Lenders, investors, managers, and sometimes employees and politicians all take part of the hit—and assets pass from weak hands to strong. Everyone learns important lessons and starts afresh.

But by rushing to the rescue, the IMF is preventing this cleansing process and, in the current case of Asia, blowing a chance to inject freedom, imagination, and competition into economies that suffer from too much government control.

The IMF is also creating a classic problem of "moral hazard"—helping imprudent countries actually encourages more imprudence in the future.

Look at Mexico, which received a $50 billion bailout in 1995. Yes, Mexico is in better shape than it was two years ago [1995], but the rescue almost certainly gave governments in Asia a sense of confidence that, if they got into terrible straits, the IMF would help them, too.

Even worse, the bailout encouraged investors, including U.S. mutual funds, to make risky bond and stock purchases in countries with overheated, shaky economies. And, of course, it's postponed Mexico's own economic reforms.

Lately the IMF has been shoveling money at Thailand, Indonesia, and now Korea. The IMF itself has put up $35 billion for the three countries (roughly 18 percent of its funds come from the United States, with less than 6 percent each from Germany and Japan).

But the IMF doesn't act alone. It's the lead bank in a bailout consortium that includes the World Bank ($16 billion) and the United States individually ($8 billion). A total of $113 billion has been put up, with no end in sight.

IMF money typically comes with strings attached: requirements for higher interest rates and lower government spending, for instance. The Korean bailout will try to go even further. "Banking and financial-sector restructuring is absolutely at the heart of the program," says Stanley Fischer, the IMF's number two.

There's no doubt Korea (which will get $55 billion in bailout money) needs it. Like most other Asian nations, Korea practices command-and-control capitalism—a version of the Japanese business-government partnership model that still seduces America's liberals.

In Korea, banks made massive loans, at the government's direction, to the *chaebols*, or conglomerates. The banks also owned large chunks of stock in Korean companies. So when a conglomerate like Kia Motors got into trouble, the banks were hit by a double whammy—though the government tried to cover the losses up.

"Korea," said a recent editorial in the *Financial Times*, "needs a thorough clean-out of both its banking system and the balance sheets of its industrial companies. . . . Government patronage of industry must end, and there needs to be an effective competition policy to curb the power of big companies."

Absolutely. The question is whether the IMF and its fleet of lenders can accomplish those ends better than the free market, which would create a new Korean economy through loan defaults and bankruptcies.

At a symposium at the American Enterprise Institute, Lawrence Lindsey, a former Federal Reserve governor, said unequivocally that "we would get much more done in Korea without the IMF bailout."

Deregulate Korea's banking system and let its banks be bought out by American ones. That would do more to fix the economy than all the billions the IMF can throw at the problem.

IMF officials aren't evil or stupid, but they do suffer from a kind of superhubris, or overweening pride, that international institutions tend to breed. And they often forget that they're using other people's money for their good deeds.

That money won't last forever, and Congress is not in the mood to provide more.

An article in yesterday's *Post* [8 December 1997] characterized this reluctance to back the IMF as evidence of "globalphobia," or "a retreat from the internationalist consensus that has governed U.S. economic policy for 50 years." It also cites the defeat of fast track and the new antagonism toward free trade.

Isolationism is certainly rearing its ugly head, but to oppose IMF bailouts is not to oppose free market internationalism. On the contrary. Without the IMF and the World Bank, Asia would be more open, not less. The conflict is not so much between globalists and isolationists as between those of us who want the future to take its own vivid course and politicians who try, vainly, to guide it along a path of their choosing.

The Asian countries have a lot going for them: a diligent workforce and high savings rates, for starters. But they will never achieve their promise unless they jettison the top-down control and xenophobia that have landed them in their current mess. The way to end the old ways is to allow markets to punish the perpetrators. "Capitalism without failure," says American Enterprise Institute economist Allan Meltzer, "is like religion without sin."

The IMF, using the hard-earned money of U.S. taxpayers, is trying to prevent that failure. It's the kind of charity that helps no one.

REBUTTAL

The Mission of the IMF

William Lassetter and Shailendra J. Anjaria

The following two letters to the editor of the Washington Post, *written in response to the preceding selection, "Who Needs the IMF?" appeared on 23 December 1997. William Lassetter lives in Charlottesville, Virginia. Shailendra Anjaria is the director of the fund's External Relations Department.*

LETTER ONE

James K. Glassman's judgment of the IMF ["Who Needs the IMF?" op-ed, 9 December 1997] is a little simplistic. The failures of financial systems such as happened in Southeast Asia and Korea are the result of two processes. One, as Mr. Glassman discusses, is the misallocation—or even misappropriation—of equity and debt capital to nonproductive or marginally productive uses. The other, which he does not mention, is a loss of confidence on the part of investors and creditors and the consequent flight of capital in a last-out-takes-the-hit panic.

The mission of the IMF should be to address directly the second problem (capital flight). The IMF, in such cases, is the creditor of last resort that supplies capital at secured market rates on the basis of good faith rather than good credit. The conditions that it imposes should be designed to be a convincing demonstration that the first problem (misuse of capital) is being addressed with full intent and good faith and that good credit will follow in due course.

In the process, the IMF should ensure that the losses entailed as a result of bad investments, both to local and foreign investors, are fully exposed to a free market's corrective influence. Nobody should be forgiven his investment sins—least of all the rich and powerful made so through those very sins.

But it is in the interest of the world that economies, where they will, are stable and productive. And if the IMF can accomplish that as creditor commanding a good return with good assurance, then we have lost nothing, and gained much.

WILLIAM LASSETTER

LETTER TWO

James K. Glassman misunderstands the recent role of the International Monetary Fund in Asia. His claim that by making its financial resources available to Korea, the IMF is stifling reform, competition, and economic recovery is just wrong, and his advice to allow "the future to take its own vivid course" is plain dangerous.

In its IMF-supported program, the Korean government has committed itself to liberalize trade, open wider the doors for foreign entry into its domestic financial sector, cease the directed lending and subsidies that favored privileged corporations and aided the system of *chaebols* (huge conglomerates), and take many other steps to open its economy much further to free market forces.

Is American taxpayers' money wasted in footing the United States' share of the bill for IMF assistance to Korea and other countries? The IMF makes loans, not grants. The interest on loans goes back to our shareholders. Successive Democratic and Republican administrations consistently have supported an IMF of adequate technical and financial clout because, as President Reagan put it to the world's finance ministers and central bank governors assembled in Washington for the IMF annual meetings in 1983: "The IMF is the linchpin of the international financial system. Among official institutions, it serves as a counselor, coaxing the world economy toward renewed growth and stability. At various times in its history, the IMF has provided important temporary balance of payments assistance to its member nations—including my own. At times, it must play the 'Dutch uncle,' talking frankly, telling those of us in government things we need to hear, but would rather not."

The IMF was set up in 1945 and has among its goals the promotion of world trade, thereby contributing to growth among nations. IMF financing is to be made available to members to help them deal with balance of payments problems. Mr. Glassman ignores history by asking the world to follow his vivid course, which, unfettered by international assistance to Korea and concerted action through the IMF, would produce deeper industrial collapses and more widespread loan defaults and bank failures. Such a future course would lead us back to the past, to the 1930s era of competitive devaluations, punitive trade barriers, and closed capital markets—an era in which all economies, including that of the United States, would be worse off.

SHAILENDRA J. ANJARIA

REBUTTAL

Give the IMF Some Credit

Robert Solomon

This letter to the editor of the *Washington Post*, written in response to James Glassman's article, "Who Needs the IMF?" appeared on 5 January 1998. Robert Solomon is a guest scholar at the Brookings Institution in Washington, D.C., and a former director of international finance at the Federal Reserve Board.

James Glassman's diatribe against the International Monetary Fund ["Who Needs the IMF?" op-ed, 9 December 1997] is full of misconceptions about the fund's original purposes and present functions.

The IMF was not set up primarily "to help guard the world's currencies under the Bretton Woods monetary agreement" and did not change its aims after par values for currencies were abandoned. Its original purpose, which still holds, was to help countries in need to finance balance of payments deficits so that they would not take actions that would harm their trading partners.

Mr. Glassman would substitute bankruptcy for that function. Of course, countries do not go bankrupt. He also claims that IMF credits to Asian countries are "blowing a chance to inject freedom, imagination, and competition into [those] economies." That is precisely what the IMF is trying to accomplish in Korea.

Mr. Glassman trots out the well-worn "moral hazard" argument: The potential availability of IMF loans encourages countries to act "imprudently." What he ignores is that IMF credits come with policy conditions that borrowing countries find painful to accept and implement.

Korea's economy is badly in need of reform, given the degree of government intervention in it. Mr. Glassman believes that the free market could accomplish those reforms better than an IMF program. How would the free market have dealt with the problem that Korea was running out of reserves and that without IMF financing it might have resorted to trade restrictions that are hardly consistent with free markets?

VIEWPOINTS

Why We Need the IMF

Robert J. Samuelson

This selection was originally published in the *Washington Post* on 11 February 1998. Robert Samuelson is an economics columnist for the *Post* and *Newsweek*.

The case for the International Monetary Fund is that the world economy needs a "lender of last resort." This concept usually applies to a nation's economy. It holds that a central bank—the Federal Reserve for the United States—can stop banking panics when losses at a few banks cause depositor runs. It does this by making loans available to all banks so that scared depositors can withdraw their funds. Seeing that they can, they are reassured. The panic subsides, avoiding the dire consequences of a banking collapse: a drying up of credit, a drop in the money supply, a loss of purchasing power. In the 1930s, the Federal Reserve's failure to do this job brought on the Depression.

The IMF plays a similar role for the world economy. It acts as a backstop for countries that exhaust their foreign exchange reserves: the dollars, yen, and marks that nations use to conduct trade. When this happens, the IMF makes loans to them in these currencies. The loans buy time to restore a sustainable balance in their overseas payments without an abrupt halt to imports. The global advantages are obvious. One country's imports are another's exports. So, if too many countries reduce their imports, the process can feed on itself and trigger a worldwide slump. The huge loans organized by the IMF for Asia's ailing economies—now exceeding $100 billion—aim to avoid that.

All this is now relevant because the Clinton administration is urging

Congress to approve a new $18 billion U.S. contribution to the IMF. This may well be the most important legislation that Congress debates in 1998. A rejection would symbolically repudiate the IMF and, quite probably, undermine its efforts to contain the Asian crisis. But approval isn't preordained. "Anything that smacks of foreign aid is controversial," says Representative Jim Leach (R.-Iowa), chairman of the House Banking Committee. "But anything that leads to recession is explosive."

In hearings before Leach's committee, both views surfaced. Raymond Bracy of Boeing testified that the company already expects Asian airline customers to delay deliveries of sixty of three hundred planes ordered for the next three years. Dean Kleckner of the American Farm Bureau Federation said that farmers worry about a drop in exports to Asia. In 1997 these totaled $23 billion, or 40 percent of U.S. farm exports. But the IMF was also criticized for rescuing—potentially at taxpayer expense—countries and private banks from their own folly. These are serious objections.

It is not countries that are spared the pain of their errors. All the Asian nations engulfed by the present crisis (Korea, Indonesia, Thailand, Malaysia, the Philippines) face recessions and higher unemployment. There have already been food riots in Indonesia. Even with IMF loans, overborrowed countries must slow their economies to reduce imports. At most, the IMF cushions the shock and provides breathing space for economic repair. The real question is whether, in doing so, the IMF protects private banks from losses on bad loans. The answer is yes.

The Asian crisis occurred because these countries received huge inflows of foreign capital that created speculative booms and import surges. The capital inflow included large investments in local stock markets and funds used by multinational companies to build factories. These investors have already suffered big losses. Local stock prices have plunged; many new factories won't soon, if ever, be profitable. But the capital inflows also included billions in short-term bank loans on which Japanese, U.S., and European banks have yet to suffer losses.

Countries have traditionally been loath to permit default on bank loans—even though many were made to private companies or banks—for fear that one default would dry up all future bank credit. So Asian nations have repaid many maturing loans by depleting their foreign exchange reserves or tapping the IMF loans. Or banks have converted short-term loans (usually less than a year) into longer-term loans. Just recently, banks lending to Korea converted up to $24 billion of short-term loans into loans with maturities as long as three years. The implication, though, is that many of these loans will be repaid with the proceeds from the IMF loans. This is bad policy for two reasons.

First, forcing repayment of all debts may deepen the present crisis. The debt burden needs to be lightened; otherwise, countries will be compelled to run huge trade surpluses (to generate foreign exchange) for years. If too many countries have to do this, all may not succeed. Their economies will stagnate; global trade will suffer. Second, there is the problem of "moral hazard." If banks (or other investors) can reap profits on risky investments but are saved from losses—by the IMF—they will make more risky investments in the future. The solution to today's crisis may become the seed of tomorrow's; capricious capital flows will continue to destabilize the world economy.

Though well known, these problems are hard to solve. In theory, the IMF might insist that banks write down their loans by, say, 25 percent. But no formal mechanism exists for such a renegotiation; many banks with many loans would be involved. Some economists say that the IMF should just step aside. Don't lend at all. Then debtor nations and creditor banks would have to renegotiate. Banks would write down loans because countries couldn't afford to pay. Perhaps. But there's a huge danger. It is that, once the IMF's safety net was withdrawn, banks and other investors would flee other developing countries (Brazil, Russia, Mexico). Fear of panic could provoke the very panic that the IMF exists to prevent.

All lenders of last resort face a similar dilemma. Too much easy credit will spawn future crises. But stingy credit risks making this one much worse. The IMF is tiptoeing through a minefield. Somehow, it ought to prod banks to write down loans, but it needs to be subtle enough to maintain confidence. It may or may not succeed. Congress shouldn't make the job harder by having its largest member—the United States—refuse new support. It's worth noting that the United States has never lost anything on its IMF contributions; almost all IMF loans are repaid. The larger reason for acting is that the Asian crisis won't resolve itself. If the IMF didn't exist, we'd have to invent it.

Time to Terminate the IMF

Anna J. Schwartz

This selection first appeared in *Cato Commentaries*, published by the Cato Institute in Washington, D.C., on 6 October 1998. Anna Schwartz is a research associate at the National Bureau of Economic Research in New York City.

The bailout model of the International Monetary Fund and the U.S. Treasury is an abject failure. Instead of rescuing the financially distressed Asian and Russian economies, the bailouts have worsened their situations.

When the IMF was created in 1944, its well-defined purpose was to enforce the rules in a fixed exchange-rate system about altering a country's exchange rate when fundamental adjustment was needed, as well as to provide temporary resources to deal with a country's balance of payments problems. With the collapse of that system in 1971, the IMF lost its purpose. The switch to floating exchange rates eliminated its exchange-rate regulatory role and changed the character of balance of payments problems. Since the early 1970s, the IMF has been seeking to reinvent itself. Until the 1995 Mexican bailout, it had pretty much decided that it would promote its purpose as providing advice and information to its members, which number more than 180 countries. That, however, proved to be only an interim stop on the road to acquiring a new identity.

The IMF's role in the 1995 Mexican bailout planted the idea that the fund should serve as an international lender of last resort. The problem with this program is that its advocates have little understanding of the meaning of a lender of last resort.

Central banks have the capacity to serve as their banks' lenders of last resort. They can create high-powered base money (currency in circulation plus reserves), they can act quickly, and they can decisively stem a banking panic. The IMF lacks each of those features. It cannot create high-powered money. It can issue special drawing rights (SDRs) to central banks that can monetize the SDRs in their national currencies. But the IMF cannot issue SDRs without authorization by its membership. It cannot act quickly.

The decisions of its executive board are subject to the votes of executive directors who consult their national authorities. To provide money to a borrowing country, the IMF first engages in lengthy negotiations of a reform program. A national central bank can promptly provide liquidity to the money market without prior external approval. Moreover, a national lender of last resort rescues solvent banks temporarily short of liquidity. It does not rescue insolvent institutions. The IMF has no such inhibition.

The IMF reinvented itself again after the Mexican bailout in 1995. The lesson the fund took from the bailout was that it needed a stockpile of money if it was to act as a lender of last resort in the next financial crisis, given that it lacks the capacity to create high-powered money. In early 1997 the IMF announced a plan to raise cash to rescue a country in distress by creating a special $28 billion fund. By 1998 that proposed line of credit was increased to $47 billion. In addition, the IMF decided to increase the quota that each member contributes. For the United States, the total contribution amounts to $18 billion. That amount is what the administration is now asking Congress to appropriate. Since mid-1997, the appeal to Congress to allocate funds to the IMF has been based on the plight of the Asian countries.

Short-term renewable loans denominated in foreign currencies were the undoing of Mexico in 1994; yet the Asian countries welcomed the same form of credits two years later, and the lenders came off scot-free in 1995, as the banks probably will in 1998, because of the IMF. A big pot of IMF money is clearly the wrong response. Bailouts are not needed, especially in today's world of deep capital markets that are ready to lend to liquidity-constrained countries at interest rates that reflect credit risk.

As the financial turmoil in Russia this summer [1998] proves, money infusions have not bought Russia's compliance with pledges to convert a command economy into a market-oriented one.

Within Congress, the IMF faces two groups of opponents: liberals who seek labor and environmental reforms in the countries to which the IMF is prepared to lend as a quid pro quo for supporting the increase in funding and conservatives who seek concessions related to abortion legislation or the way in which the IMF operates. Congressional opponents of whatever stripe should not demand a quid pro quo but should reject the increase in IMF funding on principle.

The countries in Asia that are experiencing financial problems will either adopt measures to reform their banking systems, to eliminate political domination of credit allocation, and to earn restoration of their creditworthiness in international capital markets or they will not. To do so requires political resolve, not the IMF. Not to do so means those countries will fail to grow out of their problems. The world financial system will not be undermined if the IMF does not bail out those countries. Low-income countries have gotten into trouble financially many times in the past two centuries. Investors who lost money in ventures in those countries were hurt, and the countries involved had setbacks. The world did not collapse.

The IMF is weak on crisis prevention. It says that it warned Asian countries and Russia against bad policies but that they rejected its advice. If the moral authority of the IMF as a source of sound advice cannot win the respect of its client members, it is in the wrong business. Reform of the IMF is not the answer. It should be shut down.

Why We Need the IMF

David Rockefeller

This selection was originally published in the *Wall Street Journal* on 1 May 1998. David Rockefeller is a former chairman and CEO of the Chase Manhattan Bank.

Since the outbreak of the Asian financial crisis, it has been open season for attacks on the International Monetary Fund. We have been told that the prospect of IMF bailouts caused the crisis and that the IMF's existence, if continued unchanged, will result in many more financial disruptions. Distinguished former cabinet officials, writing on this page, have asked "Who Needs the IMF?" And this newspaper has added its editorial voice to the chorus.

Here's a more balanced perspective: In a globalized economy, everyone needs the IMF. Without the IMF, the world economy would not become an idealized fantasy of perfectly liquid, completely informed, totally unregulated capital markets. Investors and lenders would still make decisions on the basis of imperfect information, and they would have to take into account the absence of an international lender of last resort. This would be a serious, perhaps devastating, defect. In fact, we got a good sense of life without the IMF in the 1920s and 1930s. The results included widespread competitive devaluation and trade wars in response to balance of payments problems, followed by a plunge into global depression and world war.

Without a guarantor of international liquidity, many good loans would not be made. Fundamentally sound private investment projects in emerging markets can be dragged down by decisions external to the businesses involved. Even prudent government policies can be waylaid by unforeseeable shocks. Either way, fundamentally good investments will run into temporary liquidity problems. In a world of flexible exchange rates, such temporary problems can be magnified by accompanying drops in the value of the domestic currency. IMF programs finance the adjustment necessary to give these countries and firms time to let their fundamentals pay off.

CREDIT UNION

Thus, the IMF is the sovereign nations' credit union. It imposes strict conditions on countries' policies for bridge loans to get through hard times. Only a multilateral institution like the IMF could exert the discipline required without causing an unacceptable affront to a country's sovereignty. The benefits to the borrowing nation are that the adjustment program will be less painful and any resulting contraction less severe. The benefits to the lending countries are not only the availability of those credits to themselves, if and when they need them (as even the United States has), but a smaller contraction of world demand associated with the borrowing country's adjustment.

Some have claimed that these IMF conditions have been misapplied in the Asian crisis, demanding either too much austerity or unjustified structural reform. But IMF conditionality is highly pragmatic. Since the current crisis was not caused in large part by macroeconomic policies but by financial fragility and lack of transparency, the conditions were designed to respond to those causes. The fund has been ready to renegotiate its programs and to loosen austerity (such as the inflation target for South Korea) as matters stabilized. There always is room for improvement in individual IMF programs. But attacks on the basic idea of IMF conditionality are thoroughly misguided.

Events in emerging markets have spillover effects on the world economy as a whole, including the United States. Growing economies provide greater opportunities for investment and exports, so an institution that sustains productive capital flows to developing countries also sustains our own economic growth. More important, countries that run into significant balance of payments problems would have only two policy options without the IMF: default or devaluation. As seen in the interwar years, either can induce reactions by other countries that make a bad situation worse; together, they can make the global economy rapidly spiral downward. This chain of events is precisely what the IMF was created to prevent.

A cycle of competitive devaluations is the most dangerous potential chain of events the IMF prevents. Imagine that an emerging market in trouble over its balance of payments decides that it must export its way out and so devalues or depreciates its currency. Economies with similar exports and markets find themselves competitively disadvantaged, so they too devalue, hoping to offset the first country's currency gambit. Yet, if many countries pursue this strategy simultaneously, none of their positions improve significantly, while their purchasing power drops along with their currencies. It must be considered a triumph of the IMF's rapid response to the recent Asian crisis that no ongoing spiral of competitive devaluation has arisen despite the pressures on Hong Kong and China and even on Brazil and Russia.

All these virtues of the IMF have been forgotten in the rush to condemn one of its inherent costs: the creation of moral hazard. Moral hazard exists whenever insurance is provided against any kind of risk. Anyone who has worked in the banking industry knows that government guarantees, or even the perceived possibility thereof, can create perverse incentives for financial risk taking. The prospect of a rescue can encourage investments that otherwise would not be made. This increases the herdlike behavior of global capital since financial firms often watch what other investors do more than they watch the performance of the actual investments. This tendency certainly contributed to the surge of capital flows into South Korea, Indonesia, and their neighbors, and the subsequent drain of that capital.

It is a huge exaggeration, however, to suggest that the so-called bailout guarantee played more than a minor role in creating the Asian crisis. It is absurd to believe that any country would risk a national currency crisis simply because the tender mercies of the IMF were waiting to rescue it from its follies. The pain imposed by IMF programs deters crises rather than bringing them on.

As for private investors who put money into these economies—in the form of foreign direct investment, equities, commercial paper, and even many foreign currency loans to nonbank businesses—significant losses have been taken in every single country. Market discipline has in fact hit all domestic investors and their intermediaries in these countries hard. Many government and financial officials who contributed to the problem have had their careers ended as well.

TOO MUCH PROTECTION

There was indeed too much protection for the loans of some foreign banks. Here the IMF needs to move toward greater reliance on private financial workouts than excessively large rescue programs. Substantial burden sharing by all foreign creditors must also become an integral part of all future IMF programs. But saying that there is room for increasing the degree of market discipline is not the same as saying that market discipline is entirely lacking, let alone that its absence caused the Asian crisis.

In any event, such a moral hazard cost hardly outweighs all the benefits of IMF programs. The relevant comparison is between the explosive growth and macroeconomic stability we have experienced in the postwar decades, with the IMF in existence, and the much slower growth in the developing countries and far greater worldwide instability we saw in the interwar years or in the late nineteenth century. Only part of the differences can be attributed to the IMF, but it is illogical to ignore its contribution while attributing to it total responsibility for the few short financial crises of the past decades.

Kill the IMF

Doug Bandow

This selection first appeared in *Fortune* on 25 May 1998. Doug Bandow is a senior fellow at the Cato Institute in Washington, D.C., and a former special assistant to President Ronald Reagan.

When American business talks about capitalism, it usually means free markets for everyone but itself. Thus, the Chamber of Commerce, the National Association of Manufacturers, and big exporters like Boeing are lobbying Congress to approve roughly $18 billion in funding for the International Monetary Fund—a backdoor method of seeding foreign economies with money to buy U.S. goods.

Congress should say no. The IMF has long impeded economic growth in poorer countries, and its new penchant for bailouts is likely to further slow reform while putting U.S. taxpayers at risk.

The IMF was created in the aftermath of World War II to help countries meet balance of payments shortfalls. When that original role disappeared along with fixed exchange rates in the early 1970s, the fund showed an agile instinct for self-preservation by shifting to the economic-development business. Persistent failure in that new incarnation didn't stop the IMF from expanding into the markets created by the collapse of communism. Now the fund has taken another step and become the bailout king. Last fall [1997] the United States agreed to a $100 billion increase in the IMF's capital base; fund managing director Michel Camdessus is pushing for $60 billion more.

The real test of any aid agency is whether its clients move from dependency to self-sufficiency. Bryan Johnson and Brett Schaefer of the Heritage Foundation figure that, in the end, more than half of the IMF's borrowers between 1965 and 1995 were no better off than when they started. A third were actually poorer. Almost all were deeper in debt. Eighty-four countries have been borrowing from the fund for at least a decade.

Although the IMF sets conditions for its loans, it usually focuses on narrow accounting measures—currency devaluations, for example—that often bring borrowers' economies to a halt. Moreover, the fund is shamelessly eager to lend: It responded to Indonesia's recalcitrance by promising "considerable flexibility" and by constantly renegotiating its loan agreement.

Nor are the IMF's conditions ever enough. Economic reform is a continuing process, yet the fund buys only onetime compliance. And the fund has routinely aided the worst examples of socialism and state capitalism—including Romania's Nicolae Ceausescu—even as it turns liberalization into a foreign import, prompting nationalist resentment against "economic imperialism" such as that now raging in Indonesia and South Korea.

The 1995 Mexican bailout marked the IMF's entry into a new line of work entirely—one reflected in U.S. Treasury secretary Robert Rubin's argument that "the financial stability of the world is at risk." Of course, if the world is ready to topple into the economic abyss, there won't be much the fund can do about it—the $23 billion it lent last year [1997] was just a tenth of the private capital flow to developing states alone. The IMF doesn't create resources; it only reshuffles them. What's more, as the IMF, backed by the United States, piles international loan on international loan, it risks transferring instability from the foreign to the American domestic stage.

Nor do the IMF's loans aid the reform process: In the short term, the money cycles back to private creditors; in the longer run, fund programs subsidize inefficient and corrupt political systems. Over the past two decades the IMF and other lenders have bailed out the Mexican economy four times, allowing the government to delay painful reforms. Significant elements of crony capitalism seem likely to survive in both Indonesia and South Korea as well.

Fund supporters argue there's no alternative. Actually, unsubsidized economic failure imposes a far tougher discipline: Without an international bailout, countries like Indonesia would have to adopt all the changes necessary to reassure foreign bankers and investors. As South Korean president Kim Dae Jung promised, "I will make it so that foreign investors will invest with confidence." Reliance on the market's invisible hand would also help shield reform efforts from domestic xenophobia. Governments would have no one else to blame.

The main losers in a world without the fund would be the businesses that today lobby so heavily for it. The IMF's proclivity to bail out the profligate creates what economists call a moral hazard: Western investors make irresponsible decisions in the belief that they will be protected regardless of the results. In effect, the fund is promoting capitalism without loss, rather like Christianity without hell.

Financial crisis requires economic reforms, not IMF loans. As nations liberalize, private investment and credit will return. It is time to close the fund.

Appendix:
Balance of Payments Deficits and
IMF Adjustment Programs

The balance of payments (BOP) account is a statistical record of the economic transactions during a given year between residents (individuals, businesses, and governments) of one country and residents of the rest of the world. The BOP account consists of the current account, the capital account, and foreign currency reserves. The current account primarily records a country's net exports of goods and services. The current account is the cash flow element of the BOP account. If a country exports more than it imports, the current account is in a surplus position and the country has a positive cash flow. If a country imports more than it exports, the current account is in a deficit position and the country has a negative cash flow—the country's residents are not earning enough foreign currency through their exports to pay for what they buy from other countries. Countries, like people, can spend more than they take in only if they draw down their savings or borrow funds. A current account deficit, therefore, must be financed either by drawing down a country's foreign currency reserves or by borrowing funds from abroad. The capital account records a country's foreign borrowing. When a bond is sold to residents of another country, the payment, a capital inflow, is entered as a credit in the capital account. If a country's total receipts (exports plus capital inflows) fall short of its total payments (imports plus capital outflows), it has a BOP deficit and must draw on its foreign currency reserves to meet its obligations for the remaining payments. Persistent current account deficits eventually exhaust a country's credit and foreign currency reserves, just as a persistent negative cash flow for consumers eventually exhausts their credit cards and savings account.

If a country, say Brazil, has a BOP deficit—for example, U.S. dollar receipts from abroad are less than U.S. dollar payments due abroad—

Brazil can, for a time, draw on its dollar reserves. Alternatively, Brazil can borrow dollars from the IMF by exchanging Brazilian reals for U.S. dollars. The IMF uses an analytic framework, known as financial programming, to determine the amount of the loan and the macroeconomic adjustments that are needed to eventually establish BOP equilibrium. Typically, the amount of the loan is equal to a country's upcoming foreign debt obligations and the macroeconomic adjustments are intended to reduce imports and increase exports to enable the country to earn sufficient foreign exchange in the future to pay its bills, including the newly incurred IMF debt.

Conceptually, therefore, IMF loans come at the price of "conditionality," the policy adjustments that IMF officials believe will correct a recipient's country BOP deficit. The usual strategy for correcting a BOP deficit is to reduce domestic demand, and thus imports, through the imposition of credit ceilings, reductions in government spending, and tax increases. In addition, the IMF calls for the removal of export barriers. Currency devaluations are also used to promote net exports. For example, reducing the exchange rate for one Brazilian real from $4 to $2 reduces imports by making U.S. goods twice as expensive in local real prices and increases exports by making Brazilian goods half as expensive in U.S. dollars. Conceptually, IMF adjustment programs seek to rapidly correct BOP deficits.

Selected Bibliography

Beveridge, W. A., and Margaret R. Kelly. "Fiscal Content of Financial Programs Supported by Stand-By Arrangements in the Upper Credit Tranches, 1969–78." *IMF Staff Papers* 27 (June 1980): 205–49.

Connors, Thomas A. *The Apparent Effects of Recent IMF Stabilization Programs*. International Finance Discussion Paper No. 135. Washington, D.C.: Board of Governors of the Federal Reserve System, 1979.

Cornelius, Peter. *Das Prinzip der Konditionalitat bei Krediten des Internationalen Wahrungsfonds*. Munich, Germany: VVF, 1988.

Donovan, Donal J. "Real Responses Associated with Exchange Rate Action in Selected Upper Credit Tranche Stabilization Programs." *IMF Staff Papers* 28 (December 1981): 698–727.

———. "Macroeconomic Performance and Adjustment under Fund-Supported Programs: The Experience of the Seventies." *IMF Staff Papers* 29 (June 1982): 171–203.

———. *The Sources of Current External Debt Servicing Difficulties: Some Empirical Evidence*. IMF Working Paper DM/84/15. Washington, D.C.: International Monetary Fund, 1984.

Edwards, Sebastian. "The Role of International Reserves and Foreign Debt in the External Adjustment Process." In *Adjustment, Conditionality, and International Financing*, edited by Joaquin Muns. Washington, D.C.: International Monetary Fund, 1984.

Goldstein, Morris, and Peter Montiel. "Evaluating Fund Stabilization Programs with Multicountry Data: Some Methodological Pitfalls." *IMF Staff Papers* 33 (June 1986): 304–44.

Goode, Richard. *Economic Assistance to Developing Countries through the IMF*. Washington, D.C.: Brookings Institution, 1985.

Guitian, Manuel. *Fund Conditionality: Evolution of Principles and Practices*. IMF Pamphlet Series No. 38. Washington, D.C.: International Monetary Fund, 1981.

Gylfason, Thorvaldur. *Credit Policy and Economic Activity in Developing Countries with IMF Stabilization Programs.* Princeton Studies in International Finance No. 60. Princeton, N.J.: Princeton University, 1987.

Kelly, Margaret R. "Fiscal Adjustment and Fund-Supported Programs, 1971–80." *IMF Staff Papers* 29 (December 1982): 561–602.

Khan, Mohsin S., and Malcolm D. Knight. "Stabilization Programs in Developing Countries: A Formal Framework." *IMF Staff Papers* 28 (March 1981): 1–53.

————. "Determinants of Current Account Balances of Non-Oil Developing Countries in the 1970s: An Empirical Analysis." *IMF Staff Papers* 30 (December 1983): 819–42.

————. *Fund-Supported Adjustment Programs and Economic Growth.* Occasional Paper No. 41. Washington, D.C.: International Monetary Fund, 1985.

Killick, Tony, ed. *The Quest for Economic Stabilisation: The IMF and the Third World.* London: Heinemann Educational Books, 1984.

Loser, Claudio M. "The Role of Economy-Wide Prices in the Adjustment Process." In *Adjustment, Conditionality, and International Financing,* edited by Joaquin Muns. Washington, D.C.: International Monetary Fund, 1984.

Loxley, John. *The IMF and the Poorest Countries.* Ottawa, Canada: North-South Institute, 1984.

Officer, Lawrence H. "The Differential Use of IMF Resources by Industrial, Other Developed, and Less Developed Countries: A Historical Approach." *Journal of Developing Areas* 16 (April 1982): 401–20.

Pastor, Manuel, Jr. "The Effects of IMF Programs in the Third World: Debate and Evidence from Latin America." *World Development* 15 (February 1987): 249–62.

Payer, Cheryl. "The IMF in the 1980s: What Has It Learned; What Have We Learned about It?" In *Third World Affairs 1985.* London: Third World Foundation for Social and Economic Studies, 1985.

Reichmann, Thomas M. "The Fund's Conditional Assistance and the Problems of Adjustment, 1973–75." *Finance & Development* 15 (December 1978): 38–41.

Reichmann, Thomas M., and Richard T. Stillson. "Experience with Programs of Balance of Payments Adjustment: Stand-By Arrangements in the Higher Tranches, 1963–72." *IMF Staff Papers* 25 (June 1978): 293–309.

Zulu, Justin B., and Saleh M. Nsouli. *Adjustment Programs in Africa: The Recent Experience*. Occasional Paper No. 34. Washington, D.C.: International Monetary Fund, 1985.

Index

actual-versus-targets approach, 49–50
American Farm Bureau Federation, 219
Anjaria, Shailendra J., 195, 214, 216
Anwar Ibrahim, minister, 134
Argentina, 79, 121, 128
Armey, Dick, 88, 122
Articles of Agreement for the International
   Monetary Fund: on loan interest rates,
   34–35; origins of, 3, 6; political
   noninterference provisions of, 161, 169–
   71; on practice of conditionality, 66–68;
   U.S. Congress concerns with, 63
Article V (Articles of Agreement of the
   International Monetary Fund), 53
Article XIV (Articles of Agreement of the
   International Monetary Fund), 6
Asia: crony capitalism practiced in, 25,
   33–32, 132, 137; exchange rates and
   interest rates of, 152; IMF failure in,
   140; IMF on macroeconomic failures
   of, 116–17; IMF monetary measures in,
   117–19; nature of political values of,
   166–68
Asian economic crisis: bailout expense of,
   197–98; debate over IMF and, 119–23,
   131–33, 203, 210, 211–13, 216–17,
   219–20, 224–25; higher interest rates
   and, 133–35; origins of, 198
"Asian flu," 33–34
Asian values theories, 166
Assetto, Valerie, 81

bailouts: dangerous legacy of, 123–26,
   197–200, 211, 228; increasing expense
   of Asian, 197–98; Mexican, 99–103,
   106–9, 110–12, 114, 124, 197–98, 228;
   Mexican repayment of, 31; prospective
   risk of, 31–33; to Indonesia, 28, 32–33;

to Russia, 23, 138–40, 143–47; to South
   Korea, 23, 28–29, 30, 32–33, 217;
   unpenalized, 28–31. *See also* fund-
   supported adjustment programs (IMF);
   moral hazards
balance of payments performance:
   conditionality goals for, 72–73; of
   developing countries (1970–80), 46–47;
   of developing countries (1971–80), 47;
   of developing countries (1974–81), 49;
   of developing countries (1977–79), 47–
   48; eligibility for IMF credits and, 53–
   55; human rights and assessment of,
   170–71; IMF's response to poor, 57–59;
   of Latin American nations (1987), 48;
   summary of IMF programs on, 52
Banco de Mexico, 101, 103
bancor payment, 5
Bandow, Doug, 34, 53, 55, 63, 78, 195,
   227
Bank for International Settlements, 156
Bank of Korea, 118
Bank of Thailand, 129
Barro, Robert J., 94, 112
Bartley, Robert, 89
before-after approach, 44–46, 75
Boeing, 219, 227
Bracy, Raymond, 219
Bradbury, Ray, 113
Brady, Nicholas, 80
Brazil, 79, 113, 114, 120, 121, 158
Bretton Woods conference (1944), 3, 6,
   25–26, 63, 216
Bretton Woods system, 35, 170
Brunner, Karl, 72, 179
buffer stock financing facility (BSFF), 17
Bulgaria, 118
Burma, 83

Elsevier Science: "The International Monetary Fund and the Developing Countries: A Critical Evaluation" by Sebastian Edwards in *IMF Policy Advice, Market Volatility, Commodity Price Rules, and Other Essays,* eds. Karl Brunner and Allan H. Meltzer, vol. 31 (Carnegie-Rochester Conference Series on Public Policy, 1989).

Financial Times Ltd.: "Power unto Itself" by Jeffrey D. Sachs (*Financial Times,* 11 December 1997).

The Heritage Foundation: "The International Monetary Fund: Outdated, Ineffective, and Unnecessary" by Bryan T. Johnson and Brett D. Schaefer, Heritage Foundation Backgrounder No. 1113, 6 May 1997.

Indian Express Newspapers, Ltd.: "IMF Crackdown on Corruption in Projects" by Chidanand Rajghatta (*Indian Express* [Bombay], 9 August 1997).

International Monetary Fund: What Is the International Monetary Fund? by the International Monetary Fund, 1998; "The Macroeconomic Effects of Fund-Supported Adjustment Programs" by Mohsin S. Khan (*Staff Papers* 37, June1990); "Conditionality: Fostering Sustained Policy Implementation" by the International Monetary Fund in *1998 IMF Survey Supplement on the Fund,* ed. Ian S. McDonald.

Investor's Business Daily: "What to Expect from IMF? Look at Mexico" by Ian Vasquez and L. Jacobo Rodriguez (*Investor's Business Daily,* 1 April 1998).

The McGraw-Hill Companies, Inc.: "The IMF Doesn't Put Out Fires, It Starts Them" by Robert J. Barro (*BusinessWeek,* 7 December 1998).

The Nation Company, L.P.: "Mexican Handout: Bailing Out the Creditor Class" by Walker F. Todd (*The Nation,* 13 February 1995).

Nation Newspapers, Ltd.: "IMF Unlikely to Resume Loans to Kenya Soon" by Robert Shaw (*The Nation* [Nairobi, Kenya], 7 September 1997). Reprinted by permission.

The New York Times Company: "As Economies Fail, the IMF Is Rife with Recriminations" by David E. Sanger (*New York Times,* 2 October 1998); "A Bad Side of Bailouts: Some Go Unpenalized" by Louis Uchitelle (*New York Times,* 4 December 1997); "On Both Sides of the Border, Peso Ills Were Long Ignored" by David E. Sanger and Anthony DePalma (*New York Times,* 25 January 1995); "The Bad News about Bailouts" by Lawrence B. Lindsey (*New York Times,* 6 January 1998); "Critics: The IMF Is Misguided. Skeptics: Too Much Rot in Asia" by Peter Passell (*New York Times,* 15 January 1998); "Rule of the Ruble" by Jeffrey D. Sachs (*New York Times,* 4 June 1998); "A Needed, but Risky, Bailout," editorial (*New York Times,* 22 July 1998); "IMF Loans to Rights Violators Are Attacked in Congress" by David E. Sanger (*New York Times,* 22 April 1998); "The Indispensable IMF" by Paul Krugman (*New York Times,* 15 May 1998); copyright 1995, 1997, 1998 by the New York Times Company. Reprinted by permission.

News World Communications: "IMF and the Russian Missiles" by J. Michael Waller (*Washington Times,* 23 January 1998).

St. Martin's Press: Excerpt from *The IMF and Third-World Political Instability: Is There a*